PUBLISH
TO WIN

PUBLISH

TO WIN

SMART STRATEGIES TO SELL MORE BOOKS

JERROLD R. JENKINS
and Anne M. Stanton

Rhodes &Easton
Traverse City, Michigan

Published by Rhodes &Easton
121 E. Front Street, 4th Floor, Traverse City, Michigan 49684

Publisher's Cataloging-in-Publication Data
Jenkins, Jerrold R.
   Publish to win: the smart marketing approach to profitable book publishing / Jerrold R. Jenkins and Anne M. Stanton. – Traverse City, Mich.: Rhodes & Easton, 1997
        p.   cm.
   Includes bibliographical references and index.
   ISBN 0-9649401-2-4
   1. Self-publishing–United States. I. Stanton, Anne M. II. Title.
Z285.5 J46   1997
070.5/93 dc21   97-65078

PROJECT COORDINATED BY JENKINS GROUP, INC.

00 99 98 ❖ 5 4 3 2 1

Printed in the United States of America

*To all aspiring writers and publishers who believe that it
takes more than a burning desire to sell books,
but also thoughtful planning, a valuable product,
a targeted message, creative promotion, and,
above all, unwavering persistence.*
JERROLD R. JENKINS

*To Doug, my husband, who believes that anyone
can achieve whatever they want, given enough
effort and imagination.
And to my children, Katey and Johnny,
who have taught me how to see life anew.*
ANNE M. STANTON

CONTENTS

ACKNOWLEDGMENTS

WE OWE MANY THANKS TO ALL THE PUBLISHERS AND PUBLISHING EXperts who have generously contributed their thoughts and shared their experiences with us. There are too many to name, but we do want to mention David Ramsey, Richard Paul Evans, Diane Pfeifer, Ed Hinkelman, John McHugh, Gail Golomb, Gene Schwartz, Cynthia Kim, Greg Roy, Randi Kreger, Greg Godek, Veltisezar Bautista, Linda Donelson, Wally Bock, Mark Habrel, Thorn Bacon, Bruce Kletz, Jan Nathan, Jim Cox, Barbara Hoffert, Vernon Avila, Steve O'Keefe, Lori Marcus, John Storey, Bev Harris, Michael Keating, Cornelius van Heumen, Shel Horowitz, Steve Mettee, Tim Smith, David LeClaire, Stella Otto, Mary Westheimer, and Robert Friedman.

We also want to thank Sam Wells and David Hahn, both of Planned Television Arts in New York City, for their contributions to the publicity and Internet chapters, respectively.

Finally, we want to thank Jan Nathan for establishing the Publishers Marketing Association forum on the Internet, where hundreds of publishers exchange scores of ideas each day.

INTRODUCTION

BACK IN 1990, CYNTHIA AND SANG KIM WOULD HAVE BEEN CONSIDered unlikely publishers. They ran a martial arts studio in Connecticut and noticed that the older students who had mastered Tae Kwon Do were struggling to teach what they knew to the less experienced students. An exhaustive search for a book to help these novice instructors turned up nothing. So they decided to write their own book, *Teaching Martial Arts*, that stressed the significance of teaching mind, body and character skills in the practice of Tae Kwon Do. Knowing how badly *they* needed the book, the Sangs optimistically shipped off the manuscript to several publishers for consideration.

"Nobody would publish it. I'll be honest. The original manuscript *was* really bad. I wouldn't have published it either," said Cynthia Kim, laughing. "We took it to a martial arts mainstream publisher and they said there was no market. We didn't think it was true so we published it ourselves. But we did revise it significantly before we did."

The Kims, both in their twenties, were young, inexperienced, and lucky. They had accidentally stumbled upon a "niche" market of 50 million Tae Kwon Do practitioners. The early days weren't easy, however.

They intuitively believed the best way to sell the tightly niched book was through direct mail. Unaware of vendors who sold mailing lists, they went to the Hartford, Connecticut, library and laboriously copied the addresses of the biggest martial arts schools from every phone book in the country. "We targeted the biggest schools. We thought if they could afford to buy display ads, there was a bigger chance they could afford our book," Cynthia said.

In retrospect, the book's sales weren't impressive—only about 9,000 copies were sold over the course of six years. But the Kims learned from their mistakes and their firm, Turtle Press, has since published 10 more books and 30 videos, all related to martial arts. Business is good. In fact it's great. Turtle Press sells more than $500,000 of videos and books annually.

To her publishing peers, Cynthia Kim has become a model of guerrilla publishing.

"The traditional model of publisher is effectively dead," said Cynthia Kim. "No one can start a business today and hope to be a Random House. No one should try. Sure at Turtle Press, we publish books, but we also produce videos, audios, tapes, posters, special reports and a newsletter, promote seminars, and head a membership organization."

Kim said her business has succeeded where others have failed because she and Sang have established a unique philosophy:

1. Be a guru: You don't have to be a publishing guru. Be a guru in your own special industry.

2. Find a very small and underserved niche.

3. Use your books to establish yourself as an expert and support your speaking activities.

4. Be a one-hit wonder (you know, like the *Chicken Soup* guys). Quit your job, invest thousands of hours and even more money in marketing, promote the book in your every waking hour, make it your life's mission. (Okay, maybe not for everyone.)

5. Develop supporting products on the topic of your book and be an information provider, not a publisher.

6. Write something that people will pay a lot of money for (*a la* Anthony Robbins).

7. Establish yourself as the premier source for information in your industry (*a la* Nolo Press or Peachpit).

Cynthia Kim couldn't be more on target. The publishing world has changed and publishers are starting to think more expansively and creatively than ever before.

Publish to Win will help you sell your books smarter. Granted, there is no *one* way to succeed. But what is key to any publisher's success is to identify a book's prospective audience with laser-point accuracy, create a message that appeals to the audience, and distribute the message and/or the book to the prospective readers' buying hangouts.

This book will discuss marketing strategy at length. Rather than rely solely on bookstore sales and traditional promotion, we suggest that publishers consider the wide world of alternative book markets. This requires an acceptance that success doesn't necessarily translate into making the *New York Times* Book Review Best Seller List or selling four million copies through bookstores.

There are hundreds of unsung winners, people who have sold 3,000, 5,000, 10,000, 25,000, even 100,000 copies and have built lucrative livelihoods around publishing. More often than not, these successful publishers have sold their books in what's normally referred to as "alternative channels"—to corporations, through classified ads in niche magazines, through direct marketing appeals, to bookclubs, and on the Internet.

Alternative markets have become increasingly attractive because publishers get cash in hand almost immediately and once the book is sold, it *stays* sold. That compares to bookstore sales where a book that's sold today can be returned tomorrow.

Mallery Press in Flint, Michigan, has sold more than 180,000 quilting books through mail-order campaigns and back-of-the-room sales. Entrepreneur Wally Bock has made hundreds of thousands of dollars by selling niche books—police books and booklets on property management—through direct mail and classified ads. Dawn Hall, who has sold almost 70,000 copies of her plaid-covered cookbook, *Down Home Cookin' Without the Down Home Fat,* has sold her books in gift shops, grocery stores and health clubs. She also offers cooking demonstrations and classes. Her strategy is to persevere and *to keep trying new marketing approaches.*

Hurtling the Title Wave

In 1996 alone, an avalanche of 140,000 books were published, pushing the total books in print to a staggering 1.3 million. Does this mean a small publisher should forget about trying to publish a general interest book for a bookstore destination?

Absolutely not.

We will talk about strategies of independent authors who have accomplished their goals of selling tens of thousands of books. Most of these best-selling authors were initially rejected by the big New York City publishers and had to use their personal savings to fund their dream, a few even financing their venture with credit cards. Many peddled their books from bookstore to bookstore or tirelessly sold them in seminar after seminar. In the end, these authors were rewarded by fame and fortune and a certain sense of satisfaction in conquering the Goliath book industry.

What made the difference between a best seller and a bomb? The answer is marketing strategy. These authors first proved the saleability of the book in alternate markets or tightly defined geographic areas before attempting national bookstore distribution.

Avoid Proven Pitfalls

Some people say that to succeed, you need to avoid proven pitfalls as well as pursue winning strategies. The first step, no question, is a well-written book. One veteran book reviewer, Jim Cox of *Midwest Book Review*, said too many self-published books are "useless, tedious trash." Many started with useful, quality information, but were published with an inferior cover, littered with typos, or were poorly edited. Because we've produced dozens of books for independent publishers, we can provide time-tested design guidelines for books that can stand on their spines next to the best.

We'll also help you avoid the often fatal mistakes that small publishers make when selling to bookstores. Bookstores are indeed important for most publishers, but we will arm you with strategies that will shield you from high returns (books that failed to sell once they were placed on the shelves) and contracts with book distributors that produce profits so skinny they would break any company's profit line.

Unfortunately, with the explosive growth of independent publishers, it's becoming increasingly difficult—sometimes virtually impossible—to even find an exclusive, national distributor or national wholesaler to represent your books. That can be fatal for publishers planning to sell their books in bookstores. That's why some publishers have become so desperate they have *paid* a distributor to represent their books. We have discovered a couple of ways around this problem that we discuss in Chapter 7, "The Truth About Distributors and Wholesalers," and Chapter 8, "Partnership Publishing: A Well-Kept Secret."

PUBLISH TO WIN PUTS THE ODDS IN YOUR FAVOR

Book publishing is a gamble, but it's not brain surgery. You don't need an advanced degree, but you do need a burning desire to succeed and the tacit recognition that publishing is a business.

Most people enter the publishing realm out of a love for writing or the sincere desire to help and inspire people in some way. Sometimes a book simply evolves from a hobby or craft. No matter what your initial inspiration, as a publisher it's vital to strike a fine balance between art and commerce.

"A publisher who consistently disrespects the demands for quality and worth in the manuscripts he publishes will, despite temporary successes, find his enterprise dying of spiritual starvation in the end; just as a publisher who consistently ignores the commercial needs of his establishment will find before long that his cultural opportunities are negated by bankruptcy," wrote John Dessauer in *Book Publishing; What It Is, What it Does.*

This book is for people who have published a quality book and want thousands of people to read it. They can't afford failure and demand results from their efforts. This book will explain how to identify your target market and it will give you one example after another of low-cost publicity ideas that, perhaps, will spark your own publicity machine. Each alternative market will be discussed from QVC to direct mail to corporate sales.

In the final analysis, independently publishing a book is a "calculated gamble," said author David LeClaire, who decided the odds were in his favor.

"There are no guarantees," said LeClaire, author of *Bridges to a Pas-*

sionate Partnership. "We know that not all of us will succeed, not every book will be a best seller. Yet it's a gamble I'm willing to take. But you can't hit a home run if you aren't willing to swing the bat and take a risk. Smart business people look for ways to improve their odds, reduce the risk, and are pro-active about avoiding and solving problems."

THE TARGET AUDIENCE FOR THIS BOOK

This book isn't only aimed at independent publishers who are ready to expand sales with more creative and aggressive marketing strategies. It's also aimed at authors, who:

- Have found a wonderful publisher, but have been asked to handle their own publicity;
- Had their book published by a publishing firm—small or large— only to realize that their publisher is unable or unwilling to aggressively market their book; or
- Published their book through an established press and now have the opportunity to buy back their books as remainders.

PUBLISH
TO WIN

1.

INSIDE THE INDUSTRY: THE EVOLUTION OF INDEPENDENT PUBLISHING

Next to doing things that deserve to be written,
nothing gets a man more credit, or gives him more pleasure
than to write things that deserve to be read.
LORD CHESTERFIELD

INDEPENDENT PUBLISHING ISN'T A NEW PHENOMENON. INDEED, IT'S virtually an American tradition that dates back to the eighteenth century. Thomas Paine's *Common Sense* rolled off the press on January 10, 1776. The pamphlet, originally rejected by colonial newspapers as a series of letters to the editor, eventually sold more than half a million copies and helped foment the American Revolution. In the nineteenth century, Walt Whitman published at least six editions of his controversial *Leaves of Grass*— the last in 1892 as he lay on his deathbed. Whitman never profited from his ventures, but his dogged determination and unabashed promotional techniques, which included writing reviews of his own work, catapulted him to fame as an influential literary figure in his own lifetime.

Novelists Upton Sinclair and Anais Nin proved their own independent publishing ingenuity in the early twentieth century. Unwilling to compromise on the content of *The Jungle*, which one American publisher characterized as "too much blood and guts," Sinclair organized a group of his friends to publish his novel. While waiting for the press to run, Doubleday and Page offered to publish a simultaneous edition. The novel was not only a commercial success for Sinclair, but it also triggered the passage of the Pure Food and Drug Act.

With the printing of *Winter of Artifice*, Nin already had a toehold in a major French publishing house until World War II began and she immigrated to the United States. Her humble beginnings here can be traced to the purchase of a secondhand printing press she brought with the help of a friend and ran in a rented apartment in Greenwich Village. Later, when she established that her work could sell, she was courted by several major publishers who had originally rejected her work.

Independent publishers were an asset to many voices during the social upheaval of the 1960s. On the heels of the movement that defied the establishment, John Muir published his *How to Keep Your Volkswagen Alive* in 1970. This classic how-to manual sold more than 2.2 million copies and provided start-up funds for John Muir Productions, which evolved into a successful small-press operation that published the works of other authors.

Authors Ken Blanchard and Spencer Johnson burst onto the scene with *The One Minute Manager*, a snappy hand-held manual of easy-to-learn management techniques. These two enterprising individuals packaged and published the ideas taught in their seminars into a virtual textbook for the home and office that enjoyed more than two years on the *New York Times* Book Review Best Seller list.

More recently, inspirational speaker James Redfield successfully identified a target market for his book, *The Celestine Prophecy*. He sold 90,000 copies of this parable of spiritual adventure on his lecture circuit. That's when agents at Warner recognized the book's broad appeal and paid $800,000 for the world rights, an unheard-of sum for a virtual unknown. There are now more than 5.5 million copies of the book in print.

The list of other successful independent publishers reads like a Who's Who of the literary world: John Bartlett, Richard Bolles, Steward Brand, Edgar Rice Burroughs, Stephen Crane, Mary Baker Eddy, Zane Grey, Gordie Howe, Washington Irving, Spencer Johnson, James Joyce, Rudyard Kipling, D.H. Lawrence, Edgar Allen Poe, Ezra Pound, Robert Ringer, Edwin Arlington Robinson, Carl Sandburg, George Bernard Shaw, Gertrude Stein, Henry David Thoreau, Mark Twain and Virginia Woolf.

Throughout its long and rich history, independent publishing was referred to as the seedbed of the literary avant-garde. Many authors regarded it as the only alternative after commercial publishing houses rejected their manuscripts. Vanity presses and subsidy publishers were (and are still) an option, but not a smart one for they generally charge authors to publish their books, usually retain the rights to the work, and then offer little or no promotion. Offered no other choice, authors decided to publish themselves.

That "no-other-choice" feeling prevailed over independent publishing until the mid-1980s when the information age exploded and the race to feed the flames began. Unknown authors, shut out of the commercial New York publishing houses, found that demand for information was high enough to support their enterprises. At the same time, superstores were born and exclusive national distributors devoted to the small press industry sprang to life. Superstores—with the ability to offer ample shelf space—were eager to consider books from independent publishers. Master distributors sold them the books they wanted. For the first time, independent publishers found an easy conduit for national sales.

The bottom line: successful authors have proved that independent publishing should no longer be considered as a last resort. Today it may be to your benefit to *choose* to independently publish.

Do you have what it takes?

Winning in the game of independent publishing takes mental toughness.

> *Let me tell you the secret that has led me to my goal.*
> *My strength lies solely in my tenacity.*
> Louis Pasteur

"The ability to self-promote vigorously is a key ingredient for most self-publishers," wrote Suzanne Mantell in a May 22, 1995 *Publishers Weekly* article.

"They have to be really motivated to get in the door, and they have to be pounding on it nonstop. And they have to believe in their work."

How much money will I need?

Besides tireless promotion, you'll need sufficient capital to produce and market a book. Compared to other business ventures, independent publishing requires a relatively low initial investment and little overhead. The average independent publisher will spend $7,000 to $20,000 to produce a well-packaged book and a minimum of $3,000 for promotion. But as Theodore Roosevelt once said: "Do what you can, with what you have, where you are."

Our publishing firm, Rhodes & Easton, spent $1,700 promoting its book, *Deer Camp Dictionary*, which sold 5,000 copies in the first three weeks. Instead of spending big bucks on promotion, the firm decided to rely on impulse sales to the target audience of hunters and their friends. Rhodes & Easton placed the book in nearly every store that sold beef jerky, ring bologna and Old Milwaukee beer. The title and bright orange cover attracted hunters like deer to bait piles.

Knowing how much money you'll need and where best to spend it comes with realistic planning. Downsizing your plans and creativity often fill in when pennies are tight.

The importance of author charisma

You probably have bought a truly awful book in your lifetime—a "visual accident" as Jim Cox of the Midwest Book Review would call it. So why did you ever buy the book? You probably heard or read a great pitch. For many books, the author's pitch made the book a success rather than the content itself. We are not suggesting that author charisma is more important than the content, but it is every bit as important. Before New York publishing firms make a final decision on a book, they often will bring in the writer for an interview to see how the writer will come across in an interview.

But a great pitch isn't enough. It will bring in the first wave of sales, but it's word of mouth from enthusiastic readers that keeps the sales waves rolling in. Just ask Robert James Waller, author of *Bridges of Madison County*, whose book sold literally millions of copies thanks to word of mouth. The countless reviews that mercilessly skewered the book certainly didn't do him any good. Promotion may require interviews, perhaps even speeches and seminars. If you're witty, if you can make people laugh, cry and believe that your book will change their lives, then you'll probably sell warehouses full of books. And don't believe that humor is biologically hardwired. *Most* people can learn how to be funny.

So what is publishing?

Does it mean owning and operating a printing press? Putting the actual ink on the paper and binding the pages? Simply defined, publishing means owning the rights to intellectual property, whether it's words or pictures, and making the financial investment to get it into some form that a consumer can use. Publishing is managing the entire process of making a book, from the writing to the production to the marketing and shipping.

Don't limit yourself to thinking about your book as a cover encasing a few hundred pages. You can option your book to a movie production company and then ultimately sell the movie rights. You can sell foreign sales rights and possibly trademark rights for a character. You can turn your book into an audio, video, CD-ROM, and sell excerpt rights to magazines. *Newsweek*, for example, bought Colin Powell's serial rights for $210,000. Increasingly, publishers are getting paid for electronic rights and getting portions of their book published on the Internet.

Even the Net-heads are publishing books

Speaking of the Internet, many publishers fear that books will make interesting fossils someday. Not likely. Books are portable, sturdy and permanent. You can take them anywhere. You can't do that with computers. Ironically, the computer has *created* a demand for the publication of even more books. Even the net-heads that laugh over snail-mail and the reign of the dead tree are publishing books. Case in point: *The Soul of Cyberspace* by Jeffrey Zaleski and *What Will Be: Our Lives in the 21st Century* by Michael Dertouzos, with a foreword by Bill Gates.

According to *HeadsUp*, a book industry newsletter, the growth rate of computer book sales—12.1 percent—was nearly double that of general book sales in 1995. Some publishers are even "marrying" books with online content.

"One MacMillan imprint, Waite Group Press, recently initiated an interactive programming course series that puts tutorials in the hard copy book and then directs the user to its 'E-Zone' on the Net," said the article.

Books are not dead or even approaching rigor mortis. Domestic consumer spending on books is estimated to reach $31.2 billion by the year 2000, up from an estimated $19 billion in 1990—an average of 6.4 percent each year, according to the *19th Annual Edition of Book Industry Trends 1996*, a book published by the Book Industry Study Group. Publishing has evolved dramatically over the last quarter century and continues to change every day. Statistics tell the story best. In 1970, there were 3,000 recognized publishers in the United States. Today there are more than 50,000 and the number of new publishers grows at the rate of 8,000 per year, although many are one- to two-book publishers. Many independent publishers who successfully capture market share are bought out by large publishing houses.

At any given time there are about 1.3 million books in print. The numbers are staggering and yet the marketplace continues to absorb them and ask for more.

In his book, *In One Day*, Tom Parker writes that Americans buy five million books every day. According to a 1994 study published by the American Booksellers Association, book buyers buy an average of eight books over a six-month period. And a study by Maritz Marketing Research reports that adults read 10 or more books each year.

SUPERSTORES ARE DRAMATICALLY CHANGING THE INDUSTRY

While book sales are strong, there is strife within the industry. Massive superstores such as Borders and Barnes & Noble are opening in city after city. These giant superstores dwarf the once popular mall bookstores, offering up to 300,000 titles in a single store. Independent bookstores are struggling for survival by transforming into specialty stores and/or by offering more sidelines (calendars, greeting cards, etc.) Still, many have tumbled into bankruptcy. In 1990, the independents' market share was 32.5 percent. By 1995, it had slid to 19.5 percent. Even many of the well-established independents that managed to survive report that business has dropped by up to 25 percent.

Yet the superstores are spilling red ink. Borders lost $200 million in 1995 despite sales of $1.7 billion. Barnes & Noble, with sales of nearly $2 billion in 1995, lost a little more than $53 million.

Meanwhile, major publishers are finding they can do huge chunks of business by dealing only with a few superstores, instead of hundreds of independents. In fact, Random House, Simon and Schuster, and Farrar, Strauss & Giroux withdrew from the 1997 BookExpo America (formerly called the American Booksellers Association trade show)—the country's largest book trade show. The reason? Book industry experts speculate that these large publishers question the wisdom of investing in a trade show that largely involves independents when they do the vast majority of business with the superstores.

What does this mean for a small publisher? How does a small-press title compete with 300,000 other books? How does a Barnes & Noble buyer even hear of your book? Our general advice is this: national distribution in chain stores should be avoided, particularly in the early run. The return rate is significantly higher among chain stores and the profit margin is very slim. Put your books in bookstores only in areas where you're promoting the book and buyers can pull them off the shelves. In general, small publishers are better off finding alternative and more profitable channels. This is especially true with niche books, which can be successfully marketed in specialty retail stores or sold through incentive or specialty markets.

WHAT KIND OF PUBLISHER DO YOU WANT TO BE?

Before embarking on a publishing career, it's useful to think of the eventual shape of your publishing firm.

We categorize publishers by the number of books they produce and the kind of books. The first category is single-book publishers. These people aspire to publish one book and only one book in their lifetime. Some feel they have only one story to tell or one theory to share. Single-book publishers may already practice a satisfying profession and have no desire to get into publishing. They may also believe their efforts are better spent concentrating on the promotion of one book for the life of that book. The decision to publish a single book has no bearing on the sales or profit potential. Single-book publishers can sell 5,000 copies or 5 million copies. If a single book is all you plan to publish, it's useful to consider a joint venture with a more established publisher.

The second kind of publisher is the one who publishes a number of his or her own books all in the same subject area. Author and publisher Harry Knitter is a good example. Knitter travels often for business. He loves to travel and write about travel. In 1996, he published *Holding Pattern: Airport Waiting Made Easy* under his company imprint, Kordene Publications, Inc. Because travel is a multibillion dollar industry, Knitter believes his niche in the travel market offers infinite possibilities for additional books: traveling with children, selecting a travel agent, and finding the best travel bargains.

The third kind of publisher are those who want to publish his or her own books, but on various topics. Author and publisher Dan Poynter produces books both on sky diving and independent publishing.

The fourth kind of publisher produces his or her own books and also the works of other authors. Diane Pfeifer, owner of Strawberry Publishing, had successfully sold 200,000 copies of 10 books that are fun and pun-filled—cookbooks, baby shower books, and a wedding gift book—many written by her husband. Firmly established in selling books to specialty stores, Pfeifer was game to sell another line of books—elegant, floral journals and note cards. She tested out the line at a July trade gift show and was delighted to see the new line had bumped up her orders.

"I got customers I otherwise wouldn't have," she said.

And finally there are publishers who simply want to publish other people's work. You may have sent your manuscript to some of them. Many operate like large department stores offering something for everyone. Others limit the books they publish to certain topic areas, subjects, or regional interests.

You will often hear publishers labeled as small, medium, and large. However, size in these terms requires clarification. Publishers can be small in terms of the number of titles they publish or the amount of revenue they generate, but the two do not correspond directly. Our rule of thumb is a small publisher is one who publishes less than 10 titles. A medium publisher produces anywhere from 10 to 200 titles and a large publisher has a list of greater than 200.

WHAT YOU SUSPECTED ABOUT NEW YORK PUBLISHING HOUSES IS PROBABLY TRUE

Many authors seek the prestige associated with commercial or what's called traditional publishers such as Random House, HarperCollins, Simon & Schuster and Bantam Doubleday Dell. Yet tens of thousands of manuscripts arrive at the doorsteps of New York publishing houses each year. Senior Editor Eamon Dolan estimates that HarperCollins receives a total of 18,000 manuscripts annually, solicited and unsolicited. Of these, only 200 hardcover titles are published each year. Any unsolicited manuscripts from an author are immediately returned unopened with a form letter, he said.

The New York houses publish books on a wide range of topics, but if a new manuscript falls into one that is already well-covered, publishers are rarely interested in hearing why it is better. They take fewer and fewer risks on unknown authors with the exception of a book written on a subject with obviously mass commercial appeal. They concentrate on proven fiction authors and well-known names—athletes, celebrities, national magazine writers, and politicians who can produce high returns on the company's investment. Generally, if a book can't generate sales of at least 25,000 copies, these companies are unwilling to publish it.

The publishing companies have trapped themselves in an inflationary spiral, paying celebrities huge, multimillion dollar advances. Advances get absurdly higher as the companies attempt to outbid each other. When these gambles fail—Newt Gingrich's book, *1994*, (returned in droves) comes to mind—there is little money left for unknowns.

"More money is being spent on fewer titles, and a lot of people can't get their books placed. This is one reason people are going the self-published route. Another reason is the money to be made. And there's validation," said Rick Horgan, a former executive editor at HarperCollins, in a *Publishers Weekly* interview. Horgan has since moved to Random House.

Major publishers do enjoy several advantages over independent publishers. The largest, perhaps, are established contacts in the book business. When it comes to book reviewers, bookstore chains, and national media shows, these publishers are usually welcomed with open arms. Secondly, a major house can back its favored projects with a highly experienced marketing and sales staff. With years of experience and a stable of media contacts, their publicity campaigns can be enormously effective.

However, major publishers make a decision early on whether they want to heavily promote the book or let it die an early death from neglect. In the latter case, it's up to the author to generate media interviews and book signings, something most of them may not realize until it is too late and their masterpiece is being returned by the truckloads.

Here's the experience of one independent publisher, Greg Roy.

"The first two books that I wrote were published by Betterway Publications, which has since been purchased by *Writer's Digest*. I've also worked with one huge publishing house in New York City and found the entire experience so depressing that I gave up entirely on writing (it wasn't a primary income source).

"My first book became a best seller for the publisher, was highlighted in their catalog as such, and I didn't get involved whatsoever in its promotion. So on my second book, I thought I'd get more involved in the publicity and promotion. During contract negotiations, I asked the publisher for 300 free review copies. My intent was to send these to appropriate reviewers, TV/radio shows, etc., and I made that clear to the publisher.

"Now everyone knows the cost of printing. The amount of actual cash that the publisher would have had to put on the line for those 300 copies wasn't much. I was going to pay for the postage, follow-up phone calls, etc. How much would the publisher receive in return on that investment of 300 copies? We all know the value of publicity. Yet, when I made this request, you would have thought that I was asking for a six-digit marketing budget! The publisher absolutely refused. All I could get was 10 copies for free. The rest I could purchase for 50 percent of retail! Hey, my royalties were around 12 percent, and it just didn't make financial sense for me to get actively involved in the marketing, putting in my precious time and money, just so that I could get back 12 percent of the publisher's receipts.

My attitude was the heck with them. Just let the book die. And that's what it did."

Roy cited the experience of a friend who wrote two books for Random House. The first book sold like gangbusters—more than 150,000—due in part, to Random's substantial promotional budget. Yet his friend watched helplessly when Random House slashed the ad budget for his second book and sold only 12,000 copies.

"I could go on and on about the large 'respectable' publishing houses," wrote Roy. "I'll sum it up by saying that my experience was that I was at their mercy. It wasn't worth it for me . . . So I graduated to self-publishing."

Rod C. Addicus, owner of Rod C. Addicus Books in Omaha, Neb. which publishes about seven books annually, remarks there are pros and cons to New York houses.

"In 1991, I decided to let Bantam publish my nonfiction book in mass market paperback. They did a nice job. It was a true crime book based on a local regional case. But then they did not reprint after 60,000 books sold out in two months. I had stores calling me at home for months asking if I had any books; customers were asking for it. It was *beyond* aggravating!

"The point is, you do lose control. They can tie up publishing rights for years—seven in my case—and make you wait a long time for your money. On the other hand, back then I was really not ready to start my own publishing business and I did learn a lot from working with my editor at Bantam. It was a good learning experience to translate into my own business. And granted, I didn't have to put out any money. They paid me. Still, in the end, if I had self-published, I probably would have made $30,000 to $40,000 more on the book, given its success in the region."

Besides losing the publishing rights to his book, the author has little to no say in the book's design unless it's negotiated in the contract. There have been many authors disappointed with a dud title, a badly designed cover, paper that looks like newsprint, or print that's too small to read. Unless authors stipulate approval of specific production aspects, it's out of their control.

Commercial publishers certainly have their place in the market, but their inability and unwillingness to change their practices have left the door of opportunity wide open for independent publishers to satisfy the diverse demands of consumers. Independent publishers have commandeered count-less niches with creative marketing and invaluable books.

Which route is best for you: Choosing a traditional publisher or independently publishing?

One of the most frequently pondered questions are the advantages to hook-ing up with a publisher or independently publishing. Of course, the answer is: it depends on your individual circumstances.

Will a New York house do you right?

In the right circumstances, a New York publishing firm is a writer's best choice. Let's say that you have no savings, an excellent full-time job, pos-sess little business savvy, know nothing about promotion nor do you care to, aren't particularly aggressive, but you are a brilliant writer. In fact, you're a writer with a national reputation and have decided to write a novel or nonfiction book with broad appeal. In this case, it makes sense to find a publisher. The publisher can oversee the editing, production details and the marketing campaign so that you can get to work on your next book.

It's not a panacea, however. Most authors can't get the attention of a big publisher. If they are lucky and do sign on, they find the money comes much slower than they expected. And don't count on much, if anything, from royalties. Experienced authors realize that their advance will likely be their only revenue from the book. The more money the publishing house thinks your book will earn, the higher the advance. What is an advance? The amount of money a publishing house pays up front for a book—usu-ally on acceptance or publication. A writer keeps the entire amount no matter how few books are sold. If and when royalties on the books exceed the advance (plus a substantial amount set aside as a reserve for books returned by the bookstores), a writer begins receiving royalty checks.

Larger publishing houses typically pay advances of $10,000 and up and royalties of 8-15 percent of the book's listed retail price (depending on quantity sold).

Usually the amount of your advance from a traditional house will pre-dict the amount of marketing the firm will commit to your book (the lower the advance, the less promotion you can expect. A $10,000 advance probably means very little promotion. For what's called a "midlist book," a New York City firm will send out press releases to the top 300 media and that's it. With a $75,000 advance, the house could go either way. Above that, they usually do invest in an aggressive marketing campaign. In general, a mid-size publisher will promote your book more aggressively, but pay a lower advance.

It is possible to come out a winner even with a big publisher. Make sure your contract spells out what you expect for publicity: i.e., all-expense-paid 10-city tour, review copies sent to library journals and major media, expenses paid for all TV appearances, etc. Many times the publisher will ask for the option for first dibs on your next book. We advise not agreeing to this as it eliminates any sort of auctioning process.

A fairly accurate account of how publishing works is portrayed in Olivia Goldsmith's *The Bestseller*.

Large publishers specialize in books with broad appeal, as opposed to "niche" books, because the market is much bigger. In almost every case, they will reject a niche book appealing to a highly defined market, i.e., a book on running a natural yeast bakery or coping with a schizophrenic child.

To secure a publisher, you normally must find a literary agent who will serve as an intermediary between you and the publisher (a large house will only work through an agent, smaller houses are willing to work directly with an author). An agent will help you put together a book proposal, mail it to the most likely publishers, negotiate an advance and royalties for a fee of 10 to 20 percent, and review your contract to avoid costly pitfalls (some authors make it a point to join the National Writers Union, which reviews members' contracts). Increasingly more authors are requiring that the contract stipulate an author's rights to buy his or her own books at an author discount and sell them through their own outlets.

If your book appears highly desirable, the agent will set up an "auction" of sorts and award the book to the highest bidder.

You can usually get the attention of a publisher or agent by first publishing an article on the subject in a national magazine and including the article and the media's follow-up response with your query. The more enthusiasm you can prove, the better chance you'll have in getting the book sold. Once you have a publisher's interest, you're typically asked to provide three chapters. With a fiction book, however, you'll need to write the *entire* work before securing an agent.

Persuading a good agent to represent you isn't easy, and you'll have to write a query letter similar to what you'd send a publisher. There are many good books on writing a successful query letter, including Michael Larsen's *How to Write a Book Proposal* and Jeff Herman and Deborah Adams' *Write the Perfect Book Proposal.*

HOW DO YOU IDENTIFY A GOOD LITERARY AGENT?

One way is to look at the books that are similar in spirit and subject matter to the one you want to write. Call the author (the publishing firm can usually provide a phone number or call directory assistance in the city where the author lives). Explain to the author that you've written a book and are looking for an agent. Ask about the agent, the author's feelings about the agent, the agent's address, etc.

Also, check out these three excellent resources: Jeff Herman's annually published, *The Insider's Guide to Book Editors, Publishers, and Literary Agents*, the *Writer's Digest* annual directory of agents, The Jenkins Group database of 540 agents (800) 706-4636, and the *Literary Market Place*. Also, try this Internet website to help you collar specific agents: http:// www.accumail.com/. Or do a search on the Internet by typing, literary+agent—you'll get an extensive list of agent names and specialties. Some even answer their e-mail.

WHY GO WITH A SMALL TO MEDIUM PUBLISHER?

Unknown authors and writers of niche books can get completely lost in a big publishing firm, but could potentially perform as a best-seller in a small- to medium-size house. Smaller publishers are far more likely to do niche-type marketing and will promote a book much longer than their big sisters in New York. The drawback of smaller houses is that they pay significantly smaller royalties and advances. Advances range around $3,000 to $10,000— averaging $5,000.

Also royalties from small houses are significantly lower. Some do pay 8 percent to 12 percent of the *list price*, but a new industry practice is to pay that same percentage on cash receipts—the amount the publisher receives for the book. Generally, the cash receipts equate anywhere from 35 to 100 percent of the book's list price, more or less, depending on the sales channels the publisher chooses. The advantage of a smaller house is they assume the risk for publishing a book, all the details on the business end; the publishing house typically cares as much as you do about making your book a success. They are also more likely to pursue alternative channels such as corporate sales.

WHY INDEPENDENTLY PUBLISH?

Independent publishing is free enterprise. It's guerrilla marketing at its finest. Independent publishers can take more risks than major publishers because they know their markets well. Independent publishers can control their own destinies. They can manage the publishing process from the moment of conception to the day the book hits the shelves.

Control is number one on the list of reasons to publish independently. After all, if *you* don't believe in your book, why should another publisher? And if you really do believe in your book, why sell it to someone else? As the independent publisher, you will edit the content, choose the title, pick the cover design, determine the price, plan the promotion, and collect all the profits. And nobody will do it with more attention and care than you will.

The second reason is speed. You have a target market; you believe there are thousands of readers who need your book. Who can afford to pursue the time-consuming task of courting major publishers while their manuscript collects dust mites? For the most part, big publishers are lumbering giants, slow to get a book finished and into stores (there are a few striking exceptions, such as the myriad of books on the O.J. Simpson trial). On average, though, it takes 18 months for a book to go through the publishing process.

If you can strike while a trend is hot, you can greatly boost your chances for success. With proper planning, you can leapfrog from writing to selling in six months or less. Fewer stops along the chain of command mean the process moves along faster and, usually, the first to the marketplace wins.

Another benefit for the independent publisher is profit. Conventional wisdom suggests that as an independent publisher you can earn up to 50 percent of a book's cover price compared to the much smaller fraction collected as royalties.

Another reason to independently publish: consistent and continued marketing will build steady demand for your book and generate greater income over a longer period of time. That contrasts with New York houses that give a book about three months to perform and then retitle it, *R.I.P.*

Another huge advantage to independently publishing a book is that you possess *all* rights. Not only publishing rights, but audio rights and foreign sales rights. Compare that with the typical agreement of sharing rights sales with a small publisher.

Finally, independent publishers are more flexible. They do not rely solely on bookstores to supply the target audience with their titles. They *find* consumers where they live, work, and play.

THE IDEAL INDEPENDENT PUBLISHER

No one can predict success, but the highest odds are in the court of the niche book publisher. Large publishers often reject special-interest books because the profit potential is too paltry. You might be surprised at what a publisher might consider a "small" market. Randi Kreger, who proposed a book on borderline personality disorder—a book that she said will appeal to the six million people afflicted with the disorder plus another 18 million people who care for these people—was told by several publishers that they considered the market too small.

Have you written a uniquely slanted book that's spiritual in nature, soul reviving, or philosophical in tone? Over and over again, these kind of books have been rejected by New York houses only to rise to the top. Here's a short list: *The Girls with the Grandmother Faces, The Five Rituals of Wealth, Zapp: The Lightning of Empowerment, Just As I Am, Mutant Message Down Under, The Celestine Prophecy,* and *When I Am Old Woman I Shall Wear Purple.*

Books with a broad market appeal have a much tougher road to travel. Those who have succeeded have often sold their book—often inspirational—through seminars or speeches or a groundswell of demand that began in their hometown.

Before sitting down and writing that self-help book, however, be aware that it's one of the most popular genres of small presses—and most of these books are either trite or terrible.

But if you truly believe your book is a diamond in the rough, don't despair. There are ways of determining if you really do have a best seller on your hands before investing a huge fortune. Let's get started.

2

WHEN YOU THINK YOU HAVE A SPECTACULAR BOOK IDEA . . .

*The person who is swimming against the stream
knows the strength of it.*
WOODROW WILSON

BEFORE YOU TAKE THE PLUNGE INTO INDEPENDENT PUBLISHING, YOU should know that the current is strong. Book reviewers, distributors, and bookstores are unkind to neophytes and will quickly dismiss a self-proclaimed independent publisher or an amateur-looking book. Do your homework on the front end, and you'll be thankful once the book is in print.

READ THE FUNDAMENTAL HOW-TO'S

There are no stupid questions in this world, but a sure way to raise the ire of veteran publishers is to ask a fundamental question that's well-covered in the independent publishing world's classics:

- Dan Poynter's *The Self-Publishing Manual*
- Tom and Marilyn Ross's *The Complete Guide to Self-Publishing*
- Avery Cardoza's *The Complete Guide to Successful Book Publishing*.

These books emphasize bookstore sales and traditional publicity efforts. Read them. In addition to marketing advice, they comprehensively cover book production and management angles. Here are additional resources:

- An absolute must-have reference book is the *Literary MarketPlace*.

- Best picks for marketing guides include: *Publishing to Niche Markets* by Gordon Burgett and John Kremer's *1,001 Ways to Market Your Book* and *Book Marketing Made Easier*. Kremer offers a wealth of ideas and systematic worksheets; Burgett's is the best book written on selling to tightly defined markets.

- For industry overviews, read John Dessauer's *Book Publishing; What It Is, What it Does* and editor Elizabeth Geiser's, *The Business of Book Publishing*.

- For inspiration, read *Inside the Bestsellers* by Jerrold Jenkins with Mardi Link and *For All the Write Reasons* by Patricia Gallagher.

- Option resources: *How to Make a Fortune in Self-Publishing* by James E. Neal, Jr., *The Prepublishing Handbook* by Patricia J. Bell, *Book Publishing Encyclopedia* by Ronald Ted Smith, and *A Simple Guide to Self-Publishing* by Mark Ortman.

REACHING OUT

Besides reading books, we strongly advise talking to living, breathing publishers, a practice which in the 1980s took on the term "networking." Fortunately, independent publishers are a friendly lot and are often willing to take time out to give advice.

Talking to these publishers about your idea will help you crystallize your reasons and expectations for independently publishing a book. As an independent publisher you may enjoy your autonomy, but you'll lack the information, resources, and teams of specialists afforded by large corporations. There's no opportunity to walk down the hall and ask, "What do you think about such-and-such?" There's no one to tell if a firm is headed by a rip-off artist or a marketing genius.

Independent publishers also complain that running their own companies has afflicted them with severe myopia. They are so engrossed with the day-to-day details that they've lost perspective on the book industry as a whole.

How to get out of the tunnel? The absolute easiest way is to get on an Internet mailing list, an electronic forum of sorts where people of similar interests post messages to the group as a whole. These messages show up in your e-mailbox. Here are a couple of suggestions:

Publishers Marketing Association Forum: This is a feisty list, where publishers ask for help and share advice. Lots of the input for this book came from participants on the PMA Listserv. This is a must-join. Be prepared, though, for about 50 to 70 e-mails a day. To join, send an e-mail to listserv@hslc.org. In the message block, type: *SUBSCRIBE PMA-L yourfirstname yourlastname.*

John Kremer's Book Market Online, a high quality but less trafficked list, focuses on book marketing. Subscribers are invited to share information and help solve problems. Send e-mail to majordomo@bookzone.com. You don't need to fill in the subject line, but in the message block, type: *subscribe bookmarket.* If you want it in digest form, type: *digest book market.*

Finally, if your interest is in audio publishing, join the Audio Publisher's Association. Send an e-mail to listserv@hslc.org. Leave the subject line blank. In the message area, type: *subscribe audiobooks yourfirstname yourlastname.*

If your book is new age, join the NAPRA New Age Bookstore Network. Send to majordomo@pacificrim.net. Leave subject line blank; in the message area, type: *subscribe napra-bookstore.*

Another resource: independent publishers and writers groups in your area. Bounce off your book idea unless you feel they might steal it. (If you're the only one uniquely qualified to write the book or it's taken you years of research, don't worry about theft). They can also give you the ins and outs of printers and regional distributors.

Don't limit your networking contacts to publishers. Seek out writers, editors, graphic designers, agents, distributors, printers, booksellers and marketing and public relations professionals. Again, proceed with caution. While you want to get feedback on your idea, you don't want someone to rip off your idea.

Build the foundation for your network by reading trade publications such as *Publishers Weekly*, *Small Press* magazine, *Publishing Entrepreneur*, John Kremer's *Book Marketing Update*, *Subtext* published out of Darien, Connecticut, *Bookselling this Week*, *PMA Newsletter* published by the Publishers Marketing Association, and the *SPAN Connection* published by the Small Press Alliance of North America (SPAN). They can give you a good handle on who's who and keep you up to date on best sellers and buy-outs. In addition to providing the inside track on industry trends and technology, they include lots of tips on marketing and production.

To expand your network, attend conferences and seminars. Although this event isn't intended for publisher wannabes, the BookExpo America (formerly called the American Booksellers Association Convention and Trade Exhibit), held annually in Chicago, is by far the largest in the country, hosting literally hundreds of publishers and booksellers. There are also smaller regional trade shows held throughout the country, which many publishers find more valuable than BookExpo America because they're not as frenetic. Besides giving you a feel for the industry, trade shows are a perfect place to check out the catalogs of small and large publishers alike.

Once you become a publisher, consider yourself a member of a special club. You'll find that your colleagues are witty, smart, and supportive. Association memberships provide a ready-made network. The two biggest are the Independent Publishers Network (IPN), organized by The Jenkins Group, Publisher's Marketing Association (PMA), and Small Press Alliance of North America (SPAN). The smaller publisher associations are listed in the Encyclopedia of Associations.

DECIDING ON A BOOK IDEA

There is nothing so useless as doing efficiently
that which should not be done at all.
PETER DRUCKER

Every book published falls into one of three categories: information, entertainment and a combination of the two. When authors create a non-fiction or how-to book, they are providing information for the reader. They are imparting knowledge, research, instruction, data, facts, assistance, advice, intelligence, or wisdom. On the other hand, fiction provides an escape, a diversion, a source of fun, or amusement. And, of course, there are books that straddle the fence between the two: accounts of how or why that are laced with humor, or fictional stories heavily intertwined with real-life backdrops. Tom Clancy, a former insurance salesman, is a good example of the latter. Before he wrote his first fiction book, he heavily researched the military field, combing 300 books for background data.

Your publishing strategy will depend on the nature of your book. A nonfiction, niche book is probably the easiest of all books to sell for an independent publisher. Books on rubber stamping, how to backpack with a baby, or passing a standardized public school test would all be considered niche books. What's even easier to sell than nonfiction books are nonfiction books written with a hint of wit or humor. Northern Michigan author Dick Mallery, who signed a six-figure advance with Bantam, Doubleday, Dell to publish a bird-feeding book for beginners, explained to a *Traverse City Record-Eagle* reporter why his book was worth the steep advance.

"It's going to be like *Bird Feeding 101*, kind of a textbook attempt in a tongue-in-beak fashion at feeding birds," Mallery said. "Most other books have made the subject as dry as toast, and we're going to change all that."

Arthur Naiman wrote one of the most entertaining books ever on computers, *The Macintosh Bible,* and was rewarded with sales of more than 400,000 copies. Interestingly, he had already published 12 books with several traditional publishing companies, but complained that editors had stripped his work of his quirky humor. His unusual blend of reference and comedy justified his hefty price tag of $32 and pushed *The Macintosh Bible* to the top-selling computer book ever written on the Mac.

IS IT POSSIBLE TO INDEPENDENTLY PUBLISH FICTION?

Yes, but it's difficult. Big-name fiction authors are dominating the market like never before. That said, there are outrageously successful exceptions such as *The Christmas Box* and *The Celestine Prophecy.* These authors sent their manuscripts to several entrenched publishing firms, but a long line of rejection letters persuaded them to independently publish. Marketing independently published fiction is, in fact, so difficult that most authors will sign up with a major publisher after "proving" their book is marketable.

Speaking of big-name fiction authors, when John Grisham (one of the richest, if not *the* richest writer today) tried to sell his first best-selling novel, *A Time to Kill*, he was rejected by more than 100 publishers. It was finally picked up by a very small press, which printed 5,000 copies. The press did very little to promote the book, so Grisham took matters into his own hands. He bought 1,000 copies of his own book and spent weekend after weekend visiting Mississippi bookstores, garden clubs, and libraries. Word of mouth kept building, and the first printing sold out. Ultimately, Grisham landed a contract with a major publisher, which sold more than 10 million copies of the rejected novel.

Many of the successful independent publishers today, such as Marcella Chester, the author/publisher of *Cherry Love*, are selling fiction books by focusing on a subject matter that allows for *target marketing*—the same strategy employed by nonfiction book authors. For example, *Cherry Love*, a novel about a woman who was raped, appeals to certain types of women's catalogs, the women's studies departments at universities, rape awareness advocacy groups, etc.

If children's fiction and poetry are your interest, be forewarned that they are the most speculative and risky of all book markets. There are several reasons why. The juvenile market has resisted price increases, and, with four-color the norm, production costs are much higher for children's books than general trade books. A publisher needs to print and sell huge numbers of children's books to become profitable. Not only is there a built-in downside for profits, children today fill much of their leisure time with movies, videos, television, and video games and have little time left for reading books. Plus, there's already a glut of children's books. While we would never want to discourage a publisher from trying to market a great children's book—a few independently published books do indeed succeed each year—we want to offer a realistic picture of the market.

The most important decision you will make as a publisher is the subject of your book. If it's nonfiction, the subject must be original or offer a fresh slant. To find out whether a book already exists on the topic, you'll need to do some research.

📖   📖   📖

Getting the Wheels Turning on a Great Novel

Any experienced fiction writer knows how difficult it is to find a publisher. It's even difficult to find a good agent to pitch a novel to a publisher. The strategy of many a good writer: self-publish to gain enough attention to attract a good publisher.

Jack McBride White, for example, could be called the reluctant independent publisher. He first tried the traditional route. He sent his book, *The Keeper of the Ferris Wheel*—a coming-of-age account during the Vietnam war era—to several agents, who rejected the subject as unmarketable, according to a 1996 *Writer's Digest* article.

An agent finally agreed to represent the book, but she failed to sell it after a year. She rejected his second novel attempt, the article said.

White told *Writer's Digest* reporter Robin Gee that he knew he had a good book and that it ought to be published. So he bought a few books on the subject of self-publishing and printed 2,000 hardcover copies.

He found the book extremely difficult to market. He sold only a few books at readings in Washington, D.C., where he lived, and only a few local bookstores were willing to take the book. Sales were dismal and White was nowhere near to recouping his investment. Realizing that he had to do more to draw attention to the book, he entered the book in the *Writer's Digest* 1993 Self-Publishing Awards competition and won. He also sent the book and a letter to *Washington Post* reviewer David Streitfeld, who responded with a column, the article said.

The award and column finally attracted the interest of two publishers, including Donald I. Fine who brought the book out in hardcover in 1995.

White told *Writer's Digest* that he doesn't necessarily recommend independent publishing, but a confident writer must be prepared to do anything to make things happen.

"If you really believe in your work and you're really passionate about it, I think you should explore every possible avenue, like writing letters to guys at the Washington Post, entering contests, self-publishing, banging your head against whatever door you find, and someday something will open up."

Getting Lucky Online

We won't kid you and tell you that any author can be this lucky, but Franklin White's story does prove one point: the more you can get the word out about your book to the right people, the better chances you have that good, maybe even great, things will happen.

Franklin White self-published his first novel, *Fed Up With The Fanny*, and decided to talk about it on an American Online site called Book Central, according to a February 17, 1997 *Publishers Weekly* article.

The monthly chat forum was hosted by Laurie Chittenden, a young associate editor at Simon & Schuster. White wrote that his book centered around the relationships of an African American man and four African American women. He talked about his specific concerns about self-publishing and mentioned the book was beginning to do well. Later that week, he called Chittenden to "touch base" and sent the book to her to read for herself, the article said.

"I read the book immediately, fell in love with it, shared it with other people at Simon & Schuster, and they loved it. And we bought it," Chittenden said in the article.

Fanny will be published in the spring of 1998, and White is now at work on his second novel.

📖

Booksellers Conjuring up a Success

Swain Wolfe's first self-published book, *The Woman Who Lives In The Earth*, was carried to success on the good word of independent booksellers. Like his book, the events were almost magical.

His manuscript first came to the attention of independent bookseller Barbara Theroux, owner of Fact & Fiction, a Missoula bookstore, completely by accident. The manuscript was from Farrar, Straus & Giroux and included a letter of rejection. When Wolfe, who worked down the street from the bookstore, came to pick it up, he chatted with Theroux and asked her to read it and to give him her opinion, according to a Dec. 18, 1995, *Publishers Weekly* article.

Well, Theroux loved it, and ushered Wolfe's self-published books into her store in January 1993. So did independent bookseller Lisa Gesner, who said the book literally fell on her lap when she was cleaning up after an event at the Boulder Book Store. Coincidentally, Wolfe called Gesner the next day and offered to give a reading at the store, the article said.

Theroux was such a fan of the book, she helped Wolfe launch a word-of-mouth marketing campaign. They sent galleys to 75 to 100 independent bookstores and to book-review journals. They took the feedback from the booksellers and quoted the best on the jacket cover, then shipped jackets and ordering instructions (through Pacific Pipeline) to 700 more book stores, all independents. Wolfe followed up with phone calls, offering to give readings. He also made it easy for the booksellers, by designing postcards and broadsides to advertise the event. Fifteen of the bookstores took him up on his offer, according to the article.

After eight months, Wolfe had sold out his first printing of 2,200 copies. In total, he went through five printings and sold 8,100 copies, gaining a broader audience each time. The bookstore owners were his greatest ally. At the Boulder Book Store, for example, Gesner placed Wolfe's books in the recommended reading section with a "glowing shelf-talker," the article said. Gesner also sent letters to other bookstores saying how much she liked the books and how well it sold. Five booksellers liked it so much they sent copies of the book to HarperCollins. But it wasn't until Harper publisher Jack McKeown stopped by the Boulder Book Store that he discovered the book. He asked Gesner what self-published books were selling best, and she told him they couldn't keep Wolfe's book on the shelves. The end of the story, like all fables, was magical. HarperCollins bought the book in a deal that included an audio book and a second book—still unwritten—testifying to their faith in the author's talents. The amount remains undisclosed, but as Wolfe modestly says in the article: "It got me out of debt, and I'll get to write for awhile."

📖   📖   📖

RESEARCHING YOUR CHOSEN SUBJECT

There are a number of ways to research existing books. First, check out *Books in Print* published by R.R. Bowker. This publication lists all books in print—about 1.3 million—by author and by subject. The book (also formatted on a CD-ROM) is generally available in libraries.

For *Deer Camp Dictionary*, for example, Rhodes & Easton checked *Books in Print* and found books on deer hunting, most of them very serious. They also called up deer-hunting magazine editors and asked if they'd seen anything similar to the *Deer Camp Dictionary* idea.

Has an article been published on the topic recently in a major magazine? Call the writer and ask what kind of books he came across during his research.

Consider the bibliographies compiled by nonprofit organizations. Is your book about exercising for a healthy heart? Call the American Heart Association and ask for its bibliography on heart books.

Get on the Internet and find the mailing lists that relate to the subject. Ask the participants if they've ever heard of a book similar to the one you want to write and if they think there's a need for it. (For details on locating a mailing list, turn to Chapter 20, "How To Sell And Publicize Your Book On The Internet.")

While you're on the Internet, visit www.amazon.com—an electronic bookstore that publishes the majority of books in print. Once you've ascertained that no other book has been written on the subject, or at least none from your unique perspective, you can test market your idea.

IS THE AUTHOR MARKETABLE?

Although a book's subject matter is important, the author's marketability ranks extremely high when considering a particular book project. Is the author outgoing and charismatic? Will the author "give good interview?" Does the author have sufficient credentials? How many books can the author sell through seminars and classes? This is a key point because it lowers the break-even point of sales since these books are sold at full price. Given an over-saturated book market, an author who can't promote a book does not bode well for success.

DEFINING YOUR TARGET AUDIENCE

Your marketing strategy must be driven by one thought: Who is your audience and how can you reach them?

When you think of your book, think "positioning." Write a description of the book and the audience to whom it will appeal. Address these questions:

- How is your book better than the competition?
- Is it more comprehensive, easier to read, more practical, less technical, does it cover an area that, so far, has been left untouched by others?
- What are the discretionary spending patterns of your target audience?
- What related organizations and associations do they belong to?
- Are there enough buyers to profitably sell to? Where do they buy books or merchandise related to the book?

- Who will buy the book? Are there enough of these people to support your endeavor?

- How will this book help them solve problems, achieve goals, or enhance their lives?

- Is their need so great that they would be willing to pay the price of your book?

- What is their socioeconomic status?

Once you define your potential buyer, you must answer this single question: *How many people belong to my target audience?* Here are some resources to help you answer that question.

- There are more than 10,000 catalogs in circulation. We include a partial listing of "catalogs of catalogs" Chapter 17, "The Art Of Getting Your Books Into Catalogs."

- To research magazines, check out *Consumer Magazine* and *Agri-Media Rates and Data*. Both provide information about magazines' rates, editorial focus, and circulation numbers.

- Contact government departments and/or nonprofit groups and associations for available lists and rental/sales prices. Your research should answer the question: *What are the total number of people in the intended market?*

- The *Direct Marketing List Source*, published by Standard Rate and Data Services, features thousands of list providers. It provides detail on how the lists can be subdivided, the form of labels, use restrictions, the number of names listed, sometimes by category.

- The *Statistical Abstract of the United States* published by the U.S. Census Bureau may shed light on your intended audiences.

- Get into the "heads" of the target audience. A good way, suggests author Gordon Burgett, is to join the associations of your targeted readers. He explains in *Publishing to Niche Markets* that "You will have a better, more intimate sense of the group's problems and needs, you will have a better understanding of its buying practices and preferences, you may have access to the group's leaders or others more knowledgeable about the topic of your book, and you may have preferred access to the group's newsletter, mailing list, convention or meeting plans, and other 'inside' information."

CAN YOUR BOOK MAKE MONEY?

Because profits are so marginal selling to bookstores and promotional expenses so high, many publishers are now rejecting trade books that can be sold *only* in bookstores.

The advice shared in a July/August 1988 issue of *Small Press Review* by industry analyst and publisher Len Fulton seemed prescient, considering the realities of the 1990s:

" . . . my advice to small publishers has always been to arrange their planning for distribution in a sort of tier: (1) Develop and use a mailing list, and sell it at full retail price; (2) Develop a relationship with jobbers who buy small quantities at a shorter discount and pay reliably; (3) Then, if you still have stock to risk, consign some of it to reliable distributors and have them sign an agreement that this stock belongs to you, not them, that they are merely warehousing it (this helps protect your stock if they go bankrupt); and (4) Sell to bookstores on a special-order basis.

Some books, of course, will not do well with a direct-mail approach. But as you explore a book project, do seriously consider rejecting it if it fails to fit in at least three alternative markets, including: direct mail, libraries, academic market, foreign markets, book clubs, specialty retailers, over the Internet, or to corporations/organizations.

3

TEST BEFORE YOU INVEST.
IT NEVER HURTS TO ASK.
AND ASK. AND ASK.

No man really becomes a fool
until he stops asking questions.
CHARLES P. STEINMETZ

TEST MARKETING A BOOK SOUNDS A LITTLE STRANGE—HOW CAN YOU test market something that hasn't been produced yet? But it's possible to test an idea for a book or even a modest print run. We're going to discuss four strategies: planting articles in the media, conducting a survey on the Internet, sending out questionnaires to the target readers or book buyers, and test marketing with a short print run.

PLANTING ARTICLES

Many an author has found herself writing a book after receiving a huge media response from an article or a speech. They used the evidence of this response to get a foot in a publisher's door. If they can prove to a publisher that an article has hit a nerve and would make for a phenomenal best seller, they have already made the sale. Planting articles also works extremely well for niche books, said Wally Bock, president of Bock Information Group, which specializes in niche publications to police supervisors. "I work on the enduring belief that no one can predict what the market will do," Bock said.

Bock will write an article on a specific topic to gauge the target audience's reaction. He'll even take the same article and lead with different headlines to see if the response varies. Obviously, the most popular headline usually becomes the title of the book.

He places the articles in trade magazines, on the Internet's various libraries, and in industry newsletters—all royalty-free and copyright free.

"If people start calling me, I've got a good idea," Bock said. "Nine out of ten times, I don't. But I'd rather find out writing an article than writing a book."

Bock's first press run averages 500 copies. If the book sells, he'll proceed with a full press run. If it doesn't, he hasn't lost that much money. About one of the eight books he test markets at this quantity qualifies for a full-print run.

Publishers need to ask prospective customers and book buyers for their reaction to a book and then *objectively* assess their reaction. Too often, authors/publishers pursue their project with the blind faith that reviews and advertising will make their books a success, said marketing consultant and writer Herman Holtz.

"Author Joe Karbo reduced test marketing to a fine formula that made great sense. He ran his initial advertisements for a small book titled *The Lazy Mans Way to Riches* before he wrote the book," Holtz said. "Had he gotten only a handful of orders at $10 each, he would have returned the money with apologies and abandoned the project. But he got enough orders to tell him that he had a winner. He then wrote the little book, about 160 pages, and had it printed.

"This is not always a practical plan for the typical publishing project, of course, but it illustrates my point," Holtz said.

INTERNET SURVEYS

Even if you're not terribly comfortable with the Internet, consider publishing a test-market survey on the World Wide Web. This can serve several purposes: you can measure interest in the book and find out where your target audience would like to buy it and you can gather and tabulate surveys to be used in the book itself. Finally, you can call the more interesting respondents and include their comments in the book. It's wise to keep the names of your e-mail correspondents and promote the book to them after it's published.

In the survey, indicate that you are thinking of writing a book on the topic. The elements of your note should include:

  • A short description of the book.

  • Tentative title(s).

  • A table of contents.

  • The author's background and credentials.

  • The number of pages.

  • The target audience.

  • The mission of the book.

Then ask what you want to know:

  • Would they buy such a book?

  • What else would they like to see in the book?

  • Which title do they like best?

  • What are *their* most pressing problems in the given subject area?

  • Where would they want to buy the book?

  • What would they be willing to pay for such a book?

If you want to run results of an unscientific survey within the book's text, ask questions in a form that could be tabulated for the book. Try to pose the questions in as unbiased fashion as possible. If the survey is humorous, more people tend to fill it out.

We give this advice with a caveat: there are literally millions of websites on the Internet. If you try this, you must either hire a professional to promote your site or learn how to do it yourself. (We offer detailed advice on how to do so in Chapter 20, "How To Sell And Publicize Your Book On The Internet.") No one will come to your web site unless you draw them there and set up links throughout the Internet. The cost of getting the survey adapted to the Web ranges from $50 to $500. Hiring someone to promote the site costs about $500.

It's important a survey isn't overly long. You'll get better results if you offer an incentive such as a random drawing for a $100 gift certificate or a gift related to the book topic. Finally, ensure respondents that the surveys are strictly confidential and that their name and address are optional.

Also consider joining the various newsgroups, folders, or topics. An Internet mailing list is a file that stores a group of names and their e-mail addresses with a common interest. Members will get all the e-mail messages each day from the participating subscribers. A newsgroup is exactly the same as a mailing list in appearance, but it's accessed by using a newsgroup reader program provided by your Internet Service Provider. There are about 100,000 mailing lists and the numbers grow each day, writes Michael Mathiesen in *Marketing on the Internet*.

You can even create your very own mailing list. There are several reasons to do this: to gather material for the topic you want to write about, to solicit input on what the book should include, and to find potential book buyers. Mathiesen explains clearly and concisely in his book how to set up a mailing list. It isn't difficult nor is it expensive, but it is time-consuming to maintain.

If the Internet sounds complicated, it isn't. Randi Kreger, co-author of *Get Off the Emotional Roller Coaster* (to be released by New Harbinger Publications in fall 1998), was completely new to the Internet. Yet most of her book research and test marketing was conducted on the Net and on America Online. She simply learned as she went along.

Kreger's book is about coping with someone who has borderline personality disorder. Here's her story.

Kreger initially became interested in the topic of borderline personality disorders when someone in her life was diagnosed with BPD. People with this disorder blame, rage, and generally try to cope with their pain by getting others to feel it for them. Out of the hundreds of published studies about BPD, Kreger could find only one book that addressed the topic of helping friends and partners cope.

Kreger realized that thousands of others needed a book for support and guidance; BPD afflicts an estimated 6 million people. Another 18 million lives are affected, assuming each person with BDP has three close friends or family members.

Her hunch was confirmed when she logged onto America Online and searched AOL folders and Internet newsgroups for information about BPD. Both borderlines and non-borderlines—the friends and family members of the borderline—were desperate for information. Their only resource was a 300-page technical book geared to psychiatrists.

"People had a hard time finding even basic information. Can it be cured? How do you cope with someone who blames and criticizes you all the time?" Kreger said.

Kreger teamed up with a psychotherapist, Paul Mason, and together they gathered information for a book proposal. They combed the research and interviewed borderlines, non-BPs, and therapists they found on the Internet.

"People on the Internet really open up because it's totally anonymous," said Kreger. "It's like a colossal recovery support group in the biggest church basement in the world. People were eager to tell their stories and grateful that someone was finally addressing their needs."

Kreger created two Internet mailing-list support groups for non-BPs. With the help of volunteer programmers she "met" on the Internet, she assembled an extensive World Wide Web site. The site, BPD Central, promoted the upcoming book. It also invited Web surfers to give Kreger their Internet addresses so that she could notify them when the book came out. She began amassing a mailing list of hundreds of potential book buyers.

But the New York publishers weren't as excited about the book as Kreger and Mason. They were looking for books with mass appeal and didn't consider a potential audience of 24 million—6 million borderlines, 18 million non-BPs, and 750,000 mental-health professionals—large enough. So Kreger and Mason considered self-publishing.

This is where the lists really paid off. Kreger asked list members if they would buy a book for non-BPs, and, if so, how much they would pay. Because members were so supportive of the project, she also asked them if they would lend her the interest-free funds to independently publish a book.

"Self-publishing can easily cost $20,000," said Kreger. "We knew we couldn't do it on our own. At first, we hesitated to ask people for money. None of them had ever met us in person. But it was either that or give up the book."

The results were staggering. All together, list members offered to lend her $25,000. A graphic designer offered to produce the book for free. In response to the question about what they would pay for such a book, several people said, "Whatever you charge."

"I was overwhelmed by the response," said Kreger. "Like me, the non-borderlines on the Net had spent years in pain searching for answers. They really wanted to make sense of their experience by helping others."

Kreger also sent an online survey to 500 clinicians she found by performing a member search on America Online. About 7 percent said they would purchase the book. This was important because the members of this specialized audience were relatively easy to reach. More importantly, they could refer the book to clients.

"Seven percent of a total audience of 750,000 is a lot of book buyers," said Kreger. "Even if only half that number actually bought the book, the revenue potential was enormous."

Ultimately, Kreger and Mason decided not to independently publish after finding a publisher at the 1996 American Booksellers Association's trade show.

Although Kreger now had a publisher, she was concerned about how to help people on the Internet who wanted material immediately.

"By now, Paul and I had developed a 10-step program for people who cared about someone with BPD who would not seek help or admit that they had a problem," said Kreger. "There was no way I could ask the hundreds of people on my list to wait 18 months for the book to come out."

In addition, Kreger knew she was losing sales. Each time she sent a message to her list, several bounced back. That meant that recipients were changing their Internet addresses without informing her.

So Kreger and Mason decided to publish a 24-page booklet for non-BPs and promote it on the Internet and via publicity. They priced it at $10.

Kreger proceeded to write the booklet, but realized it would have to be twice as long to include the necessary information. So this time, she que-

ried her mailing lists about whether she should cut the information or hike
the price. Ninety percent suggested she hike the price, which she did to
$15, including postage.

Within 30 days after publication, she and Mason sold 220 copies via an
800 number, e-mail, and mail order. And they collected pages of unsolicited praise from grateful readers.

"One person who used the techniques in the booklet told me that this
was the first time in her marriage that her borderline spouse opened up and
made himself vulnerable," she said. "And after reading the booklet, many
people ordered more for therapists and other family members. A woman
from Finland ordered five copies."

Kreger considers herself a facilitator as well as an author.

"Many of my ideas about how to cope came from the borderlines themselves," she said. "For example, I asked them how loved ones should react
to out-of-control rages. They told me that fear of abandonment lay behind
the raging, and they suggested ways that non-BPs could protect themselves while still being sensitive to the borderline's needs."

Kreger gives this advice for would-be Internet marketers:

"Selling on the Internet is about developing relationships. Trust is crucial. You can't just post messages on newsgroups and mailing lists offering
something for sale. People will chop your head off. They want to know,
'Are you here to make a buck or are you here to help me?' If you appear to
be there simply to make a buck, they'll fill your mailbox with flames (in-
sults).

"But by the time I actually had a booklet to sell, I had already established my credibility. People knew who I was. Not only were people willing
to buy, they were eager to help by promoting the book in their community."

Kreger's long-term dream is to conduct seminars with her coauthor
around the country and educate both therapists and consumers about this
pervasive, debilitating disorder. "I'm like the non-BPs on my list," she
said. "I wanted to create meaning out of my own painful experience.

"If I added up the time I've spent and divided it by the money I've
made so far, I'd probably made 50 cents an hour. Financially, I would have
been better off sticking to my public relations and marketing business.

"But that's not what this project has been about. It's about following a dream, and clinging to it despite the difficulties and the naysayers. And when I get messages from people who tell me that I've helped them tremendously, it's all been worth it."

TEST MARKETING USING THE U.S. MAIL

Can you trust your friends to give you an honest opinion about your book? Not likely, said author Gordon Burgett, author of *Publishing to Niche Markets.*

"They would rather tell you what you want to hear than what they really feel," he wrote.

His advice is to mail a survey to a limited number of people whom you've defined as your target audience. He suggests contacting a list renter and explain what you're doing. Normally, a rental list costs $100 or more. He suggests asking for a test sample of 50 to 200 now for a low introductory price. Of course, if they don't agree to that, you'll have to rent the list at the full price or find names from another source.

Good sources, he suggests, are members' names from associations, club rosters, or from professional listings in phone books. Again, the Internet can be a good source for names. Check out the website, www. bigyellow.com/. It can provide names of narrowly defined businesses by state.

Burgett advises that the best way to protect your book idea from getting stolen is to avoid mentioning it to association officers, all media folk, seminar speakers, or authors in the field.

As to the direct-mail piece, he suggests: "Keep the number tested small and select, make your presentation to them professional in tone and appearance, imply that the book is nearly ready for release, and tell them only what is necessary for them to make a valid response," he wrote.

What to send them? Describe the book, tentative titles, contents, length, purpose, your targeted reader. Again, ask them what you want to know. Would they buy the book with your proposed title (or ask them to choose their favorite of three titles)? Would they pay your asking price? Do they have any comments?

Your responses should probably arrive within a couple of weeks. Take the percentage of affirmative responses and multiply it by the estimated number of people in your estimated total market. Take that number and multiply it times 50 percent of the list price. The numbers will tell you whether your project is worth the gamble.

Some people are test marketing their books by first producing smaller or more rudimentary versions of the final product. We don't believe this is a true test since the product doesn't look as polished or professional as a book would.

Another thing to consider: if people are in an artificial survey environment, they usually respond to questions taking the high road. For example, let's take a book on Bach's music with two proposed covers: one with a naked woman, covered only by the violin and her long hair, or a cover with a stylized violin. Your respondent would probably go on record saying he liked the stylized violin best. Yet if they were *really* browsing, they'd likely be drawn to the sexier cover. So when you're trying to test a cover, place the books in as real a retail setting as you possibly can.

TEST MARKET THE FIRST PRINTING

We believe that the book's first printing can serve as a test market. Print between 3,000 and 10,000, but no more, even if you have unlimited resources. There is truly no way to predict the popularity of a book except by getting it out there.

For her first printing of the best-selling *Mutant Message Down Under*, Marlo Morgan ordered only 300 copies. Reader response was so overwhelming that Morgan hit the lecture circuit. Ultimately, after she sold 370,000 copies, HarperCollins purchased the rights for $1.7 million.

Richard Paul Evans originally printed only 20 copies of *The Christmas Box* just to share with his family. When his Salt Lake City neighbors and friends started asking for copies, he printed 3,000 and sold the books mainly in the West. By the time Simon and Schuster bought the hard-cover rights, he had sold 700,000 copies.

With *Deer Camp Dictionary*, Rhodes & Easton printed 7,500 and kept the distribution confined to northern Michigan, the hunting destination for literally tens of thousands of deer hunters each year. Fashioning the book as an impulse buy, Mark Dressler, publisher of Rhodes & Easton, priced it at $8.95 and provided every store with a blazing orange point of purchase display.

The response was even better than he predicted. A beer distributor bought 1,300 books, several gas station chains bought several hundred books at a time, and party stores snapped them up, ordering the required minimum of one dozen. Three weeks after the book's release, 6,000 were sold. Promotion was minimal, save for radio interviews and signings at party stores, restaurants, and bars.

For a minimal investment, Dressler discovered that the book hit the mark and can now present a proven sales record to stores throughout the country. He plans to spend next summer setting up distribution in eight more deer-hunting states so that by September, it will be just a matter of shipping out the books.

"It's the whole idea of being creative. For this book, we're approaching marketing in a completely lighthearted way," Dressler said.

4.

THE BUSINESS END OF THINGS

Knowledge comes by taking things apart (analysis).
But wisdom comes by putting things together.
JOHN A. MORRISON

As a publisher, you'll need to build a marketing plan to use as a business road map, and perhaps to show investors. Let's start with the four Ps: Product, Place, Promotion, and Price to serve as the framework of your business proposal.

PRODUCT

You want to create a saleable product to a specific audience. Plan your pitch and packaging. The latter is more of a consideration for books sold in gift stores, or a children's book sold anywhere. A packet of seeds, for example, with a child's book on gardening. A bag of balloons attached to a book on how to give the ultimate birthday party. For sales estimates, draw on your marketing research on size of audience and the response of the test market.

PLACE

What is the best way to distribute your book? List your marketing channels in order of profitability and how many books you expect to sell in each. Ask yourself:

+ Where will your audience shop for your kind of book?

+ Is your book more of an impulse buy or a book someone would invest in to solve a specific problem?

+ An impulse book belongs in specialty stores, whereas the latter will likely do better in bookstores.

Your answers from the questions above will drive your marketing channels. Each channel, of course, comes with its own advantages or disadvantages.

+ Catalog and book clubs buy bigger quantities of books at once, but the profit margin is slim.

+ Specialty stores. We're talking here about every retail store that's not a bookstore: gift stores, cooking stores, and hardware stores, for example. They pay 50 percent of the list price and these stores *keep* all the books they sell. Also, little promotion is required since purchases in these venues are prompted by impulse.

+ Selling direct to readers. For niche books, consider direct mail or classified magazine ads. However, to keep the profit margins high enough, you'll need to offer a package of complementary products— two books and a video, for example.

+ Premium sales. One of the most lucrative of all channels, corporations typically pay about 50 percent of a book's list price for quantities, they pay quickly, and there are no returns.

+ Bookstore sales. Broad-interest books do best in general bookstores and require a distributor or wholesaler. Bookstore sales are great ego boosters and some authors are naturals for promoting books through this outlet. They are great publicists and know how to write an enticing press release. They love giving TV and radio interviews and the interviewers love them. On the downside, the books will get quickly returned by bookstores if they don't sell, the profit margin is small, and the competition is fierce.

- Back-of-the-room sales. Many of the most successful publishers are what the industry calls "promotable authors." Take an author of a spiritually motivating book, for example. When they speak, they exude an inner quality that the audience wants to possess—a confidence in their sense of self and their beliefs. They have a story to tell and they do it well. The audience believes they can get a piece of that person by buying his or her book. It's interesting to note that several of the best-selling authors began selling their books on the lecture circuit: Betty Eadie, author of *Embraced by the Light*, Marlo Morgan, author of *Mutant Message Down Under*, and Jack Canfield and Mark Victor Hansen, coauthors of *Chicken Soup for the Soul*.

Speaking in a natural, motivational, and charismatic way is one side of the equation. Finding an audience is the other. Authors need to go where their readers are. Tim Smith and Mark Herrick, author and illustrator, respectively, of the *Buck Wilder Small Fry Fishing Guide,* sell books at elementary schools, give presentations about fishing at state and national parks, and sell their book to 4-H clubs to use as teaching tools. They ride in any parade that will have them. They're trying to get fishing-pole manufacturer Zebco to package their books with kid-sized fishing poles.

"We don't even think bookstores," said publicist Laura Jolly. "They're nice, but if we focused on bookstores, we'd just have to compete with thousands of other titles."

Marketing strategies are sometimes borne out of sheer necessity. James Redfield, author of the *Celestine Prophecy*, packed his books in the trunk of his Honda Accord and sold them to new-age bookstores across the South. Redfield said he wouldn't have enjoyed the same early success in superstores. His books only sold so well, he said, because of the high recommendations of the bookstore owners with whom he developed personal relationships.

PROMOTION

What is your marketing budget? What type of advertising and publicity do you plan? Your strategy will be determined by the number of books you want to sell and your targeted primary and secondary marketing channels. Generally, publishers budget $1 for each book printed. We'll discuss promotion in detail in Chapter 9, "Creating Publicity That's Smart, Cheap, and Effective."

PRICE

What is the price people will pay for your book? Some publishing veterans will tell you to price your book eight times the unit cost of printing. We take a modified view. We believe you ought to price your book at what the market will bear. First, consider your audience. A business manual that will likely be purchased through a corporation or by a highly paid professional will command a much higher price than one that's geared to teenagers, who generally have to scrape together their hard-earned minimum wage dollars.

Price your book no higher than your closest competition *and* no lower. Price it higher, and the buyer may choose the cheaper book. Price it lower, and they'll think your book is a cheap imitation and choose the pricier book. In general, the book price must be eight times higher than the unit cost of printing, but that's a generality. It depends on your mode of distribution and promotion costs.

The length of the book also plays a role in price. Generally, people believe the longer the book, the higher the price it can command.

Let's say that you want to write a book on herbs. Refer back to the research you did with *Books in Print* and Amazon.com. Check to see how much the book closest to the quality you envision would run: let's say it's 6x9 inches, soft cover, 288 pages, color insert, and runs $16.95.

If your book is a very close match with the competition in terms of depth, breadth, and physical attributes, set your price at $16.95.

If you are publishing a book that is technical in scope, one-of-a-kind, comprehensive, and is aimed at professionals—an insider's book, for example, that discusses the legal ramifications and legal strategies related to drunk-driving charges in all 50 states—you can charge a very steep price.

Our point is this: production costs are relevant only when deciding what price your book can't go *below* in order to be profitable. But if thousands of people will pay $100 for your book because it is so vital and so necessary to their existence, it doesn't matter what the production cost is. Demand drives the top end.

The "eight-time rule" comes into play with books that are priced at the low end. Clearly, the small gift books that you find at Hallmark and other gift stores, priced at around $5, are making marginal profits. That is, unless the publisher is producing huge quantities, which a small publisher can't afford to do. We advise that you do a very careful cost analysis to determine your margins before pursuing a book with a tiny price tag. As Lee Iacocca once said: Small cars, small profit. Big cars, big profit. The same thing applies to books. Small books, small profits. Generally, most books priced at $18 and above will enjoy healthy profit margins. A book priced below $6 generally will not.

Once you've established the price, you're ready to do a break-even analysis to answer the question: How many books must be sold to recover a target profit and cover expenses?

First, break down your projected sales numbers by category: direct mail sales, bookstore sales through a distributor, back-of-the-room sales following a seminar, on the Internet, through a distributor to gift shops, via home-shopping channels, etc. Let's take the herb book example. Think of who would buy the book and where they would buy it. How about garden catalogs, garden centers, gardening classes, direct mail offers, in bookstores, and seminars (that you would run).

Next, build a pyramid of sales, starting with the highest volume quantity at the base and the least at the tip. Multiply each quantity by the expected revenues after discount in each category. A discount is the percentage taken off the retail list price. For example, a 60 percent discount equates to 40 percent of the retail price. Following are discounts, *in general*. An exclusive, national distributor (one who has exclusive rights to distribute your book to bookstores across the country) typically takes a 67-percent discount, or would pay $3.30 for a $10 book. Catalogs and retail stores will take an average 50-percent discount. Library distributors take a 55- to 60-percent discount. Regional wholesalers take a 55-percent discount. If you sell the books yourself through direct mail or seminars, assume a 50-percent profit after mailing expenses.

Here's an example of a sales pyramid, using a $20 book:

Exclusive distributor (68-percent discount)
4,000 books x $20 x .32 = $25,600

Catalog sales (50-percent discount)
3,000 books x $20 x .50 = $30,000

Garden retail stores (50-percent discount)
2,000 books x $20 x .50 = $20,000

Books sold directly through your own seminars and classes
1,000 x $20 x 1.0 = $20,000

Total revenue = $95,600 or an average of 47.8 percent of retail price

In general, the more your marketing mix relies on a national, exclusive distributor, the higher your retail price must be—up to 10 or 11 times the unit cost. That's because you receive such a low return per book *and* the bookstores have an absolute privilege of returning any books they don't sell.

TIMING

In addition to the four Ps, consider timing. What is the optimal date for the book's release?

Some publishers purposely plan a holiday book, knowing that it extends the life of a book. Each year, magically, their book is revived, Christmas after Christmas, Valentine's Day after Valentine's Day. Holiday books are on the shelves two or so months before the actual holiday. Other books require more thought in terms of timing. Comfort-food cookbooks, for example, do best in winter, while the sales of pasta and salad books blossom in warmer weather. Never underestimate how soon you must propose a book. Catalogs, for example, usually have finalized their Christmas offerings by February. Book trade shows focus on holiday books in July (even if your book isn't done by then, you must promote it then). Read trade magazines in order to get an idea of deadlines and upcoming trade show events.

For detailed instruction and worksheets on developing a marketing plan and forecast, read John Kremer's *Book Marketing Made Easier.* We consider it a must-read.

Our advice: creatively think of alternative channels that won't entail book returns, will return more ample profits than a national book distributor, and will require minimal promotional dollars. Not only will these channels increase your revenues, they may lower your printing costs: if you receive an advance order from a book club, an overseas distributor, a catalog company, a government agency, or a corporation, for example, it will lower the overall unit cost in a press run.

On the production side, there are ways of saving money without skimping on quality. Dan Poynter's *The Self-Publishing Manual* is an excellent resource and well worth your time to read.

5.

THE MYTH: "IT'S WHAT'S INSIDE THAT REALLY COUNTS"

Don't make excuses, make good.
ELBERT HUBBARD

THE BIGGEST MISTAKE MOST INDEPENDENT PUBLISHERS MAKE IS TRYing to do the entire book production themselves. It makes sense to conserve your production dollars, but not to the point that the final product suffers.

The fine pen of an editor can turn an average book into a smooth piece of writing. Book designers will ensure that your book will look professionally produced. Publishers must begin with sufficient capital to turn out a competitive product—the same rule that applies to any business endeavor.

PACKAGING YOUR BOOK

You've heard by now that people *do* judge a book by its cover. Not only its cover, but its length, its title, its subtitle, the description on the inside and back cover, the promotional blurbs and who says them, the author's photo, even the paper quality. Bookstore browsers will process some or all of these elements and make a snap judgment. To buy or not to buy. Consider this: your book is a product, just like jeans and cereal.

"Going to the bookstore is a lot like going to the grocery store with shelves of product screaming, 'Pick me up! Pick me up!' If something catches your eye, you have a tendency to look at it more closely," Van Baker, president of Design Etc., said in a *Small Press* magazine article.

So important is appearance that Random House completely redesigned a book that it had originally thought was destined as a best seller, *A Civil Action* by Jonathan Harr, simply because its content was so good. In its first iteration, the title was written in large, block type on a plain cover with the intention of making the book look like a legal textbook. The only other information on the cover was the author's name.

The cover was simple, but too simple. The book bombed, at least in the eyes of Random House. It sold almost 57,000 copies, but Random House had to warehouse nearly an equal amount. So in January 1996, they relaunched the book taking the attitude that the book was indeed a product that required savvy marketing. The second version of the cover was far more dramatic. Against the backdrop of a swinging gavel, is this: "'Compelling' - John Grisham." And this: *"A Civil Action*, A REAL LIFE LEGAL THRILLER." *And* a gold emblem that states: "Best book of the year."

In addition to the cover meeting the standard of aesthetics, *book industry professionals*—those who will decide whether to review or distribute your book—will check to see if your book meets industry standards.

It's not the book cover that industry professionals are judging, it's the publisher, said University of Oregon design instructor Roy Paul Nelson in a fall 1996 *Small Press* article.

"An appropriate, well-done cover gives reviewers, distributors, booksellers, consumers, and others in the chain of the book business confidence that the publisher is serious about trying to sell a title and has a dependable business sense," he said.

Designing a book, however, is as much about marketing as it is about aesthetics and looking professionally produced. It should speak to your target audience. If the book is about home decorating, the cover should be pretty, feminine, and inviting. If it's about camping in the mountains, it should have a rugged look. What colors and graphics most appeal to your readers? Research shows men prefer colors in this order: blue, red, violet, green, orange, white, and yellow. Women like colors in this order: red, violet, blue, green, orange, white, and yellow. What sort of words triggers a buy from your target audience? A struggling author once joked that a title that includes the word "soul" will automatically sell 10,000 books no matter what's inside. Other kinds of audiences like action-packed, sports-oriented titles, and graphics. Some like patriotic themes. Have you ever noticed Tom Clancy's books are usually designed in red, white, and blue? Cookbook graphics immediately convey the kind of audience they expect: a red-checkered table cloth conveys "down-home good." A title like "Silver Palate" translates into highbrow tastes.

You not only need to design a book to appeal to the target audience, but also for all of the channels in which you believe most of the books will be sold—direct mail, hardware stores, bookstores, catalogs, gift stores, corporate gifts, etc. Go to the type of store where your book will sell, and find the book section. As you stand there, imagine how your book would look next to the others. You need to check out the various channels in order to determine how covers vary in each. Gift-store books, for example, have a completely different look than those books that sell in a bookstore. They tend to be shorter in length, include more illustrations, and have more fanciful or gifty-looking covers. A gift book can sell in a bookstore, but that's generally not true the other way around.

No matter how you plan to sell your book, avoid text on a perfectly plain cover. That sort of design is a favorite among self-publishers who believe it looks simple and elegant (not to mention it's also cheaper to produce). Unfortunately, it usually screams: "I'm self-published!"

The following discussion will help you write, design and produce a highly marketable book.

TIPS FOR A PHENOMENAL FRONT COVER

The cover is the single most important element of the book from a marketing standpoint. A cheap-looking cover telegraphs low-quality contents, true or not. Packaging is everything. It's why a lot of moms choose Kellogg's

Raisin Bran over the generic choice, half the price. One president of a national distribution house said a poor cover is the single biggest reason for book rejections. *Again, unless you design book covers for a living, hire a professional book designer whose work you admire.* And once you hire a professional, you must stay involved. Give the professional concrete guidelines about what the cover needs to convey. It has to be simple enough that the reader can "get it" within seconds. It should be flashy enough to compete with the Simon & Schusters of the world. Use color, color, and more color. The right use of color makes images jump off the page.

Speaking of the cover, have you noticed those silky covers people just love to get their hands all over? These matte-coated covers are said to enjoy a few extra seconds in a browser's hand, but colors don't "pop" off the paper as they do with the more traditional glossy covers.

Next, your title and subtitle must be so attention-getting that they reach out and grab the reader by his lapels. Make the title BIG. In a quick breath, it must get to the heart of what the book is about. The title and subtitle together should tell the reader why this book is uniquely different and better than any other book written on the topic. How-to titles should immediately convey the benefit that the book offers. Toy around with alliteration or humorous titles.

Of course, there are exceptions to all these guidelines. Take, for example, these nonfiction titles: *Make the Connection, The Dilbert Principle,* and *The Zone.* In the case of nebulous titles, a tag line is absolutely required in order to clarify the book's purpose.

What makes a great title? There are no clearly defined rules. Take *Chicken Soup for the Soul.* You either love the title or think it's corny. Who would guess this book would become a best seller? And *What Color is Your Parachute?* doesn't adhere to any set rules, yet has sold millions of copies over two decades. But, yes, some titles will clearly kill a book, such as this fictitious title: *My Mother's Trip to China.*

With the understanding that there are no hard and fast rules, we have gathered a few guidelines for titles:

- Titles shouldn't mislead. *Clicking In: Hot Links to a Digital Culture,* for example, makes people think of a catalog of the greatest Internet sites on the Web. Actually, it's a collection of essays and interviews about the effects of the digital age on humanity.

- Titles should be informative and easy-to-read. Good examples: *The Almost Painless Divorce: What Your Lawyer Won't Tell you.* Or *Mad at Your Lawyer?: What to Do When You're Overcharged, Ignored, Betrayed, or a Victim of Malpractice.*

- Titles must work together with the graphic, each playing off the other. Don't be so attached to your graphic that you let it push the title into obscurity.

- Avoid cover type that's boring, too small, or too cluttered.

- The first word of the title should be the same as the subject to make the book easy to find in R.R. Bowker's *Books in Print*, which lists books by title, author, and subject, Dan Poynter suggested in *The Self-Publishing Manual.*

- Some have suggested modifying other popular book titles, such as all the Dummies takeoffs on *The Internet for Dummies.* Approach this with caution. It's clever at first, but in the case of the *Dummies* books, the joke became tiresome. And there's always the risk of sounding like a knock-off. Here's one title that elicited a reviewer's groan: *The 7 Habits of Highly Happy People.*

- To get ideas for your book title, check out titles of similar subjects— maybe chapter heads in books, magazines, newspapers, Internet articles, etc. Other ideas might come from recycling commercial slogans. The slogan for a Michigan outlet mall, "Cut out the middleman," might make a great title for a book on direct selling on the Internet.

- For how-to books, the title should hit the emotional hot buttons of the specific market. Avery Cardoza's gambling book titles, for example, all include the word "winning": *The Basics of Winning Slots, How to Play Winning Poker*, etc.

- When it comes to fiction books, the title needs to reflect the emotion, mood and theme of the book.

- If you're having trouble thinking of an idea, authors Marilyn and Tom Ross suggest using a computer software program called IdeaFisher. This program is actually a workshop that spurs your creative juices by asking you lots of questions about your book, chapter heads, etc., and linking up your answers with idea words and phrases. Call (800) 289-4332 for more information.

- Funny titles usually sell best even if they're on serious subjects. Take the successful business book, *Leadership Secrets of Attila the Hun* by author Wess Roberts.

- You can't copyright a title, but avoid duplicating a title. It causes confusion. Even similar-sounding headlines cause confusion. Check out the titles in Bowker's *Books in Print* and *Forthcoming Books in Print* before you finalize your title.

Here are other considerations for the cover:

- Besides a title, subtitle and author's name on the cover, consider putting the author's credentials on the *front* cover. If they're impressive enough, there's no sense hiding the author's achievements on the back cover. Next to Michael Moore's name on *Downsize This*, was written that he was the creator of *TV Nation* and *Roger and Me*. Below the name of Susan M. Lark, author of *The Estrogen Decision* was written: "Written by a female physician specializing in women's health and preventive medicine." Write a one-liner that immediately establishes the author as an expert. Elaborate on the credentials on the back cover.

- If the book has received an award of any kind, put the name of the award with brief details on a gold emblem in the lower right-hand corner.

- If someone with a substantially high recognition factor has written a testimonial of the book or the foreword, promote the fact right on the front cover. Either quote a small piece of the testimonial or write: "Foreword by Bill Gates."

How to *sell* the Book on the Back Cover

The back cover and inside cover are tremendously important. In just a few paragraphs, you can persuade the casual browser to take action and pay for your book. In several breaths this time, the back cover must describe the book, capture the spirit of the book, and spell out clearly how the book's contents will benefit the reader. Use your entire arsenal to convince the reader that your book is worth reading: statistics, testimonials, and perhaps quote someone who has already benefited by the book.

In your synopsis of the book, make the book just as alluring and lively as you can. Sound intelligent, but avoid overly long sentences and extremely difficult or overly technical words. Don't bore the reader—the worst sin of all.

- Limit the copy on the back of the book. Make it succinct with the oomph on reader benefits. Too many words on a page, and people don't read it.
- An author's photograph is optional. It's highly recommended if the author is somewhat well-known and wants to be instantly recognizable or if the author's looks are important to the subject matter (i.e., a how-to book on hair braiding, getting in shape, or applying makeup).
- The photograph should convey a specific image. Frances Weaver once said that she put an unretouched photograph of herself on the cover of her book, *The Girls With the Grandmother Faces,* because she wanted readers to know she was a "thoughtful older woman"—not a glamorous young thing. In general, a photograph should carry a sense of sophistication.
- Include a short biography that explains the author's expertise and background. It should answer: "Why should I believe this person? Is the author a living testimony to his or her ideas?"
- Seek out well-known experts, authors (of books written on the same topic), magazine editors, or the presidents of relevant nonprofit organizations or businesses to give endorsements. As you or the author write the book, try to establish relationships with at least a few of the

people you plan to ask by interviewing them for the book. If you make a great connection, ask the person to write the foreword. It's not traditional to offer money, but some publishers do offer an honorarium of $100 or so (or ask the notable person if they'd like to have that amount donated to a favorite charity.)

Some celebrities resent getting a huge manuscript dumped in their lap with the request to write a testimonial. Send a query letter first to the bigger stars. You may want to give the person a copy of the endorsements that you've already received so you can show that his or her quote will be in good company.

To make it easier for a busy executive or editor to write a testimonial, talk to the person's assistant and make a suggestion as to what kind of quote you'd like. Or write the endorsement yourself for their approval. Finally, be prepared for no response. You may have to ask 10 or 12 people in order to get three or four good quotes. Steve Mettee of Quill Driver Books, publisher of *The Pediatrician's New Baby Owner's Manual,* wrote to six different magazine editors, all of whom said they would be happy to supply a quote. But in the end, only one senior editor from *Parenting Magazine* came through, he said.

"That's why you need to ask more than one person," said Mettee, adding it's a numbers game.

At one to three lines each, the testimonials should reveal a unique benefit of buying the book. If the testimonial comes from someone impressive enough, put it on the front cover. Rhodes & Easton did just that with *Inside the Bestsellers.* The foreword is written by best-selling author Richard Paul Evans, author of *The Christmas Box.* An aspiring publisher may not know the name of book coauthors Jerrold Jenkins or Mardi Link, but they will probably recognize Evans' name and attach his credibility to the book.

WHAT THE BACK COVER OF YOUR BOOK MUST INCLUDE

Certain clues give away that fact that you're a micro-publisher, such as the omission of an ISBN number or category classification. To meet professional standards, your book must include the following elements:

- The category classification (such as humor, fiction).

- The retail price in the lower left-hand corner along with the Canadian retail price.

- The publisher's name, city and state. *DO NOT make the publisher's name the same as your last name.* It is a dead giveaway that the book is independently published.

- A logo of the publishing house. Examples include: Random House's row of buildings, Alfred A. Knopf's Russian borzoi dog, Simon & Schuster's seed sower.

- An ISBN (An International Standard Book Number—like the Social Security Number of a book), LCCN (Library of Congress Catalog Card Number—a unique preassigned catalog number essential for library sales), a P-CIP (Publisher's Cataloging-in-Publication)—used by libraries to identify the book's subject nature and how to find it on the shelf. You'll also need an ABI (Advance Book Information—notification to R.R. Bowker's *Books in Print* and several other directories. It links the ISBN and retail price with title of book along with the publisher and distributor, and an EAN bar code scanning symbol on the back cover. Apply for these numbers *before* the book is in print.

The following points are subtle, but pay attention and you'll avoid looking like a micro-publisher.

- Do not pay for an annotation in *Books in Print*. The larger publishers never do.

- When applying for an ISBN number, you can ask for 10, 100 or 1,000 numbers. Self-publishing author Gene Corpening, author of *What the Self-Publishing Manuals Don't Tell You*, suggests you ask for 100 or 1,000 instead of 10. Why? The quantity of ISBNs issued is reflected in the ISBN number (there are seven digits in the second group of numbers as opposed to 5 or 6 for those who order 100 or 1,000). Ordering only 10 numbers will immediately flag your book as independently published. "The 7-digit group is your snitch," he writes.

Production tips

Book design is an art. Again, we advise investing in the services of a professional instead of trying to lay it out yourself. Here are some general tips, however, that will go a long way in producing a polished book.

- "Foreword" is the most misspelled word in the independent publishing industry.

- Don't establish your first book-signing date prematurely. If you rush the proofreading and printing stage in order to meet the date, you'll highly regret it.

- Typos immediately convey that the book is independently published. A proofreader should check one item a time throughout the book: all the chapter headings, for example, or consistency of the drop cap at the beginning of each chapter. Other checks (besides the text itself): page numbers have a consistent typeface and are sequential; the index and table of contents match the page; chapter headers are capitalized consistently; and the white space above the chapter headers is consistent.

- Consistency of editorial style is the most common difficulty with independently published manuscripts. Authors, for example, will write *10* and later write *ten*. Buy *The Chicago Manual of Style*, read it, and adhere to it religiously.

- A sans serif in a large type-size (13 or 14 point) gives the appearance of a third-grade reader. Avoid this in adult books.

- Make sure the book is bound professionally so that libraries will find it acceptable for purchase.

Here are additional tips for aesthetics:

- White on certain colors is unreadable. In general, black on white is more easily read than white on a dark background. This is especially important for the title. It should strongly contrast with the background color, and that goes for the spine, too.

- Avoid unpleasant colors, even for screens, such as dirty gray.

- Unless you have an extremely thin book, make the spine type as large and readable as possible.

- The title and author's name should go on the spine. Big New York houses also put on the publishing house, but the name of your small press won't be meaningful to the buyer, so we suggest leaving it off in order to run the title bigger. If your title is nebulous, add a brief rendition of the subtitle to clarify what the book is about.

DESIGNING YOUR CONTENT

As you write the book, think of how you can add chapters for wider appeal, suggest publishers Marilyn and Tom Ross in the September 1996 issue of the *SPAN Connection*.

"In today's competitive world of publishing, smart authors and publishers start thinking 'marketing' when they first think about a book project," they wrote. ". . . The more promotional angles you provide for your book, the more likely sales will mushroom."

A book on coping with the holidays, for example, could appeal to a wide range of readers with the right planning. One chapter might be devoted to gay issues during the holidays, another with dealing with alcoholic relatives, still another with coping with infertility during the holidays. These three different chapters provide three different slants for media coverage or entire reprints in specific magazines.

6

THE INS AND OUTS OF SCHEDULING

Don't agonize. Organize.
FLORYNCE KENNEDY

IN ADDITION TO DESIGN AND CONTENT, TIMING IS VERY IMPORTANT in bookstore sales. When you promote a book, the books must be in bookstores. If they're not, most consumers won't have the tenacity to wait out a special order.

Everything revolves around the first six months of the publication date. In this schedule, you'll see that the books are delivered about eight weeks before the "official publication date." That's so you can get books out to the media and reviewers in order to set up interviews, book signings, etc. in advance. You can also promote them on the Internet or via direct mail or to corporations and catalogs before the "official publication date."

Surprisingly, the publication date is arbitrary. The only people who care about the official publication date are library and trade magazine reviewers who prefer prepublication bound galleys. Because they want the galleys four months before publication, tell them exactly that: the publication date is four months from the date you sent the bound galleys, true or not. Another note: send *bound* galleys only to reviewers. Yes, it's expensive, but unbound galleys usually get tossed—and then you've totally wasted your money.

The following schedule includes both production and marketing elements. It's constructed with the premise that publicity builds on itself. In the pre-publication stage, you'll first send bound galleys to book industry magazines and journals for reviews. Booksellers and libraries place a lot of stock in these reviews so they can order books in advance of public demand. Plan to use excerpts from these reviews in your promotional material that you later mail to the mainstream media shortly before your book is published and in post-publication. Good reviews beget more reviews. Good articles beget more good articles. Along the way, document and copy *everything*. They make invaluable promotional tools for yourself, bookstores (if you can get the bookseller to post it), and your distributor's sales reps.

PRE-PRESS—24 WEEKS BEFORE PUBLICATION DATE

- Manuscript is finished with, ideally, a foreword or testimonial written by someone credible in the industry. It has been sent to peers and experts in the field for comment and input.

- Title, subtitle, and retail price have been researched and finalized.

- You have selected the most affordable and most reputable printer possible.

- Your "profit and loss" statement has been finalized.

- You have found a distributor(s) or wholesaler to distribute to bookstores.

- If you are selling your books via an 800 number, find a fulfillment company, establish your 800 number and credit-card system.

- Preliminary design of cover is done with title, subtitle, and graphic.

READY, SET, GO!

- Send out manuscripts for additional testimonials.

- Write catalog copy for distributor. Develop positioning statement and marketing materials for sales reps.

- Finalize overall marketing/promotion plan.

- After manuscript input is received, correct copy and produce galleys.
- Solicit author events at various book fairs and trade shows.

APPLY FOR REGISTRATIONS

- ISBN Number—takes about four weeks: This must be done before application of the ABI.
- After the ISBN is received and retail price is finalized, complete ABI form and submit it.
- Apply for Bar Code (3 days).
- Apply for PCIP (3 weeks).
- Application for copyright *cannot* be made until book is printed.

LAY OUT ELECTRONIC TEXT FOR BOOK

- Decide trim size.
- Lay out text/consult with designer.
- Proofread text and make any final changes. Send to printer.
- Proof bluelines carefully.
- Once you receive testimonials, finalize cover elements: endorsements, text, and photo (optional). Proofread.

SEND BOOK TO PRINTER

HIRE A BOOK-PROMOTING PUBLICIST (IF YOU'RE GOING THAT ROUTE) OR:

PREPARE PROMOTIONAL MATERIAL

- A letter explaining marketing plan and strategy.
- Press release to go with galleys. Write a fact sheet to accompany the cover sheets. The cover sheet should be tailored for each specific channel: trade reviewers, libraries, book clubs, catalogs, distributor,

and magazines. (Book clubs and catalogs, for example, should be told of *actual* date book is available). Material should include:

- Benefit that the book offers.

- Brief description of book contents.

- Statistics on the popularity of the subject.

- Where the book fits in the market: Is it first-of-a-kind or what makes it unique?

- Testimonials of writers/experts/magazine editors, etc.

- Author credentials.

- List price, ISBN, page number, publication date, distributor, publisher, size, marketing plans.

- Copy of book cover.

- Make final touches to book cover and send to printer. On the overrun, consider printing promotional text on the white side of the jacket.

- Solicit author events at book trade shows: Send in applications for trade events you want to attend.

- Schedule trade magazine advertising.

- Find out deadlines for key catalogs.

18 WEEKS BEFORE PUBLICATION DATE

- Send bound galleys and promotion package (press release, marketing plan and copy of cover) to library reviewers: *Library Journal, ALA Booklist, Kirkus Reviews,* and *Choice.*

- Send bound galleys and promotion package to pre-publication trade review sources such as *Publishers Weekly.*

- Send galleys and promotion package to book clubs and query interest.

- Send galleys and promotion package to library distributors and query interest.

- Send galley and promotion package to distributor.

16 WEEKS BEFORE PUBLICATION DATE

- Direct mailing: Search and rent/buy a direct mailing list. Write and design sales material (with new review quotes included) and print in time for mailing two weeks prior to book shipment.
- Offer magazines first serial rights.

12 WEEKS BEFORE PUBLICATION DATE

- Research online book selling and decide how best to market your book on the Internet. Start teasing the book to newsgroups and announce the availability date.
- Schedule ads with *Radio & TV Report* to appear just prior to publication date.
- Plan and design bookstore displays, point-of-purchase displays.
- Prepare list of targeted media for announcement of book.
- Assemble media press kit:

News release	Copies of book reviews and articles to date
Fact sheet	How-to-order information
Copy of book cover	Business card
Sample questions (for radio interviewers)	

  Mail media kits to magazines (which have a longer lead time than newspapers and radio).
- Direct mailers: Send out your direct mailing.
- Prepare bags to mail out books and press package to reviewers and media.
- Mail media packages to specialty stores, chains, etc., and ask for orders. Add flyer and distributor information to packet.
- Plan your book-signing "event" and prepare posters and props. Prepare invitations for book signing and mail two weeks before event.

8 TO 10 WEEKS BEFORE PUBLICATION DATE

- Upon delivery of books: check quality and quantity. Notify fulfillment house of orders, quantity of books to have at its warehouse.
- As soon as the books arrive, mail book package *and* book to wholesalers, Ingram Book Co. and Baker & Taylor, and to all trade reviewers that prefer to see finished books as opposed to bound galleys.
- Contact premium markets (i.e., corporations who might want to give out the book as a gift, incentive, etc.) Follow up with a media package and book.
- File for copyright.
- Send book to Library of Congress-Cataloging Division along with copy of pre-assignment form that indicates number.
- Sign books in your hometown and give interviews to local media.
- Offer second serial rights to magazines.
- Compile all the endorsements, reviews, book club contracts, catalogs, etc., on a separate page to include in your media kit (and quote the best blurbs on your cover letter).
- Compile a list of bookstores for book signings. Mail press kit to bookstores. In your letter, propose a book-signing event—a speech, cooking demonstration, etc. Follow up your letter with a phone call to request a book signing (post-publication date).
- Negotiate audio rights.
- Tell the distributor about all upcoming reviews, scheduled media interviews, book signings, etc. (Do this throughout the life of the book!)

FOUR WEEKS BEFORE OFFICIAL PUBLICATION DATE

- Finalize book-signing dates.
- Send out media kits to TV, radio, and newspapers, *especially* locations where a book signing is scheduled. Mail books with media kits

to local, regional media, and selected media. All others on request. Make mention of date of any book signings in the area.

PUBLICATION DATE

You'll get most of your publicity within six months of your publication date. Hit it hard.

- Continue to mail books to premium buyers and follow up with phone calls.

- Contact catalog publishers and send books on request.

- Mail media kits to secondary media.

- Schedule trade show visits.

- Continue promoting book to feature editors, columnists, niche publications, reviewers, and radio stations. Do radio, TV, and press interviews. Make copies of all media hype, reviews, etc. and enclose with updated press releases that talk about appearances to date. Notify the distributor of any upcoming interviews, reviews, book-signing dates, etc.

- Go on a book-signing tour.

- Offer reprint rights to foreign publishers.

- Package your book in alternative forms, such as audiotapes or on the Internet.

- Position yourself as an expert and give speeches and seminars, making back-of-the-room book sales.

7

The Truth About Distributors And Wholesalers

You may be deceived if you trust too much,
but you will live in torment if you do not trust enough.
Dr. Frank Crane

So many publishers write and produce a book without thinking seriously about how they might distribute them. This is a mistake. Distribution is incredibly important, particularly if the book has broad appeal and requires bookstore sales.

That said, your approach to trade bookstore sales must be well thought-out because the distribution trail is fraught with pitfalls. And as we will discuss later, trust is a crucial element in a distributor/wholesaler relationship.

The reason that you need a distributor/wholesaler is that bookstores will not deal one-on-one with small publishers unless it's a bookstore in the author's hometown. Why? It's far too much hassle. Dealing one-on-one with a small publisher means the bookstore would have to cut a separate purchase order, write a separate check, deal with a separate returns policy, etc. That's logistically impossible to do with hundreds of publishers. Plus, bookstores look at distributors as a screening device—the best books make it through the distributor's door, the worst probably don't.

There are advantages to a distributor for you, too. A distributor handles all the logistical details of warehousing the books, shipping, invoicing, and collecting delinquent payments. Paperwork duties aside, the biggest advantage of your distribution is clout. The best distributors have the willing ears of the superstores and strong independents. And while the distributor is out there writing up orders, you can devote your time to publicity and promotion, writing books in the case of self-publishers, and selling books in specialty markets.

There are other reasons for getting a distributor. If a reviewer gives your book a superb review, sales will suffer if your book is impossible to obtain. Some radio hosts refuse to interview authors if their books aren't in bookstores.

Reviewers in the book industry may also require that you have a distributor in place before they proceed with a review. Linda Donelson, author of *Out of Isak Dinesen in Africa: The Untold Story,* said that *Publishers Weekly* called her to say they wanted to review her book, but needed the name of her distributor. It took Donelson a few months to research and finalize a distributor at which point she called *Publishers Weekly* with the distributor's name. A lovely review appeared a few weeks later.

Now that we've outlined why distributors, in most cases, *must* be part of the marketing equation, we'll talk about the drawbacks. First, micro-publishers find it difficult to get their book accepted by an exclusive, national distributor. Although these distributors have accepted the books of micro-publishers in the past, distributors have become incredibly selective. To be considered, publishers need more than an excellent book. They have to show the distributor they plan on building a long-term title list and present a powerful marketing plan for each book.

Some publishers feel that an exclusive, national distributor is not the way to go. They have successfully found alternative ways of getting their books into a bookstore or avoided bookstores altogether. But this will give you an overview of distributors, the problems and opportunities they present, and some pro-active suggestions in forming a winning relationship with a distributor.

WHAT EXACTLY IS AN EXCLUSIVE, NATIONAL DISTRIBUTOR?

National distributors require trade exclusivity. That means the distributor, and only the distributor, may sell to bookstores. Gift stores, outdoor stores, and libraries are typically not included in the exclusivity agreement. (Most publishers will also sign on with a distributor that sells solely to libraries.) A distributor must first and foremost get books into bookstores when and where they're needed. It's the publisher's job to pull the books off the shelf by way of radio interviews, great book reviews, newspaper articles, even TV appearances.

A distributor's job is to sell books to bookstores, from the small independent on Main Street to the superstores. Its force of 22 to 29 sales reps will walk into a bookstore with a catalog of anywhere from 50 to 5,000 titles and talk to the bookstore owner about the hottest books and the sleeper-soon-to-be-best-seller. In addition to persuading bookstores to buy its line of books, a distributor will also warehouse the books, take orders, invoice, ship the books, and provide publishers with a report of how many books were sold. The distributor will advertise its line of books in a catalog and exhibit the books at the BookExpo America trade show. For an extra fee, the distributor will help the publisher with the cover design, the book's editorial focus, and a marketing plan.

In contrast, *sales representatives* will promote a book to bookstores and get orders, but that's where their job ends. The publisher must arrange for the warehousing, shipping, invoicing, and collections. A *jobber* services airport newsstands, drugstores, supermarkets, and convenience stores with inventory maintenance, title selection, and returns. Many times a distributor will contract the services of jobbers.

Most distributors will support a publisher in the field of marketing: setting up book tours, press interviews—usually for a fee. Some will even coordinate a full-fledged three-month national media campaign for a significant fee. But these services don't let a publisher off the hook. A dull interview won't sell many books. Authors and publishers are truly their own best publicists. The listening audience has to hear the genuine excitement in the author's voice.

PROS AND CONS OF NATIONAL DISTRIBUTORS

Although distributors are critical for selling a high volume of books in bookstores, there are drawbacks. At the top of the list is they take a huge bite out of a book's retail price. Called the discount rate, it generally ranges from 62-68 percent. There's more: payments are typically made 90 to 120 days after the sale. To combat this problem, many publishers ask if there's any way to negotiate faster payment. Some publishers, for example, offer their distributors a 2 percent prepay discount if they send a check at the time they order books.

Publishers who have signed on with national distributors have also reported a very painful problem with book returns—books that are sold to bookstores by distributors and then returned to the publisher after lingering on the shelves too long. Returns can mean death to a small publisher. Cash-flow death, to be specific. If you dish out $10,000 for a print run to fill a 5,000-book superstore order, only to have most of the books returned a few months later instead of cash receipts, you'll either need capital to prop you up or you'll go out of business.

There are several theories on why returns have increased industry-wide. Booksellers complain that New York sales reps "push" books on them.

"Reps often push large orders—'20 must-titles and face-out displays for all of them'—while having no idea whether a store can actually pay for the order," Roxanne Coady of R.J. Julia Booksellers complained in a Nov. 11 *Publishers Weekly* article.

Coady reported that returns are also distressing to bookstores, costing 40 cents a book to process.

The high return rate of 1996 was fueled by slower book sales, which some blamed on distractions from radio, TV, cable TV, the Internet and videotapes, the article reported. Others blamed the significant price jump in hardback books and softcover alike.

Finally, there's a glut of books on the market so that the time books have to prove themselves is much smaller than before, according to Mark Oimet, senior vice president of Publishers Group West in Emeryville, California, which distributes 1,200 new titles each year and oversees a backlist of 5,000.

"A book needs to perform fairly quickly to continue being in the store. If it doesn't, it's coming back pretty quickly. The competition is really fierce for a reader's attention."

Secondly, orders from bookstores—particularly superstores—are often too ambitious. The theory is that superstores, with their ample shelf space, aren't as discriminating with their orders as the independents. A publisher's elation of selling 3,000 books to a Borders or Barnes & Noble turns to anger when 1,500 are returned six months later.

To safeguard against this boomerang effect, Publisher's Group West recommends that publishers, more than ever, carefully orchestrate a promotional strategy in concert with the distributor's marketing staff.

Publishers are also wise to look at past sales performance records before filling a large book order. If past performance and the current order don't match up, then scale it down. Another option: some publishers are giving the distributor an extra five percent discount in exchange for a no-returns policy. That means that once a distributor buys books, it cannot return them to the publisher for any reason other than the books were damaged during shipping.

Here are some publishers' observations on distributors, both pro and con, that were shared on the Publishers Marketing Association Forum on the Internet:

From Cynthia Kim, co-owner of Turtle Press, a martial arts book publisher: "Getting a distributor was the best move we ever made. It opened doors that we would still be kicking at otherwise. What does it mean to have our books in the chains? A steady check every month, low returns, a way to reach customers we wouldn't otherwise meet, a big ego boost for our authors, and little need for big bucks promotion once you get a foot in the door.

"We *do* make considerably less profit on trade sales than on direct sales, so I think the market penetration provided by a distributor is more important than the direct financial benefits, at least for us."

From Rich Adin of Rhache Publishers in Gardiner, New York: "We find that having a distributor is absolutely necessary to get into the major bookstores. While the small, local independents are happy to take books from local publishers on consignment, the bigger stores are not. . . . On the other hand, distributors are killing publishing. They charge the publisher a warehouse fee, a fee to get listed in the distributor's database, a fee for being in the distributor's catalog, a promotional fee, and so forth. Then the discount rate is very high. In our case, 68 percent."

Adin added that after all distributor-related costs (including the cost of withholding money pending returns) and fees are factored in, the effective discount rate is 80-85 percent.

From Linda Donelson, author/publisher of *Out of Isak Dinesen in Africa: The Untold Story*: "If you wish to work within the bookstore system in the U.S. at present, by far the most efficient way is to be connected to Ingram. Bookstores rely on Ingram almost exclusively, especially for rush orders. It is precisely for this reason that a distributor is useful.

"What do I pay my distributor? Such shocking amounts of money that the only possible reason I would want to continue with them is for the fame of being an author.

"Technically, my distributor gets 63 percent. But they have so many ways of juggling the books, I shudder to think what they really get. They keep 20 percent of gross as 'returns retention.' They confabulate the number of books in their warehouse. For the past 18 months, 700 copies of my book have been in limbo—out somewhere on consignment, unpaid for (according to them), still counted as inventory. Their monthly report lists these books in stock, but if you call the warehouse, the numbers are not there.

"Sales of books are reported a month late, so the payment period is set back from the 90 days in the contract to 120 days. A 10-percent fee is charged for all returns. And on and on it goes . . ."

From Karen Harris of Meritas Group, which published the cookbook, *Granny's Drawers*: "Establishing distributor relationships has been an *essential* element in *Granny's Drawers'* success. Distributor sales have accounted for more than 80 percent of our total sales. To date, returns have been minimal, with only one chain sending us returns representing only 4 percent of the total orders."

Lisa Pelto of Boys Town Publishing wrote: "The distributors and wholesalers are not 'eating at your book's price' or 'taking discounts.' They are providing a service to you that you could not do on your own or you wouldn't need their service. Bookstores and libraries *want* to order from one source so they get one invoice (this is not always the case, of course). If you know the majority of your market buys product through distributors, you should accommodate their purchasing patterns. Price your product so you can make a profit at the discounted price."

The consensus of publishers is that you don't *have* to accept a distributor's terms as given. You do have the power to bargain or move on. Don't be so desperate as to accept a bad deal. If a distributor has asked for a 68 percent discount rate, it should be all-inclusive. That means no fees for storage, catalogs, initial set-up, new titles, maintenance, and loss and damage.

"This is a free country," wrote Veltisezar "Velty" Bautista, owner of Bookhaus Publishers in Farmington Hills, Michigan, whose distributor, Publisher's Group West, pays him a 60 percent discount with minimal additional fees.

"Shop around. But do get a master distributor (granting that your books are geared toward the general market) to distribute your books to wholesalers, dealers, and bookstores. Then get the two library distributors, Quality Books and Unique Books. Then get small dealers. The bottom line is the net sales at year's end."

IS A DISTRIBUTOR RIGHT FOR YOU?

So here's the scenario with a distributor. They order books from you, don't pay until four months after you ship them, and they only pay about 32 cents on the book's retail dollar. Plus, you can get *all* those books back, and you'll have absolutely no recourse.

Do you need this? First, take a hard, honest look at the book you've written.

Niche books—say a book on doing business in China—don't belong in trade bookstores across the country. They would sell much better to corporations and through direct mail.

Other books are much too narrowly defined geographically or subject-wise for a national distributor to handle. A publisher of a book on cross-country ski trails in northern Wisconsin should find a sales representative who specializes in servicing regional bookstores and ski stores and explore alternative channels, such as selling the book directly to readers through classified or display ads in cross-country skiing magazines.

There are some publishers who choose two or three smaller, nonexclusive distributors who cater to their specific market and don't require exclusivity.

Other publishers—of bigger houses, usually—hire their own sales reps to solicit orders and a fulfillment company to handle warehousing, order handling, physical distribution, invoicing, and collections. In our opinion, it's well worth the money to hire a fulfillment company since it handles the most time-consuming and expensive tasks of the publishing business.

Some publishers, spurned by distributors, will configure joint ventures with a bigger publisher in order to get a national distributor.

Some publishers believe the ultimate answer is to sell books over the Internet. In fact, an ordering service for bookstores called AllBooks was created in response to frustrations with distributors. At the time of this publication, the program was just taking off.

WHAT ABOUT DEALING DIRECTLY WITH WHOLESALERS?

Some small publishers decide that they can generate the orders themselves and decide to deal directly with a national wholesaler or a network of regional wholesalers. The job of wholesalers is to warehouse books and ship out bookstore orders. Wholesalers historically have been considered passive order-takers since they do not employ a sales force that solicits orders from bookstores.

Why deal directly with wholesalers? One reason is to get a much better return on each book sale. While distributors pay only about 33 percent of the book's retail price, regional wholesalers generally pay 50-60 percent of the retail price. A national wholesaler pays 45 percent of retail. If you're a publisher with strong marketing muscle, you may want to consider this strategy. To connect with a wholesaler, simply call them, describe your book, and if there's interest, forward the book and supporting material.

Two great resources for pursuing this option include:

- Marie Kiefer's *Book Publishing Resource Guide*, which includes scores of wholesalers and their specialties; and

- *The American Wholesale Booksellers Association Directory and Cus-*

tomer Handbook (call (219) 232-8500, ext. 25). Includes a small list of members with their discount schedules, type of books and cassettes carried, returns policy, contact names, and a general overview of wholesalers.

Don't confuse regional wholesalers with national wholesalers. The two biggest national wholesalers are Ingram Book Company and Baker & Taylor. B&T, with a list of more than 55,000 publishers, sells most of their books to libraries and schools, although they also service many bookstores. Ingram, which stocks more than 350,000 titles in seven warehouses across the country, services virtually every bookstore in the country. Ingram is *the* national wholesaler for trade bookstores, and it can be very selective in the books it stocks. To be absolutely blunt, it's expensive for Ingram to work with hundreds of tiny publishers and they're not terribly warm to them. In order to be considered for acceptance, *generally* you must find an exclusive national distributor to represent your line of books. There are some exceptions, but that is Ingram's standard policy. Your contact at Ingram is Edward Thornhill, Public Relations Manager, One Ingram Blvd., La Vergne, TN 37086-3629; Phone: (800) 937-5300, ext. 7635.

It is easier to get into Baker & Taylor, which charges a $100 set-up fee for new vendors. Write or call: Julia Quinones, Publisher Services, Baker & Taylor, 652 E. Main St., Bridgewater, NJ 08807-0920, Phone: (908) 218-3803.

A WINNING STRATEGY

There are some publishers who use no distributor, but are carried by Ingram as a "vendor of record." That is, Ingram will warehouse books and fulfill bookstore orders for these publishers, even though they have no exclusive national distributor. This is a nice arrangement for promotion-minded publishers who drum up consistently impressive book sales. The customers are pulling the books off the shelves; Ingram keeps the shelves stocked. You'll need to fully prepare before approaching Ingram. Show them all of your promotion material—media kits, press releases, clips, bookmarks, ads, etc. Also show them a solid history of sales. Again, your contact is Edward Thornhill at (800) 937-5300, ext. 7635.

The key to this strategy is to geographically marry intense promotion with bookstore distribution. Begin locally and fan out your selling efforts regionally. A local bookstore will almost always stock a book by a home-town author. You must promote your book intensively in your hometown to move your books quickly off the shelves through lectures, seminars, radio ads (if your budget allows), and radio, TV, and newspaper interviews. Service the bookstores as a distributor would, checking weekly to make sure your book is adequately stocked and the cover is turned out if sales can justify the privilege. (You should well consider using a fulfillment house for invoicing, shipping, and collection duties.) Present the local bookstore's sales statistics to other bookstores in order to prove you have a winner, and gradually fan out your effort. Books that are hot do indeed capture Ingram's attention.

📖　　📖　　📖

Building Demand One City at a Time

"As I stood putting gas in my Jaguar, the cold damp January wind chilled me and seemed to dampen my spirits even more. I hoped the attendant inside would not run a telephone check on my gold card. If he did, they probably would turn me down."

So begins David Ramsey's account of falling from financial grace. While in his 20s, he made tons of money in real estate "from nothing" and ended up losing nearly everything. His problem: he had built his fortune atop a layer of debt. The experience was shattering, but also life-changing. It evoked in him compassion for people who were hurting not only in the arena of money, but also in marriage and career. It caused him to think about what money meant for other people: he realized it was rarely a source of joy.

Ramsey and his wife, Sharon, opened a financial counseling firm in 1990. Over the course of seven years, the firm saw 10,000 clients—most of them in financial crisis—who were led step-by-step to financial solvency. Ramsey's advice was so effective that he began speaking on what he called the "Twelve Steps to Financial Peace" in seminars. At about the same time, he taught his financial principles to college-age, fellow churchgoers.

"Then the big people wanted to hear it, too. I did a lot of counseling in our ministry. I went back to real estate for a living, and ended up counseling people who were in foreclosure or bankruptcy. They told me, 'You ought to write this stuff down,'" he said. "I knew the statistics of self-publishing. Nashville is a publishing town. A lot of people said it couldn't be done."

In 1992, Ramsey and Sharon printed 1,000 copies of *Financial Peace* at the ridiculously high cost of almost $5 a copy. He couldn't get bookstores to carry it, so he walked into a video store and asked the owner to take a few copies on consignment.

Although the video store was his only account, Ramsey was committed to creating such a demand that "consumers would jerk *Financial Peace* off the shelves."

To begin with, Ramsey started speaking once a week to any Nashville group that would have him.

He also, as he puts it, was "blessed from above." Over the years, he had appeared as a guest on an obscure radio show answering bankruptcy questions. Just at the time Ramsey published his book, he was asked to take over as the show host. "The silly thing took off," Ramsey said. "That has really helped. It's like a three-hour infomercial every afternoon."

Ramsey's strategy of stirring up demand worked beyond his wildest dreams. The video store "sold 500 copies of his book in a heartbeat" and the audience for the radio show began growing. Ramsey took evidence of the book's success at the video store and persuaded a couple of Christian stores to accept several copies (the book has a Christian aspect). They, too, successfully sold the book and Ramsey took the impressive statistics to Davis-Kidd Booksellers, Tennessee's largest bookstore chain.

"I'd continually stop by and bug them. Finally, one of the stores bought three and they sold those three in two days."

After selling 7,500 books, he went to Ingram and asked if they would serve as his wholesaler. They agreed after his sales hit 10,000.

Ramsey's overall plan was to create demand city by city in the state of Tennessee. He didn't want books on shelves in cities or states where no one had ever heard of him because he "didn't want to ship a bunch out only to get a bunch back." He consciously decided not to use a distributor because he didn't need or want national distribution.

In doing business, Ramsey followed one other principle (this piece of advice is in his book): "Don't borrow money. That way it doesn't take long to save money."

Once Davis-Kidd's chain of four stores had signed on, it was easy getting other bookstores to carry *Financial Peace*. "That gave us huge credibility. It was like landing Barnes & Noble." With a total of 95 bookstores in the state eventually agreeing to stock the book, *Financial Peace* sales zipped up the charts; one store sold 900 books in one month. *Financial Peace* became Waldenbook's No. 7 seller for the southeastern region. Every two weeks, Ramsey or one of his staff would call each of the bookstores to ask about sales and orders. If they were in town, they'd stop by and ask the books to be displayed face out: "Since it was selling, we could get that," Ramsey said.

Meanwhile, Ramsey and his wife were shipping out several thousand books through mail order and from his radio show referrals. In line with his marketing strategy, Ramsey focused on the local marketing effort and didn't bother trying to get reviews or media attention from the national media.

After 35,000 copies were sold, Ramsey revamped the book, adding three chapters, adding a few new forms, and packaging it with a national quality cover. He sold another 100,000 within a year, the lion's share in the state of Tennessee.

That's when Viking Publishing approached him with a buy-out offer. Ramsey wouldn't give the specific dollar amount, but you can bet it was a nice financial piece.

📖

Richard Paul Evans, *The Christmas Box*

Unlike David Ramsey and 99.9 percent of independently published authors in this country, Richard Paul Evans had no problem creating demand for his book, *The Christmas Box*. His problem was keeping up with demand. At first.

Richard Paul Evans enjoyed the rare experience of receiving orders for his book before he even had *plans* to publish it. Just before Christmas of 1992, he wrote the novella, *The Christmas Box*, as a gift to his two daughters. Divinely inspired to write the touching story of a family moving in with an enigmatic, strangely sad widow, he was a bit surprised that the story had turned out so well. His wife, in fact, was moved to tears. Encouraged, he ran off 20 photocopies for friends and family. A few weeks later, he began getting phone calls from complete strangers who confessed that his Christmas story had miraculously changed their lives.

"I took a steno pad and started writing down names. I realized my 20 copies had been read more than 160 times," Evans said. "A few weeks later, a clerk from a bookstore was trying to track me down and calling all the R. Evans in the phone book. By the time she called me, she had her line down. 'Hello, Mr. Evans, did you write a Christmas story?'

"I said, 'Yes I did.' 'Good, good. Where do we order it?'" 'You can't. The book has never been published.' She was dumb struck. 'Well, we had 10 orders this week. That's pretty good for any book. But for a Christmas book in February, it's unheard of. Maybe you should publish this book.' And I thought, 'Maybe I should because I saw how the book was affecting people.'"

Evans, an advertising executive at the time, sent the book to tiny, local publishing houses, which promptly rejected it. So Evans decided to independently publish the book, designing the cover himself and "finding someone with better punctuation than myself" to proofread the manuscript. He optimistically printed 9,000 copies.

"I was really naive. I didn't think 9,000 copies was that much. I just thought you should be able to sell 9,000 of anything. So I started taking it to bookstores and they didn't want the books either. No one has heard of you. An adult Christmas story? So the printer, feeling sorry for me after taking all my money, gave me a list of local distributors."

He reached the president of one of the distribution companies, who agreed—after hearing Evans' pitch, "Let me tell you what this book is doing to people" . . . to read the novella over the weekend.

"I called him Monday and asked, 'What do you think?' He said, 'I was really moved. In fact, my wife was dying to read it because I was crying. We think we're going to do really well. We think you might sell as many as 3,000 copies.'

"I thought, great. If 20 copies affected so many people, think of what 3,000 copies will do. And if they don't sell, I'll have Christmas presents for the rest of my life."

By mid-November of 1993, the distributor had sold 3,000 copies which retailed at $4.95 apiece to Utah stores. Given the pace of sales *before* the Christmas season, he told Evans to print up whatever he could afford. Evans prayed for an answer and was inspired to print 20,000; common sense told him to print 5,000. So he compromised at 10,000. By December 10, all 9,000 of the original copies had sold out. Three days later, 10,000 more left the shelves of Utah's bookstores and people were clamoring for more.

"Here's an important marketing lesson," Evans said. "If you really want to sell books, tell people it's either censored or sold out."

In 1994, Evans decided to take the book nationally, and that's when he faced the grueling challenge of hand-selling bookstore to bookstore as an independent publisher.

"So many writers think of the limousines and the glory. The reality is it's in the trenches. It's at book signings, where no one shows up," he said. "I was in Scottsdale, Arizona, and I was at this bookstore for 45 minutes, and the only thing anyone said to me was this man, 'Could you please move' because I was in the way of a book he wanted. His wife bought a book from me, and he said, 'Man! You'll buy *anything*.' Twenty minutes later, they walked in and asked for 10 more copies. He said, 'There's something really weird about your book. There's something mystical about it.' I said, 'I know.'"

Another time, Evans was at a Denver book show and was excluded from a table of authors who were signing books on stage for the book sellers.

"There was an empty chair at the table, and I looked at it for a moment. I thought, 'If I don't do it, no one will. How much does this book mean to me?' I picked up my books and I sat down, and the organizer saw me and made a beeline over to me. I looked up and said, 'Sorry I'm late.'"

She let him stay. The point is, Evans said, he was scared to death, but his book mattered to him. Through all the indignities—he once was kicked out of an Arizona bookstore after the owner learned he was Mormon—he kept reminding himself of the book's effect on people. Mothers and fathers who had lost a child, even terminally ill cancer patients, would tell him how *The Christmas Box* had helped buoy them through tragic times.

To promote the book nationally, Evans sent himself on a 21-city tour from September through December of 1994, staying at cheap motels and driving whenever possible. Sales were excellent, but Evans was running out of money because book profits were continually funneled back into promotion, printing and travel expenses.

By December 1, 1994, Evans had shipped 250,000 books—a tremendous number for any self-publisher, although he had received shockingly little notice from the national media. As he explained: "Being self-published is a little bit like competing in the Olympics without a country. They make you run on the outside of the stadium, and no one is really watching anyway." Finally, the ultimate break came along: *People Magazine* ran an article on Evans during the first week of December, pushing *The Christmas Box* to No. 2 on the *New York Times* Best Seller list, only the second time in history that an independently published book appeared on the prestigious list. At long last, publishers finally took notice.

Evans was deluged with offers, shortly after which he made his smartest move, he said: finding a talented agent, Laurie E. Liss. She placed his book in a bidding war among 14 New York publishers. Three heart-pounding days later, Simon & Schuster agreed to pay $4.25 million for hardcover rights. Evans, who wanted the book to be accessible to everyone, insisted on retaining the softcover rights. Both the hardcover and the softcover editions ultimately climbed to No. 1 on the *New York Times* Best Seller list on Christmas Eve, 1995, a first-ever achievement in book history.

Evans' advice to independent publishers when it comes to distribution in bookstores: let the readers hear the excitement in your voice.

Design: Don't dress your book in ugly clothes. Look at the fonts of Hyperion and Simon & Schuster books and copy them. Make sure your cover can compete with the best of the New York houses.

Marketing: Consider each region a target market and grow regionally. If a book can't succeed in a control group, it can't succeed nationally. Bolster the public relations with cost-effective advertising. Evans advertised locally on bus-boards. Nationally, he gave 250 books away in national radio promos and ran radio ads with the tag line: "If you read only one book this Christmas, it must be this one."

Editor's note: Evans' remarks were quoted with his permission from the Maui Writer Conference, 1996.

📖   📖   📖

THE POWER OF INGRAM

Why is it so important for Ingram to stock your books? The catch is this: Ingram publishes a CD-ROM that enhances R.R. Bowker's *Books in Print*. It shows the books that are carried in Ingram's warehouses, as well as those that aren't. If your book isn't on that CD, there might be problems. Clerks electronically search it when they look up books, along with lists supplied by Baker & Taylor and maybe two or three other regional warehouses. If a bookstore clerk can't find your company on a warehouser's CD, it means the store has to place a special order, do separate paperwork, and cut a separate check. Some bookstores feel it costs more money than it's worth and tell the customer they can't get your book. Period. No sale. For this reason, some publishers have resorted to "buying" their way into Ingram by signing up with the Sarasota, Florida-based Small Press Alliance (a division of BookWorld Services, Inc., a distributor) for $500. Small Press Alliance acts as a fulfillment service of sorts for small publishers and gives the publisher the needed credential for acceptance into Ingram. Dina Fullerton of BookWorld said this doesn't mean Small Press Alliance will accept any publisher who comes through the door, but only publishers who have produced quality books.

Despite all the advantages of getting carried by Ingram, you can expect headaches. This is what Marilyn and Tom Ross had to say about Ingram in the January 1997 issue of *Span Connection*.

"Ingram . . . seems to be on a mission to alienate independent publishers. Many of us have groaned when they returned books on the one hand, while reordering them on the other. Additionally, they have stopped payment on greatly past-due checks, seized inventory from small press exclusive distributors in lieu of paying the presses what is owed to them, and refused to fill a large order from Waldenbooks when the small press had already paid for endcap displays. They wield enormous power."

WHY DOES A DISTRIBUTOR CHARGE SO MUCH?

Distributors' discount fees are undeniably high, but consider that the bookseller and wholesaler are also taking their cut out of the pie. Also, consider how much money and time it would take for you to accomplish the same job of selling, invoicing, collecting, and shipping. Finally, a distributor carries a lot of clout when making appointments with bookstores or collecting on delinquent accounts. Some distributors charge a lower percentage—say 58 percent—but typically charge the publisher additional fees for each service, so it generally evens out. The fees might include: warehouse fees, exhibit fees for Book Expo America, a catalog listing fee, shipping fees, or insurance fees to protect against damage in the warehouse.

"Some people say I want the lowest percentage humanly possible, but it may come back on the other end," said Greg Godek, who sold 1.4 million copies of *1,001 Ways to Be Romantic* through the distributor, LPC Group. "There's nothing wrong with that. But don't make a decision on incomplete information. I, myself, like to make life as simple as possible." Godek's advice: *Price your book high enough to make some money.*

Lisa Pelto, consumer marketing manager of Boys Town Press, a publisher of 109 titles, said that a publisher not only has to look at the retail price, but also the cost of production.

"When I started looking at this three years ago, the cost to produce a book was nearly 40 percent of our retail cost. Now we shoot for 23-28 percent. That means exterior services like indexing, CIP, cover design, interior layout, and printing," she said.

Shop around. If your book is truly marketable, there are national distributors who will take a discount in the low 60s and charge very few additional fees.

Choosing a distributor

There are a lot of sad stories of national distributors going belly up, causing their small publishers to sink with them. Yet some publishers are so anxious and thankful to sign on with a distributor, they fail to get the full story on a distributor's marketing competence or financial solvency.

Doing your homework involves talking to other publishers: at regional meetings, book fairs, publishers' conferences, everywhere. Publishers also freely share information on the Publishers Marketing Association Forum on the Internet.

Another strategy is to visit the places where you want to sell your book. Have you written a book about vegetarian cooking? Visit the main bookstores, as well as health food co-ops and vitamin stores—anywhere that you think your book could be sold. Introduce yourself to the owner as a cookbook author/publisher and ask who distributes their cookbooks. Attend the BookExpo America trade show (formerly known as the ABA trade show) in Chicago, if possible, where each distributor typically takes up an entire aisle. Publishers are stationed with their respective distributor. A good way to get into the BookExpo is with a reporter's pass (even if you're not a reporter, find a publication who'd like an article on the show and they will get a pass for you).

If you can't get to trade shows, ask the distributors to send catalogs.

Examine the titles, the graphics, the topic area, the writing. Can you see your book in it? Does it have the same spirit of your book?

The biggest distributors obviously carry a huge range of books. Catalogs from more specialized distributors might focus on offbeat topics: vegetarian cooking, women's issues, gay and lesbian studies, Eastern religion, new age, and more. The best known are New Leaf (Atlanta, Georgia) and Bookpeople (Oakland, California). A smaller distributor may not reach as many bookstores, but may give your book more care and personal attention.

Once you find a distributor you feel would work for you, call three of the publishers randomly picked from the catalog. Dominique Raccah, co-CEO of the Chicago-based LPC Group, a major small press distributor, offered these suggestions when interviewing publishers about a specific distributor:

- How accessible is the management? If something goes awry, will there be a living, breathing person to talk to, or an endless queue of voice mail?

- How many books do they sell? Pick actual titles and ask for real numbers.

- How prompt are payments? The trade standard is 120 days after the sales report date.

- Are their shipments timely? A 72-hour turnaround time is fairly standard. With the trend of stores and wholesalers stocking less and reordering more, a quick turnaround can make a huge difference in sales.

- Are there any unforeseen expenses working with this company?

- Ask about any hidden problems and benefits to working with this distributor. For example, does the distributor have poor relations with a particular superstore, embarrassing employee turnover, bad phone service, or a habit of publishing catalogs late?

Also, ask about the distributor's returns policy. If you're lucky, the distributor doesn't allow returns. This is highly unlikely, however, unless it is a specialized distributor.

Besides finding a good fit with a distributor, you must be convinced of the distributor's integrity. Like it or not, you will have to trust the distributor to give you an accurate accounting of your sales (although the distributor's contract typically allows for an audit at your cost), to enthusiastically promote your book, to keep accurate track of your inventory, to ship your books in good shape, and, very importantly, to pay you when your money is due. Cash flow is already a tough issue in the publisher/distributor relationship. If you ship books to a distributor in January, you can't expect any money until three or four months later. Your cash flow will get really ugly if your distributor is suffering from its own cash flow problems. Cash flow has chronically dogged distributors because they sell books on very slim margins. Distributors who are undercapitalized and/or poor business managers will likely not survive in the industry and several have already gone under, said Ciaran Mercier, a book distribution consultant based in Middletown, California. Besides cash flow problems, there have been reports of distributors who have:

- Misused the funds of book sales.

- Falsified their sales reports.

- Consistently made late payments to the publisher.

- Forgotten to put a book in their catalog.

- Made a mess of the inventory reports.

- Declared bankruptcy.

How do you choose a trustworthy distributor from the get-go? Word-of-mouth is the best way to avoid a loser. When you're talking with the publishers represented by the distributor, ask what their experience has been with the distributor's payment history. Does the distributor pay fully and on time? Are the inventory reports reliable? Has the distributor pulled any erratic punches?

When you talk to store owners, ask questions to get a feel for the distributor's reputation. Do they service the accounts frequently and accurately? Are they in good financial shape? Are they easy to work with? Once you've made your top picks and there's interest on both sides, ask the distributor for bank references. Follow up with calls to the bank's operations officer and tell you'd like to do a credit check on a customer. You can attempt to ask other questions (although you probably won't get answers), such as: What's their general balance (five-figure, six-figure)? How long have they banked there? Also, order a Dunn & Bradstreet report.

INTERVIEWING THE DISTRIBUTOR

A big distributor has the advantage of reaching more stores with a large national sales force. Larger, more established distributors, in general, carry more clout in the marketplace and can command meetings with chain-store buyers. Despite these advantages, consider a specialized, nonexclusive distributor if your book focuses on a specialized subject.

As you talk to various distributors, listen carefully to what they say.

 • Do they get excited about your book?

 • Do they talk about the sales they will make, the markets they'll reach? Or do they make you feel like they would be doing you a favor by taking your book on? If so, do yourself a favor and keep searching.

Here are a few more criteria to consider when scoping out distributors:

 • Does the distributor have a booth at the BookExpo America show? It may seem like such a basic, but there are distributors who attend, but don't exhibit their books.

 • Is the catalog well organized and nicely designed? (See the list of distributors at the end of this chapter to request catalogs.)

 • Does the distributor have a tight relationship with the superstores, including Barnes & Noble (B Dalton, Bookstar, Bookstop, Doubleday, Scribners), Waldenbooks/Borders (Brentanos, Readers Market), and Crown? Despite a higher return rate from chain stores, they do account for 40-50 percent of the market. If you can do well in the major chains, you are well on your way to success.

 • Besides superstores, ask who else they sell to. How many accounts? Where are they located? Ask about the specialty stores they visit, jobbers, the wholesalers they use, and on which chain stores they focus. Once you've narrowed your choices, there are more specific financial questions you'll need to ask:

 • What percentage of retail do they pay for each book sold? This is often negotiable. If it sounds too high, walk away.

- Are there any extra charges of doing business?
- Where do they warehouse the books, and is there an extra charge for it?
- How fast do they pay?
- Will they do fulfillment of your own orders, and how much will they charge?
- Who pays shipping?

This sounds like an awful lot of research, but it's worth it. Once you're in with a distributor, it's usually a long-term commitment.

SELLING YOURSELF TO A NATIONAL DISTRIBUTOR

The best distributors will only take on books that they think will sell. They'll want to know:

- Details of your marketing plan, including dollars earmarked for public relations and advertising.
- If the author is going to tour, for how long and where?
- How does the author come off in an interview? This is very important!
- Is the cover design good? This is crucial since the sales rep has just a few seconds to sell your book.

How do you approach a distributor? We've already mentioned attending the BookExpo America trade show. More traditionally, publishers will call the distributor to introduce themselves. It is best to find a distributor several months *before* the book is published. Write out your pitch and practice it so that you don't stumble. Tell them your name, the name of your publishing firm, and the name of your book. Briefly tell them what your book is about, how many pages, who it appeals to, how much it costs, and the size. Tell them why you think it's a perfect fit for their line of books and what you'll do to market it. Be sure to mention your credentials as it relates to the book—"I've been Madonna's closest confidante for 10 years." That's an extreme example, of course, but in promotion and selling, the book and the author are intertwined. The author's uniqueness and credibility are often the basis of a newspaper or magazine article or television appearance. After the phone call, mail a copy of your book, copies of reviews and articles (if it's post-publication), and a cover letter outlining what your book is about, its target audience, your credentials, a synopsis of a national marketing plan, evidence of your success to date, and your willingness to work with the distributor. Follow up a few days later with another phone call. Did they get the book? Do they have any questions? Exclusive distributors won't accept the book of a one-time book publisher unless the publisher is perceived as a very ambitious and talented marketer with enough money to put into a hard-hitting public relations campaign.

Randall Beek of Consortium, Inc., said his firm is looking for people with an ongoing publishing program of at least two books a season and a minimum of $100,000 in annual sales after returns. Yet his company has made exceptions. It took on *The Secret of Life* because it was a spinoff of an eight-part PBS television series and there was money set aside for marketing and advertising. It sold 25,000 copies.

YOUR JOB, THEIR JOB

Consider your distributor as a partner, not a distant relation. There is a lot expected from both sides. A distributor expects the publisher/author to push the book on radio, in newspapers, in magazines. They want an author who gives not good interview, but great interview.

The marketing savvy and sales success of today's independent publishers have forced wholesalers, booksellers, and national distributors to work together like a well-oiled machine. It's increasingly common for a distributor's sales reps to meet frequently with the superstores and wholesalers to ensure that enough books will be on the shelves when and where they are needed. A single television appearance can pull thousands of books off the shelves, so the distributor and wholesaler need to be kept apprised week-to-week, and sometimes day-to-day, of an author's media stops. It's also imperative that the author/publisher keep in constant contact with the distributor so that books are on shelves when the demand hits.

In terms of marketing materials, the publisher has to meet deadlines in terms of producing tip sheets and sales kits, and printing the books.

Sales representatives, armed with sales catalogs and other promotional materials, go out and sell the new and backlisted titles. Consortium, Inc., like most other reputable distributors, will evaluate your tip sheets (a double-sided information sheet that sales reps use for their presentations), your book cover, price, title and subtitle, sales kits (includes a color copy of the cover, book excerpts, a chapter or an introduction, and a tip sheet), and catalog copy. Consortium Inc.'s staff members will also determine whether the book will work best as a hard-cover or soft-cover and the optimal time to release the book. It's all part of the package.

ADJUSTING YOUR EXPECTATIONS

If you expect your distributor will sell 10,000 copies, you might be in for a big disappointment. Talk to your contact and ask for a realistic estimate.

A WORD ABOUT TIMING

If your book is tied to a particular holiday, Christmas, for example, you should start contacting distributors at least 10 months before your book is ready to go the printer. Big distributors publish spring and fall catalogs, and usually have their catalogs compiled six months prior to the publishing date. Even if your book isn't seasonal, consider finding a distributor before it's completely written. Some distributors will consider carrying a book if they see the cover design and sample chapters. Let's say that you're Madonna's personal assistant and want to write an insider's account of her first year as a mother. A distributor would take the book on in a nanosecond.

BEYOND DISTRIBUTORS

One thing to remember about distribution: there's more to life than book-stores. The more you can exploit the alternate markets, the higher profit you'll make per book. Yet, for books with a broad-based appeal, it is imperative that you use a distributor or wholesaler. You can't live with them, but you *really* cannot live without them.

Comparing Distribution Contracts

The following information compares the contract variables of several exclusive national book distribution companies. The information was provided by company executives, and was current at press time. This information is subject to change, and is intended to assist small publishers who are in the process of seeking a national distributor for their titles. All companies were asked for the same information: N/A means the company declined to provide those figures. For the most current rates, fee schedules and contract specifics, contact the companies directly.

	Access Publishers Network, 6893 Sullivan Road, Grawn, MI 49637 (616) 276-5196	**APG Trade 3356 Coffey Lane, Santa Rosa, CA 95403 (707) 542-5400**	**BookWorld Services, Inc, 1933 Whitfield Loop, Sarasota, FL 34243 (800) 444-2524**	**Consortium Book Sales, 1045 Westgate Dr., St. Paul, MN 55114 (612) 221-9035**
Categories	Self-Help, How-to, Travel, New Age, Novels, Children's	General, Metaphysical, Children's	Fiction, Self-Help, New Age, Business, Children's	Fiction, Feminism, Drama, Hispanic, Children's
Exclusive	Yes	Yes	Yes	Yes
National	Yes	Yes	Yes	Yes
International Sales	Yes, but nonexclusivity is an option	Yes, All English speaking countries	Yes, Canada, Europe, Asia, South Africa	Yes, Canada
Discount Rate	65% of list price	65% of list price (approx.)	64% to 68% of list price	22 to 26% of Net
Offer No Returns Policy		Only on certain products	No	No
Payment Schedule	110 Days	90–120 Days	90–120 Days	60 Days After Sales Report
Sales Report Schedule	Monthly	Monthly	Monthly	Monthly
Average Return	25%	23%	26%	Approx. 20%
Fee For Returns	Yes, 3% to 5% of the net credit	Yes	No	No
Shipping Turnaround	24 to 48 hours	Same day when required	24 hours	24 to 72 hours
Years In Operation	7	8	34	11
Annual New Titles	300	500	200	250 to 300
Backlist	1,500	2,500	1,000	4,000
Offer Fulfillment Only	No	Yes to select clients	No	No
Audit Allowed	Yes	Yes	Yes	Yes
Contract Negotiable	Yes, Some points are completely flexible for big publishers	No	No	On some points
Catalog Fees	Yes, $150 for full page	Yes	$1050/year average	Yes
New Title Fee	No	Yes	$390	No
Backlist Fee	No	Yes	No	No
Exhibit Fee	Only for BookExpo America, $50			
Storage Fee	Yes, 1¢ per book per month, $15 minimum	1¢ per title per month	2¢ per book upon arrival, 2¢ per book per month	Yes
Shipping Fee	For Publisher Special Orders	Yes	No	Yes
Insurance Fee	No	No	No	Yes
Bank of Record	Old Kent Bank	Trans Financial Bank	Liberty Bank, North Bradenton, Fla.	N/A
Credit Reference #	(616) 922-4240	George Fischer, CFO	Gary Franek, vice president	N/A
Internet site	No	www.bookbase.com	www.bookworld.com	www.cbsd.com/cbsd/

LPC Group P.O. Box 372 Naperville, IL 60566 (800) 626-4330	Midpoint Trade 27 West 20th St., Ste. 1102 New York, NY 10011 (913) 831-2233	National Book Network, 4720 Boston Way Lanham, MD 20706 (800) 462-6420	Partners Book Distributing Inc., 2325 Jarkco Drive, Holt, MI 48842 (517) 694-3205	Publishers Group West, 4065 Hollis St., P.O. Box 8843, Emeryville, CA 94662 (800) 788-3123
General, business, self help, sports Inbook, fiction, politics, alternative non-fiction, gay and lesbian	General, Business, Family, Children's	General, Alternative Health, Business, Sports, Academics	General, Nature, Travel, African American, Cookbooks, Sports	General
Yes	Yes for 29 Major Accounts	Yes	Yes	Yes
Yes	Yes	Yes	Yes	Yes
Yes, United Kingdom, Europe, Pacific Rim	No	Yes, Canada	No	Yes, Canada
N/A	N/A	27% of Net approx.	62% of list price	N/A
	No	No	No	
Monthly	120 Days	60-90 Days	90 - 120 Days	90 Days after invoice
Monthly	Monthly	Monthly, 6 reports/month	Monthly	Monthly
N/A	11.1%	27%	20 - 25%	30%
No	No	Yes	No	No
48 to 72 hours	One week	48 hours – 1 week	24 hours on hot titles	2-3 days
2 Years in Current Format	1	11	13	20
800	150	700	100 to 200	1,500
4,000 to 6,000	900	3,000	250	6,000
No	To certain clients	No	No	No
Yes	Yes	Yes	Yes	Possibly
N/A	No	Yes	No	No
N/A	No	Yes	No	No
N/A	No	Yes	No	No
N/A	No	No	No	No
	Only for BookExpo America			
N/A	No	Yes	No	Yes, for stock held over 2 years
N/A	No	Yes	Yes	No
N/A	Don't Insure	No	No	No
N/A	Country Club Bank, Kansas City, MO		First Chicago NBD	Bank of California
N/A	(816) 931-4060		Request From Them	Grove Atlantic
www.coolbooks.com	No	www.nbnbooks.com	No	In development

WHOLESALERS

Advanced Marketing Services
5880 Oberlin Drive, Suite 400
San Diego, CA 92121
(619) 457-2500
Tammie Johnson

Baker & Taylor
652 E. Main St.
Bridgewater, NJ 88007-0920
Julia Quinones, Publisher Services

The Booksource
1230 Macklind Ave.
St. Louis, MO 63110
(314) 647-0600
Vicki Sence

Bookazine Book Distributors
(also a distributor)
75 Hook Rd.
Bayonne, NJ 07002
(800) 221-8112
Richard Kallman

Bookmen, Inc.
525 N. Third Street
Minneapolis, MN 55401
(612) 341-3333
John Kudrle/Paperbacks, mass
market, romance, travel, etc.
Bill Mockler/All hardbound books,
adult and juvenile

Bookpeople (also a distributor)
7900 Edgewater Drive
Oakland, CA 94621
(510) 632-4700
Jeff Scott

Ingram Book Company
One Ingram Boulevard
LaVergne, TN 37086-3629
(615) 793-5000, ext. 7635
Edward Thornhill

Koen Book Distributors
10 Twosome Drive
P.O. Box 600
Moorestown, NJ 08057
(800) 257-8481
Sheila Kowalsky

8.

PARTNERSHIP PUBLISHING: A WELL-KEPT SECRET

When spider webs unite,
they can tie up a lion.
ETHIOPIAN PROVERB

THERE'S NO QUESTION THAT INDEPENDENT PUBLISHING IS A COMPLEX, competitive, and overcrowded business. The answer for some authors is what's called joint or co-publishing.

Who should co-publish? Authors who feel overwhelmed by the complexities of the publishing industry and want an experienced publishing partner. It is for the author who is aware of how extremely difficult it is to secure a national book distributor or wholesaler, and wants a guaranteed "in" through the imprint of an established publisher.

Co-publishing is also an excellent choice for someone who isn't looking necessarily for a sizeable return on their investment, but wants to author a book for professional reasons. The book would enhance the professional's credibility and attract media attention, which, in turn, would attract customers or students or clients.

Other well-known authors have decided on a joint venture because they've soured on big New York publishers:
- They wanted to enthusiastically promote the book, but the publisher wouldn't support their efforts;

93

- They were disappointed in the overall look or title of the book and wanted more control in their next effort;
- They have an established name, a loyal following and feel they can earn more money by co-publishing a book than they can with a standard royalty.

What is co-publishing?

Simply put, the publisher and author share the responsibilities of producing, distributing, and marketing the book, and, in most cases, sharing the financial risk. The author's promotional abilities are still critical to the book's success, but the publisher provides guidance, marketing support, some publicity, and a system of distribution. A partnership can take many forms, but typically the publisher and author share the cost of production and they share net returns (the actual money received for sales) by an agreed upon percentage. Say, the publisher pays 60 percent of the total cost of production (averaging $19,000), the author pays 40 percent. After the book is produced, the book's net receipts may be split by the same fraction—the publisher gets 60 percent, the author, 40 percent. In another variation, an author would put up the entire cost of the project. The publisher might then take a 20 percent commission on each book sold until the author's investment is paid, and then split all subsequent receipts 50/50.

There are other arrangements in which a publisher takes on a project *after* the book is produced and printed. A publisher, for example, may assume the responsibility of marketing, distribution and promotion with the understanding that the author will also vigorously promote the book. In return, the publisher will take 15 percent of all net cash receipts and 15 percent of all subsidiary rights sales.

Co-publishing is not vanity publishing! A vanity publisher has absolutely no stake in the success of the book. These houses are, in a word, rip-offs. Vanity presses produce chintzy books and couldn't care less about the quality of the book. Their "marketing effort" often means the placement of a cheap ad in an obscure magazine that no one reads. The reputations of the two major New York City vanity houses are so bad they are considered the "kiss of death" for any book.

A Washington physician, for example, wanted to publish a poorly conceived book and was spurned by publishers. In desperation, he paid a New York City vanity press $25,000 to produce a book. That didn't include the $8,000 he spent himself for the cover design. The press sent him 50 books and told him they'd print more on demand. He essentially spent $33,000 for a total of 50 atrocious books with not a dime of royalties to show for them. Additionally, the vanity press retained ownership of the book's copyright, which essentially prevented the physician from seeking out a publisher with true integrity.

Joint publishing is also different than literary services, whereby an author pays a fee for substantive editing, manuscript evaluation, cover design, or text layout. These contracts are very clear: there is a fee exchanged for specific services.

Co-publishing ventures have blossomed as an important part of the publishing industry because so many commercial firms, consultants, speakers, and lesser known celebrities want a professionally produced book. The ventures are rarely talked about, however, because a publishing house wants to avoid being branded as a vanity publisher.

The caveat is this. Joint publishing is often not profitable. If a healthy profit is your primary motivation, then honestly analyze the potential profitability. As a general rule, trade books by unknown authors destined for trade bookstores will most likely *lose* money in a joint venture. For example, let's say you print up 3,000 books to be sold through a national distributor (which takes a 68 percent discount rate or 32 percent of the retail price). You decide to invest 40 percent of up-front costs and receive 40 percent of net returns. For each $15 book, you'd receive 12.8 percent of the book's retail price (40 percent x 32 percent) or $1.92 per book. If every book sold, your revenues would total $5,760. If you had invested $5,800 for design, production and promotion, you'd *lose* $40. Generally, a joint venture works profitwise only for authors who believe they'll sell most of their books at a favorable discount or at full retail price—via seminars, to corporations, or to specialty markets. For example, 3,000 books sold at a full $15 price would yield $18,000 for the author (40 percent x $45,000).

A joint-venture agreement can take many forms. If you shop around for terms, you'll find publishers differ hugely in the amount they are asking for a package of publicity, editing, design, and printing of a standard 6 x 9, 250-page trade book. We found the low end ranged around $10,000, the high end was $25,000. For the best deal, shop around.

To illustrate how two joint ventures can work, we provide these two examples.

THE BEST OF SMALL PRESS PUBLISHERS, INC.

This publishing firm based in Minneapolis, Minnesota, is headed by Mark Habrel, a former small-press publishing consultant. Over the course of three years, Habrel worked with 150 author/publishers, most of whom had a good product, but—lacking a distributor—ended up permanently storing hundreds of books in their basements. The books they did sell weren't profitable enough to sustain them. Habrel felt that a production/marketing partnership would greatly bolster an author's chance of success and formed Best of Small Press in February of 1996.

A young company, BSP has published 10 books. To be accepted by BSP, a book must be well-written, appeal to a national audience (or, in special cases, a regional audience), be unique in the field (fiction or nonfiction), and show promise for corporate sales.

Best of Small Press (BSP) estimates the total project done as a self-publishing venture, then ask the author to pay 60 percent either as a lump sum or over time. The author writes the book, ensures that it's substantively edited, secures endorsements, finds someone prestigious to write the foreword and assumes publicity and promotion work. BSP designs the book, copy edits and proofreads, manufactures the book, and assumes six months of sales costs, including attending trade shows and sending out press releases and review copies. They also handle corporate sales. *Its primary job, however, is distribution.* Once with BSP, the book has an "in" with the country's two biggest wholesalers, Ingram and Baker & Taylor; it's also distributed by BSP, which services independent bookstores but is not yet on direct sales terms with the chains. BSP also telemarkets its books. Although the author and BSP work together, BSP has final say in the book's final design. The author retains ownership of the copyright. BSP has exclusive license to print for an agreed upon period of time.

The author begins receiving 50 percent of book receipts after BSP recaptures its full "earn out" of its initial investment.

As an example, let's say BSP and author Sally Smith collaborate on a $15 book with an estimated production cost of $20,000. Smith pays $12,000. BSP sells enough copies through bookstores and corporate sales to reap $8,000. Sally Smith is then entitled to half of the remaining receipts from book sales.

Author Edie Julik, who has published two children's books (one on teaching children about violence, the other about divorce) earned back her investment with Best of Small Press in less than a year. She likes the arrangement because it allows her to focus on what she does best—book sales primarily through school presentations and conference speaking—while Best of Small Press handles distribution to bookstores.

BOOKPARTNERS, INC.

Thorn Bacon, editor-in-chief of BookPartners and his wife, Ursula, president, worked for many years as a literary service, dealing with authors all over the country. Five or six years ago, he said, the distribution system was "friendly to small publishers, but it is not today," Thorn Bacon said.

"We could help an author with a manuscript, but what's going to happen to it if it can't be sold to the majors? So we made a decision, as a matter of conscience to begin this business."

In 1992, the Wilsonville, Oregon-based BookPartners was born. In 1996, they published 57 books; of those, 70 percent will earn a return of 10 percent on total investment or more based on the success of first-year sales, said Associate Publisher Lyle Nelson. That compares with the trade-book industry standard success rate, which Nelson estimates as one financially successful book out of 10 published.

BookPartners bases the split of book receipts on the amount invested up front. If authors invest 60 percent of the estimated cost, they receive 60 percent of total book receipts. The average book production cost is $19,000. Authors have invested capital from $5,000 to $45,000, with the average amounting to about $13,000. Unlike BSP, the author begins earning revenues immediately after the first book is sold.

BookPartners expects an author to be heavily involved in promotion. To support the author, BookPartners sends out galleys to review journals, 50-75 review copies, 50 press kits (at a cost of $5 apiece), presents the book at book fairs, sets up publicity for the first three months (book signings, radio and TV interviews) and even longer, if the publicity is advantageous to sales. BookPartners also writes reviews, obtains high-profile endorsements, substantively edits the book, if necessary, designs the book, prints it, and devises an overall marketing plan that specifies targeted sales and what the author has to do to achieve those sales.

The company focuses on books that "celebrate the human spirit." For each book, it conducts a market analysis in six marketing channels: top-of-the-line bookstores, libraries, the gift store market, associations and groups, corporations, and direct marketing.

"If the book has good direct sales or the author has a big mailing list of loyal readers or will sell the book through seminars, the break-even number can be as low as 1,500. If we have to sell primarily through the traditional book market, the author's break even is 3,000, our normal first print run," Nelson said.

With BookPartners, the author retains ownership to the copyright; BookPartners is given exclusive license to print. If sales dip below 750 a year, all printing rights revert to the author.

Nelson stresses that a collaboration does not guarantee success.

"We have our books that we're dissatisfied with financially; we feel bad that we didn't do better," he said. "We didn't mislead the author, but acknowledge we made a mistake in the market analysis."

Those authors with good speaking skills have a substantially higher rate of success because back-of-the-room sales reap the full retail price. Yet some authors can overestimate how many books they'll sell this way.

"Some authors have told us, 'I'm speaking in front of 10,000 people next year and I need the book in a hurry,'" he said. "Yet they don't have anything set up and they don't come close to what they projected. With these authors, we fall short of our financial estimates."

BookPartners, to preserve its reputation, will turn down a book, which is impossible to turn into a good book (or the author is unwilling to yield to certain changes). If it's a well-written book, but lacks a market,

BookPartners will give the author its best estimate of sales and advise the author that it won't present the book to the distributor. Authors who are consultants may still choose to go ahead, knowing the book will help them land consulting contracts.

Nelson said the company's biggest job is to bring an author's perception of a book—"it's a best seller" to the realm of reality.

With a partnership, an author must be willing to initiate marketing efforts. If an author wants to sign books while on a trip to Minneapolis, for example, BookPartners will provide a list of bookstores, contact names, media names and addresses, sample letters, how to stop in and pitch the book to a bookseller—but it's the author who has to schedule the book signing events, charm the bookstore owners, and enthrall the audience at book readings, Nelson said.

Peg Bracken, author of the best-selling, *The I Hate To Cook Book*, decided to go with BookPartners for her most recent book, *Getting Old for the First Time*. Bracken, who was formerly with Harcourt Brace Publishing, has written 10 books and sold an estimated 9 million copies. It wasn't money, she said, that prompted her to go with BookPartners instead of a New York publisher, but the experience of "having a good, fat input. I thought it would be fun to see a book come together from start to finish. You have a hands-on feeling that you don't have with a New York publisher. There, you let go of the manuscript, and it's in book form 10 months later."

If you are considering a joint venture, be sure to research the firms and their offers carefully. Ask your prospective partner about the:

- Number of full-time marketing employees.
- Number of full-time book editors.
- Number of books published each year.
- Average number of books sold.
- One-time fee; don't get nickel and dimed to death.

Get a feeling for the quality of the books they produce. Ask to see them. Ask for a catalog and press releases to ascertain the quality of copy they write and the overall image the company projects.

Also, ask for an explicit listing of the firm's services. The publisher's responsibilities and the author's responsibilities should be clearly drawn out. If they promise marketing support, ask for specifics: how many press releases do they send out; how many press kits; at how many trade shows will your book be represented; will they support you with a marketing plan, media lists, direct mailing lists, etc. The more you look, the better questions you can ask.

PUBLISHERS PARTNERING WITH PUBLISHERS

So far, we have discussed authors teaming up with publishers. There are also many forms of publisher/publisher partnerships. In its simplest form, publishers work out reciprocal or one-way sales deals with other publishers. Essentially, a publisher buys another publisher's books at a 40-percent to 50-percent discount. Often, this introduces entry into a brand new market at a discount more favorable than a distributor can offer. To make it a no-risk deal, many publishers ask for a mutual agreement of advance payment and no returns.

Partnerships are fluid; terms are dependent on the wishes, abilities, and financial resources of both parties. Typically, the cost of printing and marketing resources are shared. We learned of a micro-publisher teaming up with a well-capitalized publisher in order to fund a book project and establish a relationship with a distributor. It illustrates the problems and pitfalls of such an arrangement.

The story began in 1992 at Georgetown University, where Bruce Kletz was getting a master's degree in national securities studies. One of his classmates was a CIA analyst, Patrick G. Eddington. Later in 1994 when Kletz was in the early stages of forming a publishing firm, Insignia Publishing, Eddington approached him with a book idea: his personal story of learning how the CIA and Department of Defense were covering up what they knew about the Gulf War Syndrome and how Eddington attempted to persuade them to reveal what they knew.

It was to have been Kletz's first book; he originally thought he'd print up to 3,000 books and ship them out of his basement. But in the fall of 1996, the issue of Gulf War Syndrome exploded in the media and Patrick J.

Eddington found himself profiled on the front page of the *New York Times*. The next day, Bruce Kletz was also profiled as controversy swirled around the manuscript.

"We were trying to use information that the Department of Defense had declassified and published on the Internet. Later, they removed the files from their website to deflect all attempts to view the files," he said. "Varying reasons were given, including: 'They are being reclassified.'"

The CIA stalled on its approval of the manuscript so Kletz and Eddington filed suit. And to force the point that material—once declassified cannot be reclassified again under federal law—Kletz posted all the Department of Defense files in question on his own website. A day after the *New York Times* piece ran, the CIA caved in and dropped its objections to using the information in his book.

Of course, the article and ensuing appearances on major news network shows mentioned Eddington's upcoming book and soon Kletz was talking to major publishing houses about a publishing deal that would involve both Insignia and Eddington.

Why did Kletz pursue a publishing partner? Kletz was convinced the book was on the high road to becoming a best seller, but he believed an established publisher could help him achieve three key goals: to find enough capital to fund the project, to help him establish a relationship with a distributor so that when he came out with his next book "they wouldn't tell me to get in line with everybody else," and to help him learn the ropes of generating national publicity.

"I wanted to meet some of the reps, go through the public relations, set up the media tours. It's one thing to have an understanding of how to do it, and it's another to do it," he said.

Kletz discovered, however, that the major publishers essentially wanted to ignore Insignia and deal directly with the author. Yet Kletz and Eddington had already agreed they wanted to team up on the project, sharing the costs and revenues 50/50. Eddington was confident that Kletz would explore every angle outside of the normal bookstore sales—foreign rights, direct mail (Eddington was well-tied into the community of vets), foreign serialization, and grass roots promotion.

After analyzing a number of proposals, Kletz and Eddington chose Logical Figments Books, a publishing firm headed up by Burt Ward, who played Batman's sidekick, Robin, in the 1960s television series.

Ward was to provide the capital to print upwards of 20,000 books and promised to send Eddington on a 50-city tour. He also employed a network of sales representatives with established connections to the bookstore trade *and* the entertainment field—useful, of course, for publicity.

The profit split? All receipts would first go toward reimbursing expenses (Kletz was also investing in the project with an 800 number, fulfillment in and outside the trade, man-hours in setting up the tour, etc.). Once expenses were paid, profits would be divided this way: 50 percent to Logical Figments, 25 percent to Kletz, and 25 percent to Eddington.

Kletz's advice: define your goals before finding a partner. His contract, for example, explicitly stated that Figment would lay the groundwork for Insignia to fly on its own. Kletz also advised finding an attorney familiar with the publishing industry to negotiate the contract, particularly if chain store sales and national publicity are planned.

"If I were to make a recommendation, it would be don't rush out to do it unless the agreement really meets all of your goals," he said.

So how did the partnership work? It broke down, in fact, over "serious disagreements about marketing and general business practices."

Kletz bought Ward out of the contract and will publish the book himself.

"I should have taken my advice more to heart. Yes, Burt was capable of matching his strengths to my weaknesses, but there was more to the picture than just these matchups and I didn't go over them sufficiently before we jumped in.

"I stand by what I said earlier, but now I add a caution to leave no issue undiscussed, even ones you consider very basic."

WHERE DO YOU FIND A PUBLISHING PARTNER?

First of all, understand that both parties need not be a publisher, said John McHugh, a Glendale, Wisconsin-based publishing consultant.

"It's very common to see an association or a foundation co-publishing with a commercial publisher," he wrote in the March 1995 *PMA Newslet-*

ter. "Today we see co-publishing ventures between software companies and trade publishers. Also common are publishing arrangements between consulting firms and commercial publishers. Use your imagination."

To find a partner, he suggests visiting trade shows or consulting with trade associations and trade journals that are related to the book project.

THE AGREEMENT

Is your partner in place? Have you agreed on your respective strengths, have you generally defined the jobs each partner is responsible for? Now is time to draw up for an agreement. McHugh defined these elements in his article:

- The product. What is it? Define it.

- Ownership. Understand who owns the copyright and what rights are being licensed to the partner.

- Who does what? When? How?

- Details of the financial arrangements.

- When will all this happen?

- Who will work with the author? Who will pay the author royalties?

CO-PUBLISHING SYNERGY

To use that hackneyed phrase, co-publishing can be a win-win situation, but diligently pursue getting everything in writing. In the increasingly complex and competitive world of publishing, it may give you the edge that you'll need.

9

CREATING PUBLICITY THAT'S SMART, CHEAP, AND EFFECTIVE

Reach for the stars. You may not get one,
but at least you won't come back with a handful of dirt.
LEO BURNETT

Coauthored by **David Hahn**,
Senior Vice President of Planned Television Arts

PUBLICITY IS TRULY THE NO. 1 KEY TO SUCCESS FOR MOST KINDS OF books. If you've written a book about the inside story of Elvis Presley and no one knows about it, it may go the way of the King and suffer an untimely and tragic death.

Yet with the proliferation of independent publishers, writing a book isn't as newsworthy as it once was. The competition to get airplay and print space has become fierce, so you have to edge in your story with creativity, intelligence, and a sensitivity to what is news and what is not. Publicity is where guerrilla techniques really come into play. It costs no more money to write a gripping press release than a dull one that hits the circular file after the reporter glances at the first paragraph. Many of the suggestions in this chapter cost nothing or very little.

Make sure your publicity efforts are worth your time and energy. Not every book is a candidate for media coverage. If you've written a tightly focused book such as *How to Open and Run a Hardware Store,* you can expect coverage from niche trade magazines, but other than that, your marketing efforts don't belong in the mainstream media.

For books that make their homes in bookstores, however, publicity is an absolute must. A mention in the newspaper or a radio interview is a lot less expensive than paid advertising. More importantly, news stories are perceived as "Truth." People believe Oprah Winfrey when she says on her show that she's read the most exciting book in her life. In contrast, if they heard Oprah's rave review in a TV commercial, they'd assume she was paid to say it and view her endorsement skeptically.

Publishers need to strive for frequency and a variety of mediums. The common rule of thumb is that people need to hear about a product between five and seven times before they actually buy it.

How much does promotion cost? The general rule of thumb is to budget $1 for the promotion of each book printed. In general, we suggest trying to get all the free publicity and public relations possible before resorting to paid advertising. Select your advertising vehicle very carefully—choose a tightly niched magazine that closely matches the subject of your book. Not only are their ads cheaper, the reading audience will match your own. We also suggest advertising in a magazine called *Radio/TV Interview Report* (RTIR), which goes to virtually all of the radio and TV producers in the country. It's a magazine full of half-page press releases that announce books with attention-grabbing headlines.

THE ART OF BUILDING A WAVE

Media builds on media. It starts with a small wave. As attention builds, the wave builds. Once journalists think something is "hot," they write about it and jump on the wave. They are convinced that something is truly newsworthy if *other* journalists write about it. Religiously tape every appearance and save every article. Once you have local clips in hand, work on getting regional coverage—statewide newspapers or radio stations in the state's biggest cities. Enclose your clips, as well as a listing of your TV and radio appearances. Once you get regional coverage, work on national coverage, again enclosing clips. If all goes very well, journalists will be calling you or your author and publicity becomes fairly easy.

Generally speaking, there are three distinct waves of publicity: First, there are prepublication reviews, which generally appear in library review journals and book industry publications. As the official date moves closer, there is a second wave of articles in the mainstream media to announce the publication or near publication of your book. Usually, these articles either review the book or profile the author. The third wave of media is post-publication and requires greater creativity to capture the media eye. We'll include lots of examples later in this report to spark your imagination.

Publicity also comes in two shapes. The first is the traditional review. The second is called "off-the-book-page coverage"—meaning either an author profile or a news story pegged on the book's subject matter. Books on sexy or controversial subjects do best in the mainstream media. That's perhaps the reason why memoirs about *issues*—alcoholism, incest, anorexia, depression, etc.—have become so hugely popular in the 1990s. Particularly books that have been written by an attractive, articulate author who, in essence, represents a symbol of hope and transformation to those working through similar problems. Fiction writers will find this second kind of publicity harder to drum up than nonfiction or memoir writers.

"If you're a novelist, you're pretty much cooked, unless you can come up with a nonfiction thing to hook it on," literary agent Mary Evans opined in a February 1997 *Vanity Fair* article.

"Novels do break through," added book publicist Lynn Goldberg, "but rarely without prizes or a front-page review by an important writer. Everyone's looking for someone *else* to envelop a novel in royal robes. And television coverage is almost impossible until a novel becomes a best seller."

PUBLICITY'S FIRST WAVE

Before your book is officially published, strive to snag as many prepublication reviews as possible. We are referring to library review journals and trade publications, including *Publishers Weekly*. Press releases to these publications are covered in Chapter 11, "The Not-So-Quiet Sales To Libraries."

The easiest place to capture mainstream media coverage is in the author's home town. Attempt to get into every medium available, including newspapers, alternative newspapers, television news program, talk radio and on the community-access cable channel. If the book topic or the author's life is compelling, you may be able to get press coverage months before the release of your book. If not, your first media wave should be timed to coincide with the first book-signing.

The "lead" of your press release or the first paragraph should compel the reader to *keep* reading, much like a news article does. You might lead with a colorful anecdote or with a solution to a common problem or write a sentence with a surprise twist.

After the lead, the press release should include:

- The local tie-in with the newspaper's community. For releases sent to out-of-town media, the easiest tie-in is that the author will be in town to sign books.

- Provocative or funny quotes by the author.

- A summary of what the book is about.

- Relevant facts or statistics, if possible.

- Relevant topical news event, if possible.

- The press release must not assume any prior knowledge of the author or book. It should also never say the book is self-published.

- A brief background of the author. If the author's biography is compelling, elaborate—"Eve Taylor, who is blind, wrote this book while getting a bachelor's degree in physics." The reporter must perceive the author as incredibly committed to making the book a success. If the author is perceived as a hobbyist or a vanity publisher, forget any coverage. Most likely, the local coverage will profile the author as much as the book.

- The price of the book and how to obtain it.

- How to contact the author for an interview.

After you make a splash locally, fan out your publicity efforts to state-wide newspapers. As with your local news release, lead the press release with the grabbiest lead you can create (usually in terms of how it will improve the lives of the reader). It is now more important to tie it in with state or national news.

Example:

"On a sunny day last October, Harvey Smith donned a monkey costume, hung a sign around his neck, 'I will work for peanuts,' and walked the city's sidewalks. He was hired the next day at a wage significantly above 'peanuts.'

"Smith's desperate measure is no surprise given the recent reports that California's unemployment rate of 10 percent is the worst in five decades.

"The account of Smith's job-seeking strategy is included in the newly released book, *How to Find a Decent Job in 30 Days or Less,* written by Roy John, a veteran employment counselor turned headhunter. John writes about Smith and scores of other real-life examples to inspire even the most down-trodden of job seekers. Besides talking about getting a job, John also talks about ways to avoid losing one. For example, he identifies the 10 jobs that are most likely to get downsized. Would you believe bank executives are most at risk?"

Remember, the journalist is looking for a story that can improve lives, solve problems, make people laugh or cry.

Before sending a press release, study the magazine or newspaper to see how your story could fit in. Call out in your letter the specific section to which your story would fit. Personalize your letter as much as possible by naming the reporter or editor, showing familiarity with the publication, and mentioning a connected article that they previously ran. As much as possible, pick your best shots. A scattershot mailing is the easiest to conduct, but not the most effective.

Lisa Shaw of Litterature, a publisher of pet greeting cards, gives this advice: "Every press release I send out starts out with a *Wall Street Journal*-style headline (twists the brain, entices the eyes to keep reading) and then promises something to the reader in the first paragraph."

THE PRESS KIT

Opinions vary on exactly what you should send to the media. Some spend $5 per media kit, including a four-color folder, a black-and-white glossy photo of the author, scads of information, and even the book itself.

Our recommendation is to skip the $5 media kits. When you send a press release, keep in mind what the purpose is—to inform and entertain in the format of a professional presentation. Here are elements that a press kit should include:

- A cover page that focuses on the news element;
- A fact sheet (see the example on following page);
- Copies of previous articles about your book (well-chosen for the purpose of your press release);
- Excerpts of testimonials; and
- Newspaper articles that directly relate to your book's focus. These prove that the topic is newsworthy.

A successful strategy is to *fax* your cover sheet. It is more likely to be read by print and electronic reporters alike. (With an envelope, they are likely to simply toss it before opening.) A fax also conveys a sense of urgency. If the reporter calls you, then send or fax the supporting information at the reporter's request. Don't fax everything initially because it's too overwhelming and it ties up the fax machine.

GETTING NATIONAL PRESS COVERAGE

One of the easiest ways to get widespread national coverage is via the Associated Press wire. Most newspapers in the country subscribe to the AP, meaning they have paid for the privilege of taking any story—state, national, international and feature—that appears on the wire. AP writers are typically stationed around the state and scan local newspapers for stories, which they either pick up as written or they decide to revise. They could even pick up a story your local paper wrote about your book. Make sure you hire a clipping service in order to capture the articles nationally.

To get an idea of what a wire story looks like, pay attention as you read the newspaper. AP stories are always identified. Generally, you'll have to

SAMPLE FACT SHEET

Rhodes & Easton
121 E. Front St.
Traverse City, Mich. 49684

Marilyn Taylor's Muffin Madness:
Quick and Healthy Recipes for Today's Busy Lifestyles

Ship Date: 7/1/97

Author: Marilyn Taylor

Publisher: Rhodes & Easton
Trade Dist: Ingram/Partners/Baker & Taylor
Cooking
0-9649401-0-8
$12.95, Trade Paperback
7 x 8, 176 pages

Season: Summer 1997

Why this book is unique
It is packed with every recipe imaginable--from dessert muffins to muffins hearty enough to pack for a lunch.

Of the eight muffin books published within the last 10 years, none has featured as many recipes as Muffin Madness—188 in all. Also, only a few books have low-fat recipes; those that do, only offer a handful. Marilyn Taylor's Muffin Madness features an entire low-fat section.

- Not just a recipe book, Muffin Madness is filled with snippets of advice on baking tricks, nutrition, clean-up short-cuts, and running a safe, clean kitchen.

- The book is beautifully packaged with whimsical graphics and a four-color, eye-catching cover.

- A great gift at an affordable price for any muffin-lover.

Why You'll Like It
The recipes are easy, the directions are clear, and, best of all, they produce flawless muffins—consistently. There are so many recipes, you can find at least one to fit whatever ingredients are lurking about in your refrigerator and cupboards. Our favorite: Michigan's Best Cherry Muffins in honor of the author's hometown, Traverse City, MI known as the Cherry Capital of the World.

SAMPLE FACT SHEET

We also like the handwritten style of Ms. Taylor's hints; it gives the feeling that she's leaning over the counter, coffee mug in hand, telling us what works for her.

Description
Muffin Madness features 188 muffin recipes, organized into six categories.

- **Fruit Muffins:** Lemon Blueberry Muffins, Famous Cranberry Orange Muffins, and Date Nut Muffins
- **Vegetable Muffins:** Real Corn Cornbread Muffins, Paul's Favorite Pumpkin Muffins, and Zucchini Cheese Muffins
- **Grain Muffins:** Granola Muffins, The Very Best Raisin Bran Muffins, and Bettey's "A Little Bit of Everything" Muffins
- **Sweet Muffins:** Peach Upside-Down Muffins, Double Fudge Muffins, Lemon Yogurt Muffins and Chocolate Whiskey Muffins.
- **Fat-Free and Low-Fat Muffins:** Low-Fat Hodge Podge Muffins, No Oil Cherry Muffins, and Fat-Free Sour Cream Muffins.
- **Dinner Muffins**: Parmesan, Provolone, and Herb Muffins, Old-Fashioned Hot Cross Muffins, and Cornmeal, Swiss and Jalapeno Muffins.

You'll find a relevant tip footnoting many of the recipes. On the Cranberry Bran Muffins page, for example, is this hint: "To make sure your baking powder is fresh, try pouring very hot tap water over a teaspoonful. If it's fresh, it will bubble very actively."

Taylor prefaces the book with "Piping Hot Tips for Making Perfect Muffins." It includes her no-fail technique for baking airy muffins, how to convert any recipe into low-fat fare, and how to create mini-muffins and jumbo muffins.

Author information
Marilyn Taylor lives in Traverse City, MI, one of the most gorgeous corners of the earth. A native of Marquette, MI, Ms. Taylor earned a degree from Northern Michigan University. She was a TV anchor in Marquette and Traverse City, both northern Michigan cities. She's outgoing, witty, highly photogenic, and can bake a mean muffin.

Previous Books
This is Ms. Taylor's first book.

Market
Anyone who enjoys baking muffins, from the novice to the experienced baker. Will appeal especially to moms who are looking for a healthy snack or lunchtime entree that their kids will want to eat.

pitch your story to the AP reporter either as a compelling human interest story or issue-oriented. Find the AP reporter who is geographically closest to you (they're in the phone book under Associated Press—if you can't find a phone number, call the AP office in the state's largest city and ask them for the number of the nearest reporter).

After you mail a press release, make a follow-up phone call in about a week to answer a journalist's questions if they have any. One publicist's rule of thumb: she never mails out publicity that she can't follow up on.

If a story is truly hot, fax and make a follow-up phone call the same day. Don't try to pitch a story when the reporter is on deadline. As a general rule, don't call P.M. newspapers in the morning and don't call A.M. newspapers in the late afternoon or evening.

You will usually have to leave your message on voice mail and may hear nothing back. In that case, make a pest out of yourself. Leave messages daily, even twice daily, on the voice mail until you get *some* response. Perhaps, then, the reporter will call you just to unclog his voice mail—and you'll get a chance to sell your book.

GETTING YOUR STORY IN NATIONAL PAPERS

For people who have never worked with the media, just getting started can be intimidating. Who do you call? How do you get an "in" with a reporter you've never met? To answer this, picture the inside of a news room. Each week, newspaper reporters meet with the daily editor and propose a "budget" for the next week. They talk about the stories that they plan to finish and when. These story ideas often come from press releases or letters or phone calls that the reporter receives every day. Each reporter typically covers a "beat" or specific topic area: health, environment, education, etc. To justify a story, the reporter must give the editor either a *local* tie-in or a "news hook." A hook is a reason for the story. Hooks are usually pegged on a *recent* news event.

The hook for books may mean the author is making a personal appearance in town. But this doesn't always work. Someone is coming into town to sign books. Unless that someone is famous, signing books is not a news story.

Smart publishers design an attention-grabbing event. Let's say some-one is coming into town in a 36-foot RV Romance-mobile with a 12-foot mural of a couple smooching. Weird. Who would do that? How much did that Romance-mobile cost? And what about that paint job? The reporter goes to find out. That's exactly what Greg Godek, author of *1,001 Ways to Be Romantic*, had in mind when he decided to establish himself as the country's expert on romance. He would just drive into town, he said, and TV reporters would yell at him to pull over.

Reporters are also asked to give a "spin" on a national event. For ex-ample, during the O.J. Simpson case, many smaller newspapers ran articles on spouse abuse. To do these kind of stories, they need to find an expert resource. If you are such an expert, it might be an excellent time to send a press release.

Another way to attract media attention is to give a speech or seminar on a topic related to your book. To attract coverage, your topic has to be sexy, controversial, or key to improving people's lives. One of the best avenues for speaking engagements are local colleges and service clubs (such as Ro-tary and Kiwanis), which are always looking for good speakers. Michael Moore, author of *Downsize This!*, signed scores of books after a free three-hour speech that he gave at a local college that blended comedy and poli-tics. The local paper ran a front-page article the next day and a follow-up article.

Tap your creativity or borrow ideas that have worked for other publish-ers.

Realize that once a reporter—print, television, radio, or otherwise—seizes on a story idea, they usually want to talk to you *right away*! Of course, that's not always possible, but do your best. Your ability to get back with them very quickly and provide them with a press release, back-ground information, and previous coverage may break or make the article.

📖   📖   📖

Ah Ha! Dynamics Press, which markets self-help books and tapes, got a mention in the *Los Angeles Times* for its incredibly creative "Optimism Hotline." The firm rented a voice mail on a toll-free 800 number that offered unlimited calls from the U.S. and Canada for a flat fee of $30 a month. The press release read: "Stuck? Frustrated? Going Bananas? The Optimism Hotline, Toll-Free 1-800-913-9525. A Two-Minute Telephone Mental Fitness Gym for Building and Strengthening Optimistic Positive Mental Attitudes for a Healthier Immune System, and For Getting the Most out of Life. It's Free. Such a Deal."

The *LA Times* wrote: "Even the ultimate grouch, after listening to (the Optimism Hotline) might kind of want to get out there and be optimistic."

George Corman of Ah Ha! Dynamics Press said that the approach might not be for everyone, but suggested several ways it could be used to sell books. The trick is to convey free, fun, and funny messages relevant to your books. He suggested these examples: The Animal Lovers Hotline, The Health and Fitness Hotline, The Sex Hotline, The Money Hotline, The Veggie Hotline, and The Greatest Recipes Hotline. Corman adds that a key to success is finding a toll-free 800 number. Of course, mention your book and how to order it at the end of your free message.

Some people create an attention-getting persona for the press. It's a lot of fun and the author becomes a natural for media attention. During a radio interview, Greg Nachazel, author of *Deer Camp Dictionary*, told the host he'd sign books at Dick's Bar in a small town just before he took off on his own deer-hunting trip. The host, laughing in disbelief, asked him twice about the location. It was true, but it was also all part of the Joe Deercamp image Nachazel was seeking to create.

Other publishers create their own story.

📖

For a radio promo, Lisa Reid Ferguson of Carol Publishers gave five listeners a copy of her book, *Raising Kids with Just a Little Cash*, a year's subscription to her newsletter, *PurseStrings*, and two hours of consultation time with Ferguson. The families were chosen because they wanted to cut living costs. The radio station will track these families for a year (the deejay's family volunteered for the project) to see how much money they saved by using Ferguson's strategies. Ferguson didn't stop there. She pitched coverage of the story to a free-lance journalist, who frequently writes for women's magazines instead of pitching it directly to the magazine editor. That way, she was sure her proposal would get noticed.

📖

While speaking to elementary students at East Detroit Schools about following their dreams and reaching for the stars, Tim Smith, author of *Buck Wilder's Small Fry Fishing Guide*, was asked to sign a copy of his book for Jerry Linenger's little boy, John.

Tim Smith later learned that Capt. Jerry Linenger, M.D., liked to speak to students on the same subject, and was, in fact, going to reach for the stars himself on a Jan. 12, 1997, streak through space. His mission: a 4 1/2 hour visit to Russia's Space Station, Mir.

Smith's staff at Buck Wilder Books decided to ask Linenger if he'd take along a Buck Wilder book with him. As it turned out, books were prohibited under NASA regulations, but Linenger was more than happy to take along an illustration of Buck Wilder and his raccoon sidekick, both outfitted in astronaut gear. Illustrator Mark Herrick included a clever reference to the next Buck Wilder book, *Buck Wilder's Small Twig Hiking and Camping Guide*: "Dear Jerry, We hope you have a great time camping in space. P.S. Next time invite us! We love far-out places!"

The trip to space earned a mention in the *Detroit News*, the *Detroit Free Press*, and Buck Wilder's hometown paper, the *Traverse City Record-Eagle*.

"For a 'little-train-that-could' publication that aims to give kids an appreciation for nature and the outdoors, and has become northwest Michigan's top-selling nonfiction paperback, it's an amazing trek indeed," wrote Nancy Sundstrom in the *Record-Eagle* of Buck Wilder's stratospheric success.

📖

Presidents don't review books, but they sometimes help with promotion. President Bill Clinton did just that after he received a copy of the book, *Trial and Triumph: Presidential Power in the Second Term* by Al Zacher (a book, we modestly add, that was produced by The Jenkins Group). After his election for his second term in 1996, Clinton held up his book at a press conference and said, "We'll see how I do." That same day, C-SPAN called Zacher for a date on its Booknotes show, thus making Zacher the first independent publisher to make an appearance. The next day, *The Today Show* called him to invite him on their show. Just goes to show, it doesn't hurt to aim for the very top.

📖   📖   📖

CUSTOMIZE YOUR PRESS RELEASE

Whether you are pitching magazines or newspapers, it is vital to keep a close tab on the newspapers and magazines where you want to be placed. What do they write about? Which reporter writes the kind of stories you envision? Or does a syndicated columnist write in a style that strikes a chord with you? When you write the press release, mention the specific section in which the story belongs, refer to the reporter's past work, and mention connected articles the publication has done in the past.

📖   📖   📖

Lisa Shaw, the pet greeting card publisher, is a devoted reader of the *Wall Street Journal* and noticed they had run separate briefs on greeting cards and the pet industry in their front page "Business Briefs." So she handwrote a note (on her company's greeting cards, of course) that said: "I notice that you've run short pieces on greeting cards and on pets lately. Well, here's my company that combines the two." She enclosed a catalog, a couple of pet greeting cards and a copy of a mention from the *San Francisco Chronicle*. Her note triggered a one-sentence mention in the "Business Briefs" shortly thereafter. The very next day Jay Leno mentioned her company on the *Tonight Show*: "There is a company called Litterature that sells greeting cards for cats and dogs. I'm not sure that is a good idea. Do you know how dogs greet each other?"

A month later, a *Boston Globe* columnist planned to write about the company.

"Again in her case, I showed I was familiar with her work—she writes a lot about cats—and handwriting a note shows that I'm paying attention," Shaw said.

📖   📖   📖

How do you find a journalist's name who covers the beat appropriate to your topic, such as business, lifestyle, the food page, trends, computers, etc.—particularly when the newspaper/magazine is published in a distant city? One way is to network with other publishers. Call the publishers' associations in the major cities and ask for the names of feature editors and TV talk show hosts who might have an interest in your subject area (a list follows at the end of this chapter).

Also, build up contacts as you go along. If someone is writing about you, casually ask if they know of any other noncompeting medium that might be interested in writing about your book.

If you see or hear about a fantastic write-up of a book, call the publisher and ask him how they managed to get such wonderful coverage.

In truth, reporters will go out of their way to help someone they personally connected with during an interview. A publisher once wrote she won't talk directly to a reporter because she was once grossly misquoted in a newspaper article and now she insists on doing all interviews in writing. You may gain accuracy, but you risk losing a huge amount of trust and intimacy with a reporter.

Another tip is don't try to control the interview. Don't constantly say something, and then add, "But don't print it." If you don't want to see something in print, don't say it! It's risky to you, and confusing to the reporter. Also, know that reporters don't like showing you an entire article before publication for your review. You might want to offer it as a favor: "If you'd like me to review the article to check the fine points for accuracy, I'd be happy to." You may want to ask, however, if the reporter could read back your quotes. Some reporters will, others won't.

Once the article is finished (or news story or radio interview), *be sure* to send a thank-you note, pointing out what you liked about the article. The note will strengthen your bond and the reporter will be left with a good feeling about you. And that counts for a lot when you're ready to pitch another story idea.

HOW TO GET NOTICED

Most newspaper and TV reporters receive such a huge flood of press releases, they dump most of them in a waste basket without even opening them—particularly from national organizations that send out press releases frequently! This is no exaggeration. If TV producers keep a P.R. video, it's usually so they can use it as a blank.

How do you escape the waste basket?

Believe it or not, a handwritten address on an envelope will help immeasurably. It's a reporter's clue that what's inside is not just another mass-mailed press release.

A cover page that is brief often works best: "Dear So-and-So, With all the publicity on spousal abuse with the O.J. Simpson case, we wanted to let you know that the author of *Spouse Abuse: Victim No More* will be in town talking to college coeds on how to avoid destructive relationships. She'll discuss the five telltale signs that indicate a relationship is abusive and how to escape safely and forever. Evita Edwards will be speaking at Milliken Auditorium at 8 p.m., Tuesday. If you have any questions, please call the author at XXXXX. Signed, (The publicist's name)." Enclose a separate fact sheet, previous news clips, and testimonial excerpts.

Send out a short press release separately to the newspaper's Calendar of Events.

To imbue a greater sense of professionalism, some publishers go so far as having a friend serve as a publicist or giving a fictitious name of a publicist so it won't appear as a one-man show. Others say they've had no problems listing the author as a sole contact. In our opinion, it doesn't make much of a difference with news media—reporters prefer to talk directly to an author. They actively dislike publicists. However, library review journals and prestigious review media, such as the *New York Times*, are biased against small press books and are harder to sell. You may want to "hire" a publicist and put his or her name on the press release.

No matter whether you hire a publicist or not, make sure your press kit looks *professional*. Amateurish press releases make anyone seriously question the publisher's marketing savvy and legitimacy.

WHEN THE HONEYMOON IS OVER

When a book is first published, it's considered fresh, new, something to be celebrated. That lasts a couple of months and suddenly it's old news. This is when creativity really comes into play. It is now imperative to lead with a news hook.

Example: If you've written a book on getting out of credit-card debt, watch the national stories about consumer debt. If the national media is reporting that default rates on credit card payments are at an all-time high, write a press release that leads with the top five ways to get out of credit debt quickly and almost painlessly. Write the press release as if it's an article.

If you have a gripping personal story, include it within the release (of course, always write your articles in the third person). Were you once $60,000 in credit card debt yourself? Did you work four or five jobs to extract yourself from the mire? Put it in the press release. Just think: the No. 1 rule for a press release is that it must be interesting and timely.

📖   📖   📖

Publisher Grace Witwer Householder, author of *The Funny Things Kids Say Will Brighten Any Day*, has found an excellent way to get the media's attention—she and the book's illustrator often exhibit the original watercolor artwork from the book in a local library.

"Because the illustrator has had corneal transplants in both eyes, we try to publicize the miracle of organ/tissue donation at the same time. We have received a lot of good press this way," she said.

📖

Azriela Jaffe, author of *Honey, I Want to Start My Own Business, A Planning Guide for Couples* has literally created a holiday hook for her book. First she referenced *Chase's Calendar of Events*, a mammoth book available at most libraries which lists every holiday, festival, special celebration, and observance in the country.

"How can you turn this into P.R.? Because you can create your very own national holiday. So I created two holidays: 1) The first week in May is 'Acknowledge your Supportive Spouse Week.' Why? Because one of my key messages is to appreciate and recognize the key contribution that spouses make to entrepreneurial efforts. My second holiday is the Friday after Labor Day, titled, 'Honey, I Want to Start my Own Business Day.' It encourages people who are thinking about taking the leap, but are hesitating, to go for it. It also gets the name of my book out there."

To stir up P.R. for her book, Jaffe offers a national award and encourages entrepreneurs to nominate their spouses by writing to her about their spouse's valuable contribution to their business. Then, she asked sponsors to donate gifts to be awarded to the spouses who are nominated. Teleflora, for example, with a network of 20,000 florists, is considering being a sponsor and promoting the event in their flower shops. Meanwhile, Jaffe is pitching the media to acknowledge supportive spouses and the award.

"Since my book released six months ago, it gives me a fresh reason for a pitch, as I'm way past the 'new release pitch,'" she said.

A few days ago, Jaffe pitched a column idea to a *Boston Globe* columnist, who eventually bit. The idea? The "supportive spouses" are usually slaving away at a corporate job. Jaffe also wrote a column about the holiday, which was accepted by magazines and newsletters oriented toward her target market.

"Creating the holiday cost me absolutely nothing and I've found media folks appreciate the creativity," she said.

📖   📖   📖

Perhaps the biggest drawback to publicity is that you're unable to control the content. A reporter may or may not like the book or even the author. Other times they make egregious errors or fail completely to mention the title of the book or how to buy it.

The best way to correct these errors or fill in omissions is with a letter to the editor. First, cite the strong points of the article and your gratitude for the paper choosing to write on the topic. Secondly, cite the error or omission. Avoid making your letter sound like a press release, but do be sure to mention the title and the publishing company.

Dorothy Kupcha Leland did just that when the *DollReader* magazine ran a small item on the doll of Patty Reed (a young girl in the famous Donner party). The article mentioned the book, *Patty Reed's Doll*, but implied it was no longer available. After Kupcha heard about the error, she sent a letter to the editor:

"I was delighted to see your August article about Patty Reed's doll at the Smithsonian and mention of our book, *Patty Reed's Doll: The Story of the Donner Party*, by Rachel Laurgaard. Your readers may be interested to know that a reprint of the original edition (first published in 1956) is available in paperback."

Leland then told readers how to order the book and offered a free color postcard of the doll to those who mentioned the magazine's name. The magazine ran the letter in full and the color picture of the doll, which Leland had enclosed.

"For the cost of a postage stamp and some postcards, I got the equivalent of a nice big ad," Leland said.

After the journalist makes the clarification, send a thank-you note, maybe even with a small handful of flowers. It will leave the reporter with very positive feelings about you.

Journalists make mistakes, but they can get their toes stepped on, too. They want to beat their competition and highly resent working on a story only to see their most loathed competitor run a story on the same subject. The reporter feels betrayed and may ask you why you didn't mention that the *Detroit News* or whatever was also writing a story. Sometimes, a paper will pull a story rather than appear as if they're following on the heels of a competitor. Be sensitive to this. If you are in one of those rare towns that have two daily papers, give one paper a chance first and then follow up with the other paper with a completely fresh angle. This is also true of national newspapers—*Washington Post* versus the *New York Times*, for example. And city magazines versus city newspapers.

With that said, print and TV reporters don't seem as touchy about this issue.

PRESENT YOURSELF AS AN EXPERT

Within the press release—particularly one in which you are asking that the author appear on a talk show—you must present a persuasive case that the author is indeed an expert.

Connie Evers, author/publisher of *How to Teach Nutrition to Kids*, has enjoyed good coverage in the *Miami Herald, Omaha World-Herald, Chicago Tribune, Milwaukee Journal-Sentinel, Richmond Times* and the *Orange County Register*, among others. Why the success?

- As a registered dietitian, she has professional credentials in her field.

- She is a field journalist; most notably she writes a monthly children's nutrition column for *The Oregonian*, food features for *Healthy Kids*, a magazine distributed to pediatricians' offices, and trade journals.

- The timing of her book coincided with a major policy shift in the government—the USDA-mandated healthy meals and nutrition education in schools.

"You just have to have a delicious and tempting angle and be seen as a credible person with specific expertise. My prior experience definitely has aided my ability to get coverage."

Evers emphasizes that it takes time to establish your reputation as an expert.

📖　　📖　　📖

First-time author, Jim Miller, created a Best Boss/Worst Book contest to help promote his book, *The Corporate Coach*.

He promoted the essay write-in contest during a 20-city tour talking about ways of handling difficult bosses, sharing horror stories on air with listener call-ins, all the while promoting his own book. The contest not only intrigued stations which booked him during the tour, but it had a huge pay-off when he announced the winners of the contest, especially the Worst Boss submission which resulted in the book being mentioned on *The Today Show*, Charles Osgood's CBS radio show, the Associated Press, and innumerable radio interviews. The contest was so popular, Jim held it the two following years and even wrote a book based on the essays he received!

📖　　📖　　📖

PITCHING YOUR BOOK TO THE ELECTRONIC MEDIA

TELEVISION: The electronic cousin to newspapers—TV news—is similar in vein, but with obviously a much more visual angle. You need to follow the rules above, but also suggest, if possible, a visual image in your press release.

When you're going to be in town for a book signing or speech, give the TV station's assignment editor a phone call and then deliver your pitch. "I'm going to be in town for a book signing next week and have found that my book's topic, 'Pot-bellied Pigs for Pets' makes a great human interest spot." If you're smart, you'll bring your pig with you.

Local TV programming breaks down into a number of shows that are author-friendly. The basic ones are daytime talk shows, newscasts (6 A.M., Noon, 5 P.M., or variations on these), and public affairs shows that usually run on Sunday. It is important to know when to call the producers of these shows since their schedules are time-sensitive.

Producers of news shows are on hard deadlines so, generally speaking, it's best to get them three to four hours before their newscast or about 15 minutes immediately after it's aired. Watch these types of programs that appear on your local stations so you get a feel for the formats; that knowledge will be transferable across the country to stations in other markets.

The importance of attempting national TV placements cannot be stressed enough. Again, watch the shows to see if your book is suitable. While *Oprah* is always the most sought-after show, it is not the only show that can move books off the shelves! The network morning shows—*Good Morning America, Today Show, CBS This Morning, CNN, Dateline NBC, Primetime Live, Larry King, CNBC, Charlie Rose,* and *Tom Snyder*—all use author interviews as part of their programming and are proven booksellers. Take the time to research national cable systems such as USA, Lifetime, the Family Channel, and TV Food Network for talk shows. While they may not enjoy as large an audience as *Oprah*, they still can reach as many as a million people and help get the word out on your book.

Do not be intimidated by these shows either. Their producers care about ratings—not whether or not you're a major publisher or how many books you have in print. Present yourself knowledgeably and professionally and you'll have just as much chance getting on these shows as the next guy!

TV producers like short, to-the-point pitches that capture the essence of why having you on their show will make for "good TV." It may be the visual element you offer or more likely the *importance* of the subject matter you're discussing to their viewers.

David Hahn of the New York publicity firm, Planned Television Arts, offers this advice, "Broadcast producers in particular appreciate getting faxes of one or two pages that summarize the book in bullet form and make your expertise quite clear and explain what their audience can gain from the interview. Tie in your pitch with any current trends, news stories or actual print stories you can fax to them and you stand a much greater chance of booking yourself."

To prepare for a TV interview, decide on two to three main points you want to get across. Write them down and rehearse stories or examples that illustrate your main points. TV interviews are often as short as two minutes and rarely go longer than seven minutes. For that reason, practice what you have to say in that timeframe making your sentences shorter and emphatic. Don't be afraid to use colorful language, opinions, jokes. Relax and let your individuality shine. The listeners should be able to feel your passion and see it in your face.

RADIO: Radio is much easier than television because you can often give an interview over the phone—it doesn't need a visual angle.

A low-cost way of finding out if the radio does phone interviews is to simply call and ask if they do author interviews over the phone. If they fumble, quickly move on. If the answer is yes, sell yourself: "With all the current flap on credit cards, I wanted to let you know I've written a book on how to quickly dig out of debt."

Radio talk-show hosts live for controversy and self-improvement. In small towns, they may be desperate for guests. For more on how to get radio interviews, check out Joe Sabah's book, *How to Get on Radio Talk Shows.* Sabah believes that the best method of dealing with radio producers is to "Call, Write, Call." Again, radio producers, like their TV counterparts, love to receive faxes as a follow-up to their phone conversations. This means the material is fresh in their mind and they can pitch it to their hosts that day if it's something topical.

"Talk shows are *really* that . . . talk," Sabah said. "They want to talk with a prospective guest *before* the show. Paper is important, but only to follow up after the initial phone call."

If you have been successful on one show, be sure to mention that to the next producer you're pitching. Remember it's his neck that's on the line, so anything you can do to make his job easier (i.e., selling it to his boss) will move the process along that much quicker. Radio talk shows often rely on call-ins as a gauge of audience interest and if you've proven you can "light up their lines," then be sure the next station is aware of that.

Get feedback from the radio host or producer if you feel an interview went particularly well and you handled an impressive number of callers' questions. Often they will rebook you in as little as a week's time or certainly in a few months if the interview generated a ton of calls!

Besides the talk-show format found on your local news/talk station and/or public radio station, be sure to check out the possibility of doing the morning drive shows on the FM music stations. While many of these shows are music intensive, some of them have a "zoo" format which allows the hosts to do a lot of schtick that often includes interviewing authors if the book is appropriate.

The key here is to understand the demographics of the station. Orient your pitch to young women if the station is a Top-40 format or towards a baby-boomer crowd if it's a classic rock station. If your book is fun and relationship-oriented (e.g. how to kiss, great opening lines, what's proper etiquette on the first date), then you might get a lot of great airplay with these shows. Many will do telephone interviews as well. More importantly, these shows often have huge audiences.

Giveaways are often appreciated by radio shows — whether it be two copies or five copies of a book. These are free copies offered to the stations that they can give out to their audience before, during or after your interview. The advantage here is that you often get extra mentions of the book on air as part of your overall promotion with that station.

Another common outlet on local radio is the public affairs show, mostly found on FM music stations. These shows are usually taped in a studio during the week and air early Sunday morning. While these shows do not usually command large audiences, they are good outlets for books with an issue-oriented focus, such as consumer, community, health, and education. They often go as long as 15 to 30 minutes, thus giving you a lot of time to get your message across and actively promote your book.

One of the most important audiences to reach is the public radio audience. This is a proven book-buying market. Most cities have local public radio affiliates that do a variety of programming that might include authors. In addition, there are a number of shows on National Public Radio that do in-depth interviews with authors and are considered powerhouses when it comes to selling books. Chief among these is Terri Gross' *Fresh Air*, produced out of WHYY-FM in Philadelphia. Other major national shows are *All Things Considered, Morning Edition,* and *Weekend Edition*—all based out of Washington, DC. For business topics, *Marketplace*, produced out of KUSC-FM in Los Angeles, is another important national public radio show.

Other national radio shows of note are: *The Jim Bohanon Show*, produced out of Washington as part of the Westwood One Network; *The Milt*

Rosenberg Show, produced out of Chicago at radio station WGN-AM; and *The Gil Gross Show,* on the CBS Radio Network produced out of New York. All these shows include frequent author interviews.

Again, think creatively when designing a media campaign for your book. Create fun contests such as the Best Boss/Worst Boss contest; invent quizzes to go along with your interview, etc. These often provide the extra zing the producer is looking for to make the interview lively and puts you on a different level if you're competing for airtime with authors who have published similar books.

Another observation is that personnel, phone numbers, and station managers all change frequently in the radio business. Be sure to work with an updated database.

THE INTERVIEW!

Consider hiring a media coach or asking a media friend to do a practice interview. Tape it, critique it, and practice again. Remember, it's up to the *author* to make sure the book is mentioned at least once in the interview.

You'll need to practice how to mention the book in a natural way, such as "In my book, I show you there are five key things you must do to get out of debt." Or in a radio interview with call-in questions you might say, "I can only give you the short answer right now, but at my book signing today, I could show you the two worksheets in my book. I guarantee—*if* you do them, and I mean do them with all your heart—you can put your finances back on track." The deejay might wander off the subject, so be prepared to put the interview gracefully back on track without seeming like an annoying self-promoter.

Be sure to keep tapes of your first few TV interviews so you can review them and improve on any weaknesses. There's another reason to tape them. It is not unusual for the electronic media to ask to see or hear a tape before they'll consider booking you, so these tapes can prove vital to your public relations efforts.

When you sit down with a journalist, deejay, or TV reporter, you need to have fun. Forget that publishing's a business. Forget all the money that you have at stake. Enjoy the interview and tell the world how your book can keep it twirling.

Here are key things to remember:
- It might not be possible, but try to get a feel for the show before you go on. If it's "shock" radio, you might be in for a jolt. Best not to be shocked. Also, ask the program director if you can listen in on the station about 10 minutes before your interview begins. Sometimes something really catastrophic has happened in the specific geographic area that you should know about; other times, they might be discussing a subject you could tie into your book.

- During a long radio interview, you'll need to interject the location, time and date of your signing every so often. Don't break a great thread of conversation to do it, but remember that people do tune in and out. Before the show begins, remind the host of your date and time of the book signing. If the deejay doesn't mention it, make sure that you do. When the interview comes to a close, remind the listeners to come on down, meet you, and get an autographed copy of your book.

- Talk explicitly about the kinds of problems addressed in the book and how they're solved.

- Always stay positive and upbeat. If you get a question that's too tough to answer in a few minutes, just say so, give it your best shot, and explain that your book addresses the answer in much greater depth.

- If your book is controversial, anticipate getting asked tough questions. If necessary, supply your own tough questions and be prepared to answer them effectively. If the deejay gives you a hard time, give it right back to him (with humor, if possible). Listen to how other people respond when the deejay starts pushing them around.

- There are numerous radio talk shows in most every location. Try to get on as many as possible. Many authors do interviews on the same station, but on different shows. Remember! If you are interesting, knowledgeable, and funny (have lots of jokes prepared, but make them sound natural), hosts will want you on their shows. It makes them look good and helps you sell books.

- Go through your book and pick out the most startling, intriguing aspects. Highlight these during the interview.

HIRE A PUBLICIST OR FLY SOLO?

A lot of people believe they can save money on publicity by doing every-thing themselves, and some people can—particularly, if they're well-versed in the art of promotion and marketing. But many of the most talented marketers will hire a publicist. Greg Godek, for example, spent $100,000 a year on publicists to promote *1001 Ways to Be Romantic*, although Godek is a talented marketer in his own right. The biggest reason: publicists have established invaluable media contacts—particularly regional and national contacts. It often takes the force of a publicist to get through to a busy magazine editor. Sometimes a publicist's opinion can carry enormous weight. Publicist Cate Cummings of Kansas City, Missouri, sent out a let-ter for the book, *Five Steps to Selecting the Best Alternative Medicine*. In an honest, sincere fashion, she wrote that in her opinion, it was simply the best book of its kind. The ensuing response was overwhelming. Forty per-cent of those contacted responded with a request for the book, and only two in the end decided not to write anything about it.

A publicist can cost anywhere from $500 to $5,000 a month. Before choosing a publicist, make sure she or he comes with excellent referrals. Choose a publicist who specializes in promoting books in a genre similar to yours (new age, recipe books, fiction, etc.) When meeting with the pub-licist, discuss the kind of campaigns they've run successfully and evidence of creative or innovative approaches. Do they have any initial good ideas about your projects in the first consultation?

There are two ways to pay a publicist. One is to pay an established retainer fee; the other is by the number of media placements. At first glance, it seems to make more sense to pay by media placements because an article or radio interview is clear evidence that the publicist has put forth specific effort for the money. Yet there are some good reasons to hire a publicist on retainer. Here are the pros and cons:

PROS:

- You have them available to you at all times.
- You can dictate to them certain needs, wants, and desires.
- You have access to their network of contacts and databases.

- They can often get a response from editors or reporters when you can't simply because they know them.
- They'll go beyond trying to make a placement, such as setting up speaking engagements for you and thinking of creative stunts or events or gimmicks for ways of doing business.
- They can package you with other authors for TV shows.
- They set up coaching for media interviews and seminars.
- They can set up book tours, handling hotels and air fare.
- They can think of creative ways to do book signings.

CONS:

- A "retainer" agreement doesn't guarantee results—the agency gets paid the same no matter how hard its employees work. In some cases, the agency will only react to its client's instructions rather than initiating strategies on its own.
- Retainers are generally more expensive than a per-placement publicist.

Our advice is that if you have a broad-appeal book with an emphasis on trade bookstore distribution, a publicist is often pivotal in achieving regional and national publicity. But you'll need to be very clear about what you expect of them.

TRACK THE RESULTS

Advertising and publicity are expensive. Publishers need to know what's working and what's not. When someone calls to order a book, ask "How did you hear about the book?" If they order a book from your website on the Internet, ask what brought them to your website. If you advertise in a magazine, put a code in the ad and ask for it on the order form or when they call in the order on an 800 number.

Your order-taking service should be able to do the same thing. For each order they take, they should ask the question: How did the customer hear of the book?

A FINAL WORD ON PUBLICITY

Spending thousands of dollars for promotion can't make a best seller out of a bad book. But without promotion, it's very difficult to make a good book into a best seller or even to hit break-even sales. The equation requires both.

INDISPENSABLE RESOURCES:

- *Working Press of the Nation*, a comprehensive three-volume listing of every radio, television, cable station, newspaper, and magazine with circulation numbers, population served, etc. (doesn't list specific reporters' names, but does list editors). Also includes free-lance writers and photographers and a guide to corporate newsletters. Published by R.R. Bowker, a division of Reed Elsevier, Inc. in New Providence, NJ. The three-volume set runs $419.95, but volumes can be ordered separately at $229 apiece. To order, call (800) 521-8110.

- *Editor & Publisher*, 11 West 19th St., New York, NY 10011. Call (800) 336-4380. They offer the *Editor & Publisher International Yearbook* of U.S. and world newspapers with department head names (publisher, editorial page editor, political columnists, sports editor, etc.), phone, e-mail and fax numbers. It costs a more modest $125.

- There are many companies who sell media lists, including *Bacon's Information Inc.* (800) 621-0561 (lots of options, including $1,095 for a CD-ROM of 225,000 editorial contacts); *Radio/TV Interview Report* (800) 989-1400; and The Jenkins Group (the QuickSilver P.R. List on floppy disk, $200 for more than 17,500 contacts).

INTERNET MEDIA HOT SPOTS

- Parrot Media Network: (www.parrotmedia.com). This fabulous on-line source is free and comprehensive. You'll find the addresses, phone numbers, fax numbers, market data, and the names of key people of most TV stations, cable systems, radio stations, and newspapers of America. With a few clicks, it will sort out the newspapers in the top 10 markets or give you the top 100 radio stations. Glean newspapers' circulation numbers, section editors' names, radio talk show hosts, or ask for radio stations by category: Christian, all-talk, country, etc.

• The Reporters Network claims connections to more than 2,000 reporters and offers a search engine that enables searches by specialty. Find it at http://www.reporters.net.

• A related list is http://www.webcom.com/leavitt/medialist.html. This spot gives you general e-mails for newspapers (ranging from *The Flint Journal* to *The Prague Post*). It also includes a Congressional e-mail list.

• Steve O'Keefe, an Internet book publicist, has built a site that contains links to the best resources available for online publicity and promotion. Choose from 14 categories, including "Media Finders and People Finders." The URL is http://www.olympus.net/okeefe/pubnet.

• Xpress Press offers a press release delivery service to more than 750 media professionals and editors. Find it at www.xpresspress.com.

• This website takes time to peruse, but can link you to a myriad of journalism resources, magazines, newspapers and online magazines. Type in http://www.newslink.org/ajrdir.html.

PUBLISHING ORGANIZATIONS IN NORTH AMERICA

**American Book Producers
Association (ABPA)**
160 Fifth Ave.
New York, NY 10011-7000
Tel: (212) 645-2368
Fax: (212) 989-7542
E-mail: tmckee@aap.publishers.org

**American Booksellers Association
Inc. (ABA)**
828 S. Broadway
Tarrytown, NY 10591
Tel: (914) 591-2665,
(800) 637-0037

**American International Book
Development Council**
Helen Dwight Reid Educational
Foundation
1319-18th St. NW
Washington, DC 20036
Tel: (202) 296-6264
Fax: (202) 296-5149

**American Library Association
(ALA)**
Public Information Officer
50 E. Huron St.
Chicago, IL 60611
Tel: (312) 944-6780
Fax: (312) 944-8741

**American Medical Publishers
Association**
Box 944
14 Fort Hill Road
Huntington, NY 11743
Tel. & Fax: (516) 423-0075

**Arizona Book Publishers
Association**
Gwen Henson, Executive Director
957 E. Guadalupe Rd., Box 20
Tempe, AZ 85283
Tel: (602) 777-9250

**The Association of American
Publishers (AAP)**
71 Fifth Avenue
New York, NY 10003-3004
Tel: (212) 255-0200
Fax: (212) 255-7007

**The Association of American
University Presses (AAUP)**
584 Broadway, Suite 410
New York, NY 10012
Tel: (212) 941-6610
Fax: (212) 941-6618
E-mail: aaupny@netcom.com

Association of Canadian Publishers
2 Gloucester St., Suite 301
Toronto, Ontario M4Y 1L5 Canada
Tel: (416) 413-4929
Fax: (416) 413-4920

**Association of Canadian
University Presses**
c/o University of Manitoba Press
15 Gillson St., Suite 244
Winnipeg, Manitoba R3T 5V6
Canada
Tel: (204) 474-9495
Fax: (204) 275-2270

**Association of Jewish Book
Publishers**
192 Lexington Ave.
New York, NY 10016-0801
Tel: (212) 684-4990
Fax: (212) 689-1649

Publishing Organizations In North America

Audio Publisher's Association
2401 Pacific Coast Highway, #102
Hermosa Beach, CA 90254
Tel: (312) 372-0546
Fax: (310) 374-3342
E-mail: apaonline@aol.com

Baltimore Publisher's Association
Jim Sutton, President
PO Box 5584
Baltimore, MD 21285-5584
Tel: (410) 719-8827

Bay Area Publishers Network
c/o Regent Press
6020-A Adeline
Oakland, CA 94608
Tel: (510) 547-7602

Bookbuilders West
P.O. Box 7046
San Francisco, CA 94120-9727
Tel: (510) 934-1440
Fax: (510) 934-7020

Book Industry Study Group Inc. (BISG)
160 Fifth Ave.
New York, NY 10010
Tel: (212) 929-1393
Fax: (212) 989-7542

Book Publisher's Northwest
Kent Sturgis, President
c/o Epicenter Press
PO Box 82368
Kenmore, WA 98028
Tel: (206) 485-6822
Fax: (206) 481-8253
E-Mail: gksturgis@aol.com

Book Publishers of Texas Association
Pam Lange, Executive Director
3404 S. Ravinia Dr.
Dallas, TX 75233
Tel: (214) 330-8759
Fax: (214) 330-9795

Bookbuilders of Boston
66 Cummings Park
Woburn, MA 01801
Tel: (617) 933-6878
Fax: (617) 935-0132

Bookbuilders of Washington
P.O. Box 23805
Washington D.C. 20025
Tel: (202) 287-3738, x378

Canadian Book Publishers' Council (CBPC)
250 Merton St., Suite 203
Toronto, Ontario M4S 1B1
Canada
Tel: (416) 322-7011
Fax: (416) 322-6999
E-Mail: avac@pubcouncil.ca

The Canadian Children's Book Centre
35 Spadina Rd.
Toronto, Ontario M5R 2S9 Canada
Tel: (416) 975-0010
Fax: (416) 975-1839

Canadian Magazine Publishers Association
2 Stewart St.
Toronto, Ontario M5V 1H6 Canada
Tel: (416) 362-2546
Fax: (416) 362-2547

PUBLISHING ORGANIZATIONS IN NORTH AMERICA

Canadian Small Press
Second Floor
Calgary, Alberta T2P 3C8 Canada
Tel: (403) 280-0800

Catholic Book Publishers Association Inc.
333 Glen Head Rd.
Old Brookville, NY 11545
Tel: (516) 671-9342
Fax: (516) 759-4227

Chicago Publishers Association
c/o Follett Corp.
2233 West St.
River Grove, IL 60171
Tel: (708) 583-2000

Chicago Women in Publishing
43 E. Ohio, Suite 1022
Chicago, IL 60611
Tel: (312) 641-6311
Fax: (312) 645-1078

Children's Book Council, Inc.
568 Broadway, Suite 404
New York, NY 10012
Tel: (212) 966-1990
Fax: (212) 966-2073
E-mail: staff@cbcbooks.org

Classroom Publishers Association
107 Park Washington Court
Falls Church, VA 22046
Tel: (703) 532-9255
Fax: (703) 532-0086

Colorado Independent Publishers Association
P.O. Box 4008
Boulder, CO 80306
Tel: (303) 447-1971

Consortium of Northern Publishers
Lael Morgan, President
P.O. Box 60529
Fairbanks, AK 99706
Tel: (907) 474-4969

Direct Marketing Association Inc. (DMA)
11 W. 42nd St.
New York, NY 10036-8096
Tel: (212) 768-7277
Fax: (212) 768-4547

Educational Paperback Association (EPA)
Box 1399
East Hampton, NY 11937
Tel: (212) 879-6850

Educational Press Association of America (EdPress)
c/o Rowan College of New Jersey
Glassboro, NJ 08028-1773
Tel: (609) 863-7349
Fax: (609) 863-5012

Electronic Publishing Special Interest Group (EPSIG)
c/o GCARI, P.O. Box 25707
Alexandria, VA 22313-5705
Tel: (703) 519-8184
Fax: (703) 548-2867

Evangelical Christian Publishers Association
3225 S. Hardy Dr., Suite 101
Tempe, AZ 85282
Tel: (602) 966-3998
Fax: (602) 966-1944

Florida Publishers Association
P.O. Box 430
Highland City, FL 33846-0430
Tel: (941) 647-5951
E-mail: NAIP@aol.com

PUBLISHING ORGANIZATIONS IN NORTH AMERICA

**Fulfillment Management
Association**
60 E. 42nd St., Suite 1146
New York, NY 10165
Tel: (212) 661-1410
Fax: (212) 661-1412

**Independent Publishers
Association of Canada**
Doug McArthur, President
Second Floor, 839 5th Ave. SW
Calgary, Alberta T2P 3C8
Canada
Tel: (403) 290-0800

Independent Publishers Network
The Jenkins Group
121 E. Front St.
Traverse City, MI 49684
Tel: (616) 933-0445
Fax: (616) 933-0448
E-mail:
jenkins.group@smallpress.com

**Independent Travel Publishers
Association**
96 Ingham Hill
Essex, CT 06426
Tel: (203) 767-7662 (voice & fax)

Information Industry Association
555 New Jersey Ave. NW., Suite 800
Washington D.C. 20001
Tel: (202) 639-8262
Fax: (202) 638-4403

**International Association of
Scholarly Publishers (IASP)**
109 Church St.
New Brunswick, NJ 08901
Tel: (908) 932-1039
Fax: (908) 932-7039

International Prepress Association
7200 France Ave. S., Suite 327
Edina, MN 55435
Tel: (612) 896-1908
Fax: (612) 896-0181

International Publishing Management Association (IPMA)
1205 W. College Avenue
Liberty, MO, 64068-3733
Tel: (816) 781-1111
Fax: (816) 781-2790
E-mail: ipmainfo@ipma.org

International Small Press Publishing Institute (ISPPI)
121 E. Front St., Suite 401
Traverse City, MI 49684
Tel: (800) 706-4636
Fax: (616) 933-0448
E-mail:
info.entrepreneur@traverse.com

**Magazine Publishers of America
Inc.**
919 Third Ave, 22nd Floor
New York, NY 10022
Tel: (212) 872-3700
Fax: (212) 888-4217

**Maine Writers & Publishers
Alliance**
12 Pleasant St.
Brunswick, ME 04011
Tel: (207) 729-6333
Fax: (207) 725-1014

Marin Small Publisher Association
P.O. Box E
Corte Madera, CA 94976
Tel: (415) 257-8275
E-mail: msyuan@aol.com

PUBLISHING ORGANIZATIONS IN NORTH AMERICA

Michiana Independent Publishers
Kyle Hannon
Filibuster Press
55836 Riverdale Drive
Elkhart, IN 46514
Tel: (219) 522-5151
E-mail: filibstr@skynet.net

Mid-America Publisher's Association
Doug Bandos, Exec. Administrator
PO Box 376
Ada, MI 49301
Tel: (888) 308-MAPA
Fax: (616) 676-0759
E-mail: KSBPromo@aol.com

MidAtlantic Publishers Association
Summit Crossroads Press
11065 Swansfield Rd.
Columbia, MD 21044-2709
Tel: (410) 740-6920
Fax: (410) 730-9346
E-mail: SumCross@aol.com

Midwest Independent Publishers Association
Peggy Wolfe, VP Membership
P.O. Box 581432
Minneapolis, MN 55458-1432
Tel: (612) 544-5105
Fax: (612) 544-8643
E-mail: prwolfe@bitsteam.net

Music Publishers' Association of the United States
205 E 42 St.
New York, NY 10017

National Association of Desktop Publishers (NADTP)
462 Old Boston St.
Topsfield, MA 01983
Tel: (508) 887-7900; (800) 874-4113
Fax: (508) 887-6117

National Association of Hispanic Publications
301 S. Frio, Suite 102
San Antonio, TX 78207
Tel: (210) 220-1290

National Association of Independent Publishers
PO Box 430
Highland City, FL 33846
Tel: (813) 648-4420 (voice & fax)

National Association of Independent Publishers Representatives (NAIPR)
Zeckendorf Towers
111 E. 14 St., Suite 157
New York, NY 10003
Tel: (508) 877-5328
Fax: (508) 788-0208

National Directory Publishing Association
Box 19107, George Mason Sta.
Alexandria, Va 22320
Tel: (703) 329-8206
Fax: (703) 960-9618
E-Mail: ndpa@ix.netcom.com

National Music Publishers' Associations (NMPA)
205 E. 42 St.
New York, NY 10017

New Age Publishing and Retailing Alliance
P.O. Box 9
6 Eastsound Square
Eastsound, WA 98245
Tel: (360) 376-2702
Fax: (360) 376-2704
E-mail: napra@pacificrim.net

PUBLISHING ORGANIZATIONS IN NORTH AMERICA

New Mexico Book Association
P.O. Box 1285
Santa Fe, NM 87504
(505) 983-1412
E-mail: nmba@roadrunner.com

The Newsletter Publishers Association
1401 Wilson Blvd., Suite 207
Arlington, VA 22209
Tel: (703) 527-2333; (800) 356-9302 Fax: (703) 841-0629

New York State Regional Publishers Association
c/o Seaway Trail, Inc.
109 Barracks Drive
Sackets Harbor, NY 13685
Tel: (315) 646-1000

Northwest Association of Book Publishers
19996 S. Sweetbriar Rd.
West Linn, OR 97068
Tel: (503) 625-5093

Philadelphia Publishers Group
Box 42681, Philadelphia, PA 19101
Tel: (215) 732-1863
Fax: (215) 735-5399

Protestant Church-Owned Publishers Association
1100 Country Club Rd.
St. Charles, MO 63303-3364
Tel: (314) 949-3156
Fax: (314) 949-9978

Publishers Advertising and Marketing Association
c/o Cathy Collins
The Crown Publishing Group
201 E 50 St.
New York, NY 10022
Fax: (212) 333-5374

Publishers Association of the South
P.O. Box 43533
Birmingham, AL 35243
Tel: (205) 322-4579
Fax: (205) 326-1012

Publishers Information Bureau (PIB)
919 Third Ave, 22nd Floor
New York, NY 10022
Tel: (212) 752-0055
Fax: (212) 888-4217

Publishers Marketing Association
2401 Pacific Coast Highway, #102
Hermosa Beach, CA 90254
Tel: (310) 372-2732
Fax: (310) 374-3342
E-mail: pmaonline@aol.com

Regional Publishers Association
2503 Davidsonville Rd,
Gambrills, MD 21054
Tel: (410) 721-7987 (voice & fax)

The Religion Publishing Group
c/o Roth Advertising Inc
333 Glen Head Rd.
Old Brookville, NY 11545
Tel: (516) 671-9292

Rocky Mountain Book Publishers Association
P.O. Box 19013
Boulder, CO 80308
Tel: (303) 499-9540
Fax: (303) 499-9584

Rocky Mountain Publishing Professionals Guild (RMPPG)
P.O. Box 17721
Boulder, CO 80308-7721
Tel: (303) 282-9294

PUBLISHING ORGANIZATIONS IN NORTH AMERICA

Sacramento Publishers Association
Bobbie Christensen, President
P.O. Box 232233
Sacramento, CA 95823
Tel: (916) 422-8435

San Diego Publishers' Alliance
4679 Vista St.
San Diego, CA 92116
Tel: (619) 280-8711,(800) 944-5551
Fax: (619) 280-8713
E-mail: sdpa@ellipsys.com

San Francisco Bay Area Book Council
123 Townsend St., Suite 260
San Francisco, CA 94107
Tel: (415) 908-2833
Fax: (415) 908-2839

Small Press Center
20 W 44 St.
New York, NY 10036
Tel: (212) 764-7021
Fax: (212) 354-5365

Small Publishers, Artists & Writers Network
Mary Embree, Executive Director
P.O. Box 2653
Ventura, CA 93002-2653
Tel: (805) 643-2403

Small Publishers Association of North America
P.O. Box 1306
425 Cedar St.
Buena Vista, CO 81211-1306

Society for Scholarly Publishing
10200 W 44 Ave, Suite 304
Wheat Ridge, CO 80033
Tel: (303) 422-3914
Fax: (303) 422 8894
E-Mail: 5686814@mcimail.com

Software Publishers Association (SPA)
1730 "M" St. NW, Suite 700
Washington D.C. 20036
Tel: (202) 452-1600; (800) 388-7478
Fax: (202) 223-8756

Tucson Book Publishing Association
Steve Bacon, President
P.O. Box 43542
Tucson, AZ 85733
Tel: (520) 571-1111

Women in Scholarly Publishing (WISP)
The MIT University Press
55 Hayward
Cambridge, MA 02142-1399
Tel: (617) 253-5642
Fax: (617) 258-6779

Women's National Book Association Inc (WNBA)
160 Fifth Ave.
New York, NY 10010
Tel: (212) 675-7804
Fax: (212) 989-7542

10.

ADDING PIZAZZ TO YOUR BOOK SIGNING SELLS LOTS MORE BOOKS

If I have had any success, it's due to luck,
but I notice the harder I work, the luckier I get.
CHARLES F. KETTERING

AS AN AUTHOR, YOU CAN GREATLY BOOST YOUR BOOK SALES BY SIGNING your John Hancock in bookstores across the country. But it takes more than a stack of books, a pen, and a smile to move books out the door. The four keys to success are organization, creativity, planning, and promotion.

What kind of sales can you expect with a book signing? We have seen authors sell 100 copies of their book on the day of the signing. After the event, the store has then sold 5 to 10 times that number.

But don't expect people to swamp your table just because you've written a great book. People feel uneasy as they walk up to the table. They feel they're forced to make a decision, buy or not buy, right on the spot. To succeed, you literally have to lure people to you, give them a reason to walk over to the table, and make them feel comfortable once they're there. Food makes excellent bait. Some publishers even buy air-scent fragrances—

coconut or vanilla, for example—and tuck them under the table (available from California Scents, (800) 959-6025 for $2 an organic pad). When someone walks buy, a delicious smell fills the air and a curious customer is lured in.

"Food, food, food. I find that anything with sugar in it seems to pull people in enough to get them to the table," said Lisa Reid Ferguson of Carol Publishers' *Raising Kids with Just a Little Cash*.

"I now take cake made from a simple recipe in my book and a little sign, 'One-Pan, No-Bowl Banana Cake, p. 115.' But it worked even when it was just a plate of packaged cookies."

Ferguson also demonstrates another idea from her book:

"I give away 'Stick Frisbees' to the kids, which are just basically five ice cream sticks arranged into a flying form that breaks apart on contact with the wall and can be rebuilt over and over. The parents look at the book while I show the frisbee to the kid."

Tim Smith, author of the *Buck Wilder Small Fry Fishing Guide*, once found himself buried among racks of dresses and suits at a book signing, totally ignored by the shoppers. The next time he signed books in the department store (same store, but different location), he decided to beckon customers to him. He outfitted three beautiful young women in fishing vests and hats, and gave them creels into which were stuffed copies of his book. They roamed around the department store and told customers to come on over and meet the author of this wonderful book. It worked like a charm.

It is imperative to think of your book signing as an "event," as opposed to a signing.

David LeClaire, author of *Bridges to a Passionate Partnership* published by Equestrian Press, said he became committed to doing "events" after suffering through a couple of average book signings.

"When we do seminars, it's amazing. People want to buy the book because they relate to you. They think, 'Wow this is great. I want to take him home with me.' After these seminars, people are looking for something to take away."

LeClaire strives to be creative with his "event ideas."

"For example, I will be putting together a group of four authors from the area who will all do a 15-minute talk on their subject (with a common theme). All four authors' books will be available for sale during and after the talks.

"The first theme for this group will be 'Surviving/Dealing with The Holidays.' The event will be just for women in some places, since they are our primary audience anyway. The first author will talk about giving gifts (the subject of her book), another will talk about seeing humor in the craziness of the holidays (a comedian who is selling humorous books), I will talk about the impact of the holidays on your relationship, and the fourth author, who sells cookbooks, will talk about great, simple ways to prepare hams/turkeys/roasts, etc."

LeClaire offers the event to libraries, churches, service groups, and non-profits.

LeClaire has volunteered to do longer speaking engagements as the sole speaker. The sponsor sells tickets for $3 to $5, advertises the event, organizes all the details, and gets all the ticket revenues. LeClaire simply comes in, speaks and sells books.

Author and storyteller Patty Clark spends afternoons at bookstores, reading her German folk tale, *Cobweb Christmas*, and then helping children make Christmas tree ornaments.

An important point: when you're giving a mini-seminar about your book, don't tell the audience *everything* they want to know so that they feel they don't need to buy your book. *Tantalize them.* The point is to whet their appetite with a truly riveting presentation, but point out that appetite can only truly be satisfied by your book. There are several ways of doing this. Read provocative or riveting sections from your book. When someone asks a question, partially answer it, but add that your book will give them a detailed answer.

Use humor. Entertain! Sell books, but don't come off as a hustler. Invite a trusted friend to give you an honest opinion. Consider taking a speech class if you feel there's room for improvement.

Finally, you need to tell your audience in a dignified way exactly why your book is better than anybody else's. Show proof.

Other hints for effective book signings:

- Some customers may not be ready to decide whether to buy your book right on the spot. Offer an attractive, well-written flyer that might later convince them.

- Some bookstores prefer to hide their authors in the back of the store. Bad move. You need a frontal attack. The table should intercept the wave of the customer flow. Lots easier to make eye contact (which you should!).

- Make small talk with children who are unattached to their parents. When they come to detach them, greet them and tell them what a special child they have.

Think of what your book has to offer and design your event around it. Gail Golomb, author of *The Kidney Stones Handbook: A Patient's Guide to Hope, Cure and Prevention* published by the Four Geez Press, gets standing-room-only crowds at book signings. Golomb treats her speech as a performance, walking around with a mike in hand.

Golomb also believes in "events." In one such presentation, she tied her speech into Thanksgiving by using props of a traditional feast which can be poisonous to the average stone patient: cranberry sauce, more than three ounces of turkey, pecan pie/pumpkin pie, stuffing made from cornbread.

"And when everyone was hanging on the floor, totally depressed, I told them about good foods that could keep them out of the emergency room," she said.

Lots of children's book authors give readings. Great idea. The parents usually sit by their children during these kind of readings. You couldn't hope for a better audience! The only caveat is to keep your words and subject appropriate for the age level, and don't make it an obvious self-promotion.

Most signings have a "slow" period. Publisher Melanie Goldish, author of *How Was Your Day, Baby? A Childcare Journal for Working Parents*, uses the time to "meet'n'greet" all the booksellers in the store, personally show them the book and to explain to whom it might be suited.

"It makes me feel useful and wanted and gets the book some exposure with the salespeople," she said.

What's considered a "successful" signing?

Everyone probably has a different standard for a successful book signing. We have known authors who are pleased if they sell 10 copies of their book. In contrast, retired military General Colin Powell autographed more than 53,000 of his books around the country in the fall of 1995. Richard Evans, author of *The Christmas Box*, signed well over 1,000 copies of his book at each signing leading up to the holiday.

We define success as selling 50 copies in a single signing. We feel this number makes everyone involved happy: the author, the publisher, and the bookstore. If you sell 50 copies of a $15 book, the bookstore pockets $300 (assuming the standard 40-percent discount) and you'll earn nearly $450. It's a good afternoon's wage.

Besides the obvious benefit of making money, there are two other reasons why bookstores like book signings. First, it draws people to their stores who otherwise may not shop there. Secondly, people coming to meet you face-to-face may buy other books while they are there.

Make your first book signing local

Before embarking on a book tour in different cities, or even different states, break the ice first in your own hometown. The local media is far more likely to interview you for a news story or to publish a book review, which you can then include in a publicity package. You can also interview on air in a fairly forgiving environment.

Once you've exploited the local market and are ready to travel, choose a good-sized city, preferably one that has some connection with your book. Obviously, if you're just starting out, you'll have to keep your travel costs down and need to choose bookstores within driving distance.

Setting a date

Foot traffic is highest in the stores on the weekends, but think about how to tie in your book with upcoming events in your chosen locale. If you've written an antique car book, for example, call up the organization that sponsors antique car shows and ask for a calendar. Maybe you could rent some space at the show and sell your book or post flyers at the event publicizing your book signing the next day. Another example: if you've written a Christian book, find a Christian speaker you like and ask him if you could sign books (maybe even speak) in conjunction with his events. Remember! A bookstore isn't always the best place to sign your books.

Once you've determined your optimal date, we recommend reserving your book-signing date with the bookstore at least 60 days in advance. There are several reasons why:

1. To make sure no one else has scheduled an event on that date.

2. To give you ample time to notify the bookstore's publicity manager, who will likely list the event in the bookstore's newsletter and/or promotional calendar.

3. To notify the media for advance publicity.

4. To get promotional flyers designed, printed, and distributed.

5. To schedule time to get a window display set up at the bookstore.

TALKING TO THE BOOKSTORE OWNER

Once you've decided on a date, it's time to talk to the bookstore owner. Select a bookstore that's friendly to signings, but just one per city. So again, we stress networking. Call up publishers who reside in the city (or a publishers' association) and ask them for good signing destinations. Who's cooperative, who's not? What's the bookstore's contact name? What radio stations can you get on? What's the deejay's name? Newspaper and TV contacts?

Approach the bookstore owner first with a phone call. Describe your book, your proposed event, sales figures for past book signings (only if they're impressive), why the people in that particular city would be interested in buying it, your proposed signing date, and why you chose it. Emphasize whatever local angle you can think of. Was your subject matter related to a town similar to this one? Did you ever live in the town? Is the message of your book somehow applicable to the town's commerce or a current problem (i.e., massive layoffs). Follow up by mailing a promotional package, which includes a letter describing yourself and your book, a free copy of the book, reviews, a page detailing your past successes at book signings, a general outline of your publicity campaign, and a picture of yourself at past signings (surrounded by banners and/or posters). A good strategy is to ask bookstore owners to write a letter of recommendation, which you can show as proof of your past successes.

Another note: Be sure to sound like you know what you're talking about. Know that bookstores take a 40-percent discount, or be prepared to be dismissed as a naive amateur. And don't expect the bookseller to read your book. They usually have time to flip through it, but that's about it.

Once the bookstore owner has agreed to let you sign in the store, discuss publicity, which is usually a co-op effort. Many bookstores will provide a list of media contacts, put up a window display a week in advance of the signing, mention the event in the newsletter that goes out to their best customers, and advertise the event in-house with a blow-up color poster of your book with the date and time. Bookstores, however, do not provide paid advertising and don't handle the publicity end—that's your responsibility.

GETTING THE WORD OUT

The single most important element of a successful book signing is publicity. Get people not only interested in your book, but interested in you.

There are two kinds of press releases you'll need. The first is simply for media calendar purposes, so make it intriguing and short. "John O'Toule, a psychologist who has spent a career mending troubled marriages, will speak on 'Why the Holidays are Tough on Relationships' on Dec. 5 at Borders Bookstore. Married folk are invited to peruse his new book, *Saving a Rocky Marriage: Miracles Do Happen.*" Add a paragraph describing the book, a few good blurbs, and the date, time, and address of the signing. Include a phone number for more information.

This press release should go to all newspapers, radio stations, and television stations to the attention of "Calendar of Events." Call the newspaper and magazines for the specific name of the calendar, the person who is responsible for coordinating it and the lead time required. Make your letter to that person's attention. If you're short on time, just mail it: Attention, Calendar."

The second kind of press release is intended to spark a story. Your job is to convince the editor or reporter that there is, in fact, a story to write. Include a local/news angle and orient the release to how the reader can benefit: "With the recent 20-percent price hikes of propane fuel, an increasing number of people are looking for an answer to reduce their heating bills. On Friday, they can find out how. A California author will explain at an upcoming book signing how it's cheaper than ever before to convert a home to solar energy."

Be sure to enclose copies of any stories written about you or your book.

📖　📖　📖

To sell *Inside the Bestsellers*, Jerry Jenkins speaks in front of an average of 15,000 people a year at bookstores, writing groups and writer and publisher associations. Talking about the ins and outs of independent publishing, he relates stories of successful small press publishers who have cracked the market and mentions that their complete stories are told in his book, *Inside the Bestsellers*. To ensure a good audience, Jenkins tries to get booked with a radio talk-show host a day or two before the event. He also sends out a press release to local writers' groups, the newspaper's "Calendar of Events" and flyers to libraries and coffee shops. Usually, because it's a free speech, newspapers happily publish the event. The bookstores are also key in promoting the event. If they believe in you and your event, they'll do anything to get people to the speech. Jenkins builds on recommendations—one Borders store will tell another: "Jerry made lots of money for our store, he got 110 people there and sold 90 books!" After each bookstore date, he makes it a point to send the bookstore a thank-you letter.

📖　📖　📖

Here are some specific suggestions for getting the word out:

PRINT MEDIA

- Alternative newspapers: These newspapers—usually weekly freebies—happily publish cultural events such as book signings and frequently feature interviews of visiting authors, particularly if your book topic matches the interest of their readers.

- Specialty publications: These might include business journals, tourism publications, gay and lesbian newspapers, visitor and convention publications, regional "What's Happening" publications, senior magazines, and many others. Consider the reading audience when preparing your press release.

- Newspapers: We suggest sending a press release to all daily and weekly newspapers within a 50-mile radius of the signing. The press release should be sent out about two weeks before the signing. Call the newspaper and get specific names of people: features editor, book editor, and calendar editor. If you have a topic with a specific slant—Italian cooking, for example—send the press release to the food editor. Again, think of a connection to the current news of the day!

- Specialty insert sections: Many newspapers now include special-interest inserts, such as a 10-page section on technology, home and garden, or car care. Check with the newspaper to find out if any will focus on your event (the advertising manager is often the best person to ask).

- Magazines: Call the regional magazines, if any, and ask about the deadline for the book-signing announcement for the calendar (generally 60 to 90 days). Don't expect a story, however, unless there is a very strong local connection.

ELECTRONIC MEDIA

Radio: Your efforts should focus, above all, on arranging a radio interview on the same day as your book signing (or on the eve of your signing). One radio interview consistently pulls in high numbers of people to a signing, assuming, of course, that the interview is interesting.

Internet: Contact a few of the local Internet Service Providers and ask if there's a website that posts local events. If so, send in a press release. It doesn't hurt! For tips on interviewing skills, refer to Chapter 9.

THE STAGE IS SET

Books need to arrive at the bookstore about three to four weeks before the signing. This ensures that the bookstore can unpack the books and arrange them before the big day. The bookstore will also need the books to set up a window display a week or so before the signing.

How many books? Plan on asking the bookstore to purchase 150 books and tell them that you assume 100 will be moved out on the day of the signing. If you work with a wholesaler or distributor, make sure they have enough books to accommodate the bookstore's order. If the bookstore balks at this amount, remind them how successful you were at past signings, the amount of effort that's going into publicity, and the fact that books are returnable after a period of time.

Two days before the book signing, call the bookstore and ask how many books have already sold as a result of your publicity efforts. This will give you a clue as to whether your efforts are having an effect. If you are driving to the signing, make sure to carry an additional 50 to 100 copies of your title in case the bookstore sells out everything it has. Obviously, if additional books are needed, the bookstore will purchase them from you right on the spot.

Once you're there, relax and enjoy yourself. Set up your table and posters and get ready to speak. Author Tim Smith takes a life-size cardboard cutout of his book's character, Buck Wilder, and a four-color banner. Not everyone can afford this kind of display, but for certain kinds of books, it really works and is worth the investment. At minimum, bring two posters: one to display quotations on how great your book is, and the other to display a color copy of your book cover. You may want to do a third poster with an excerpt from your book. Many authors take their book cover to a copy shop, get a color enlargement and back it with foamboard.

You also may want to dress the part. Match the persona of your book. Pamela Houston, author of *Cowboys Are My Weakness*, shows up for public events dressed in cowboy boots and a cowboy hat.

Author Jerry Dennis said he never knows what to expect. His worst experiences have been at mall bookstores, where he and illustrator Glenn Wolff were placed in the aisle, making them feel as if they were giving away samples of food. At one bookstore, so many people made it a point to avoid them (thinking they had to buy a book if they made eye contact), that the duo set out a sign, "Please do not feed the authors." That broke the ice. The customers laughed when they read the sign and asked them about their book. This illustrates that people often find authors intimidating and shy away from them. Jerry Dennis said his best sales occurred at those bookstores where the store owner would personally introduce him to the customers. Yet that's not something you can ask an owner to do—it has to come from the proprietor's own gregarious nature, he said.

And one more thing. Just don't sign your name and be done with it. Ask the person who it's for and why. Make your comments personal and warm, perhaps with a touch of humor. After all, you not only want to make money, you also want to have a good time and help others do the same.

11

THE NOT-SO-QUIET SALES TO LIBRARIES

The true university of these days is a collection of books.
THOMAS CARLYLE

LIBRARY SALES IN THIS COUNTRY ARE THOUGHT OF AS RATHER QUIET. A library, it's thought, might buy one or two of your books, but no more. So why consider them at all? Ponder this: there are more than 100,000 libraries in this country. Their combined purchases in 1994 totaled $3 billion, including $1.5 billion on book purchases alone, according to *Book Industry Trends* 1995.

Librarians are also a wonderful group to work with; they are consistent in their business practices, they are loyal customers, and they are the most ardent of all book lovers.

There is another wonderful quality to libraries. The market is hugely diverse and includes not only public libraries, but corporate libraries, military libraries, hospital libraries, foundation libraries, not to mention academic libraries, which serve kindergartners through Ph.D. candidates. Specialty libraries are willing to pay full price for one- or two-book purchases, although libraries, in general, make the vast bulk of their purchases from wholesalers such as Baker & Taylor at a 55-percent discount.

It is worth any publisher's time to spend a day at a large metropolitan library to look through the reference books that list the various specialty libraries, said James Cox, editor-in-chief of *Midwest Book Review*, who's been heavily involved with libraries for three decades.

"There is a Shakespeare library in California who will buy anything written about Shakespeare no matter who the publisher is," he said. "Their endowment requires that they do that. There is a library in Boston that is mandated to buy every book of poetry that's ever been written. It's an automatic book sale. You can just send the book with an invoice enclosed."

Still, many publishers count libraries out of their marketing equation because of untested assumptions. They believe for example, that many libraries buy only one copy of each book. Although true in many instances, metropolitan libraries with a couple of dozen branches often buy up to 50 copies of a book.

It's also assumed that public libraries exclusively prefer hard-covered books. It is true that librarians prefer sturdier, hard-covered books, but cash-strapped librarians often choose a paperback because of its lower price. In fact, virtually all public libraries today buy paperbacks. Others assume libraries buy only scholarly, technical or reference books from small publishers. Admittedly, public libraries rarely buy fiction from a small press publisher, yet they will readily consider nonfiction books on most any subject if it's accurate and written by a credible author. If you have written a high-priced specialty book—say a comprehensive tome on rehabilitative techniques for wild animals —you will very likely find a lucrative library market.

Another fear: why put your book in a library and lose sales at the bookstore? Indeed, you will lose a few sales to borrowers, yet most publishers find that word-of-mouth boosts sales at the bookstore. Generally, if borrowers find an invaluable reference book, they'll eventually buy their own personal copy.

But how do you sell to libraries? Many publishers believe that librarians only buy books that have received glowing reviews in *Library Journal, Kirkus Reviews, Choice, Booklist, School Library Journal,* and *Small Press.*

Indeed, a good review is critical. Busy librarians, particularly, rely on reviews when they select books, but not exclusively. They realize that for a balanced collection, they must go beyond the reviews. After all, only a tiny fraction of the thousands of titles published each year are ever reviewed in these journals. That's why small publishers need to approach libraries more creatively than the New York houses do. Strategies include library stops on book tours, exhibiting books at major library conventions and trade shows, employing direct mail campaigns, advertising in the library industry's publications that were mentioned above, and signing on with a distributor who specializes in library sales. Experienced publishers also know the power of popular demand; if their book is requested three or four times at a library, the acquisition director usually takes notice and buys copies.

In library sales, timing plays an important role. We'll discuss library sales from the conception of the book to publication and promotion.

WRITING YOUR BOOK

Librarians are perhaps the most discriminating of all buyers. Skimp on accuracy or content and you'll forever sacrifice sales to libraries.

Your well-researched book should include citations and a complete index to interest libraries. The librarian will scrutinize the table of contents before purchasing the book. Make the contents logical and clear. Nearly all nonfiction books will need an index. There is indexing software available or find someone who compiles indices for a living. Proofreading must be done again and again by many different pairs of literate and knowledgeable eyes. Consider sending chapters to experts in the field and asking for comments of overall context (enclose a self-addressed stamped envelope for ease of return).

GETTING YOUR BOOK REVIEWED

Getting your book reviewed begins at the very basic level: your chosen topic. Your book will get the cold shoulder if your topic is trite or done to death, i.e., *Ten Steps to Happiness Through Positive Thinking*. Optimally, your book will be the first on the subject or the first to offer a dramatically different slant. If you're stepping on the soapbox about a particular issue, make sure you back up your opinion with solid research. Here's how *Small Press* Managing Editor Mardi Link screens books for reviews.

"We reject a lot of books. A higher percentage of fiction books are rejected, and that's because there are a lot of mediocre fiction titles, maybe because fiction is harder to write.

"I look at the press kits, the cover, all the materials an author sends, but really we decide on the content. However, if you hide great content inside of an ugly cover and a poor print job, it's possible it can get put into the 'no' pile.

"I read the introduction, the last chapter, the book jacket; what you put on the jacket is pretty crucial. If you're sending the galley, make sure you tell us what's going on the book cover—finished art is even better. I am susceptible as anyone to a great cover.

"On subject areas, we're generally not interested in books with a very narrow appeal, unless it's truly spectacular enough to make it worth a review in our limited space. We just reviewed a book, *Toads and Toadstools*—it's a really narrow topic on the relationship throughout history of toads and toadstools—but the author did painstaking research, the cover was gorgeous, the paper first-rate, the illustrations were beautiful, and the writing was excellent. So it forced a review.

"We receive a tremendous amount of self-help books and new age books. Some of the new age books are ridiculous. They are not based in any sense of reality whatsoever—*Health Care by Extraterrestrials*, if you can believe it. Self-help has been done and done and done. A lot are just knockoffs of the best sellers. If it's new research, or they truly have something significant to say, we'll review it, but I'm not interested in a rehash.

"We get books that are really sloppily put together. On the other end of the spectrum, we get some phenomenal art books, great works of fiction, fascinating works of nonfiction."

Once such successful book is *Common Blood Tests; What Every Patient Must Know About Lab Tests*, now in its third edition. It has done very well in library sales not only because it's a useful book for medical consumers, but also because it translates important medical terminology into language a layman can understand, said Richard Capps, product manager for Unique Books.

When to submit your book for reviews

Once your book is in book galley form, it's time to submit to library review journals. State your publication date as three to four months from the date you ship the galley (even if it isn't).

In general, do *not* wait until your book is published to send it out for reviews. Most library review journals only publish reviews in advance of publication (although a review may appear post-publication, particularly after a book has received a prestigious award).

"The competition for a review is very fierce," said Barbara Hoffert, managing editor of book reviews at the *Library Journal.* "Of the 600 we receive each week, only about 20 percent are reviewed."

To boost your chances for a review, she said, submit your book during the review journals' slower months of July, August, December, January, and February.

To entice a second look at the book, emphasize testimonials by experts and famous authors. Do you have a huge promotion budget or large printing planned? Mention that, too. Enclose copies of any early publicity about the book.

The ideal cover letter, Hoffert said, is short and sweet.

"With 600 queries to go through each week, the cover letter must be very focused to get our attention," she said.

The cover letter must quickly tell the librarian what the book is about and why it's so special.

"What does it do that no other book on the subject has done? Also, we need information on the author. The author's bio is a very important part of a cover. Librarians care very much about credentials. I might not know from looking at the cover of a book on lace-making that the author is the head of the Lace Maker's Association, so tell me.

"Your letter should include statistics on the popularity of the subject. Maybe a lace-maker magazine has a circulation of one million. We need a really concise one-page cover letter about how good the book is, where it fits into the market, what makes it distinctive."

Also include in the letter a few quotes from respected authorities in relevant fields.

A MODEL COVER LETTER AND SUPPORT SHEET

WILLOW CREEK PRESS

PO BOX 147, MINOCQUA, WI 54548

PHONE: 715-358-7010   FAX: 715-358-2807

August 12, 1996

We are pleased to be sending you a copy of **FLASHES IN THE RIVER: The Streamside Images of Arthur Shilstone and Ed Gray** for consideration for review or mention.

We think you will agree that this book captures the beauty of American fly fishing in both art and words. Get ready to be transported from the brawling rivers of the mountainous west to the storied streams of the east and all the hallowed waters in between.

If you would like more information on this book (the first in the "Images" series) or would like to set up an interview with either Ed Gray or Arthur Shilstone, please call me at 715-358-7010.

We would appreciate receiving two copies of any review or mention you make of this book.

Sincerely,

Victoria Houston

Victoria Houston
Associate Publisher

enc.

A MODEL COVER LETTER AND SUPPORT SHEET

FLASHES IN THE RIVER
The Streamside Images of Arthur Shilstone and Ed Gray
First in the "Images" Series

Watercolors by Arthur Shilstone; Essays by Ed Gray • As artist Arthur Shilstone is renowned for capturing the beauty of American fly fishing through his masterful brushwork, so author Ed Gray's word images evoke the spirit and essence of the sport. *Flashes in the River,* the first in our continuing "Images" series, combines the artist's finest paintings with the author's original, complementary essays in a visual and verbal celebration that dazzles the eye and warms the heart. • The delightful collaboration takes you from the brawling rivers of the mountainous west to the storied streams of the east and all the hallowed waters in between.

Flashes in the River is an inspiring and colorful flyfishing journey taken with two of the finest companions possible.
• **Arthur Shilstone** has achieved worldwide fame as a watercolorist. His paintings hang in international galleries as well as in private and corporate collections. He lives and paints in Connecticut.
• **Ed Gray** founded *Gray's Sporting Journal* with his wife, Rebecca, in 1975, and was its editor for 16 years. He has been contributing editor to *Esquire Sportsman* and *Sports Afield.* He now writes fiction and essays from his home in New Hampshire, contributing frequently to national magazines.

ADVANCE PRAISE:
"In the sporting art of Arthur Shilstone, what emerges is as much a feeling as a picture— soft and fresh and spontaneous, altogether the result of a roving and resourceful eye and an immensely talented hand."

—*Sporting Classics* magazine

"Flashes in the River *glitters with brilliance."*

—Nick Lyons, author of *Spring Creek*

WILLOW CREEK PRESS
PO Box 147
Minocqua, WI 54548
1-800-850-9453

SPORTS & RECREATION / FICTION
Hardcover, 12 x 9 inches, 128 pages, 70 color images.
ISBN 1-57223-040-1
Order No. 0401
$35.00

Although the book may be available at your local bookstore, many readers will find it easier to order directly from Willow Creek Press by calling **1-800-850-WILD,** or by sending $35.00 plus $4.00 for postage and handling for each book to: Willow Creek Press, PO Box 147, Minocqua, WI 54548.

The Dearborn Publishing Group, for example, began its press release on *Buying Mutual Funds for Free* with the headline: "Don't Buy Another Mutual Fund Until You Read This Book *Pay No Transaction Fees *Select Top-Performing Funds." They state the benefits for readers clearly and directly.

On an accompanying fact sheet, list these elements: title, author, size of book, hard-cover or paperback, ISBN number, copyright year, number of copies in print run (if 10,000 or more), key points of the publicity program (i.e., Dearborn Publishing Group bulleted these: Trade and Co-op Advertising, National Print Publicity Campaign, Talk Radio Nationwide, Author Seminars and Newsletter), publisher's name, distributor and/or wholesaler's name, and contact name.

Besides credentials and content, Hoffert said she's very sensitive to typos in both the cover letter and the galley.

"I distrust any book with typos. If they can't get the spelling right, how can I trust that the facts are right? The same thing with a cover letter. It doesn't make sense, but I get cover letters with typos all the time."

If you must send a galley with typos, be sure to label it: "UNCOR-RECTED PAGE PROOF."

Hoffert also advises not to bother sending the book cover design when seeking a review. She doesn't need it at this point, nor does she need T-shirts, teddy bears, or hats—just the galley and cover letter.

"I just want a book that's well-prepared and copy-edited. It's the quality of the book that really matters," she said. "Put your time and money into good research, good design, good proofreading, good copy editing."

Library review journals and prestigious review media, such as the *New York Times*, do not want to review a book that can't be easily purchased by libraries or consumers (i.e., isn't carried by the wholesalers, Baker & Taylor or Ingram). Many wrongly assume that a micro-press offering has no wholesaler and they'll reject the book out of hand. To ensure this doesn't happen to your book, make sure you list the wholesaler and distributor on your fact sheet.

There is also endless discussion among publishers on the importance of putting a publicist's name on the cover sheet. Some believe that the name of a publicist makes them look less like a micro-publisher and improves the odds of getting a review. We don't know, but it intuitively makes sense. What if you're a one-person operation and you don't have a publicist? Some publishers fake it. One publisher, for example, puts her friend's name on the press release and an 888 toll-free number, which rings into three mailbox options at her publishing firm, including one that rings into the mailbox of the "publicist." A week or so after this publisher sends out a review package, her friend—serving as a temporary publicist—makes follow-up calls asking if they received the packet, have any questions, etc., to the reviewers to pre-empt calls asking for the publicist.

For names and addresses of review journals, refer to the list at the end of this chapter. Also, talk to experienced publishers for their list of favorite reviewers.

DISTRIBUTING YOUR BOOKS TO A LIBRARY

Distributors play a huge role on the library circuit. Librarian Sarah Ormond, head of adult reading at the Baldwin Public Library in the Detroit area, said she meets with a representative of Quality Books—a distributor specializing in small press books—once a year just to see what the small presses have to offer in the areas of crafts, travel, and offbeat subjects.

The timing of contacting a distributor isn't as rigid as a library review journal, but distributors do prefer seeing a galley and finished cover art instead of waiting for the printed book. Make your pitch to distributors at the same time you're pitching the library review journals.

Unlike library journals, however, all is not lost if your book has been out on the market awhile.

"A lot of librarians are interested in newer material. In the same breath, while the copyright year is very important, if it's the only book I can obtain on a specific subject matter and it has an older copyright, I'll pick it up," said Richard Capps of Unique Books.

An older book on traditional costumes, for example, has sold very well, Capps said.

Several hundred distributors serve the country's libraries; the largest and most well-known serving the small press are Unique Books and Quality Books Inc., representing 3,800 and 12,500 titles, respectively. Both companies reject hundreds of books each month, but you can maximize your chances by following a few guidelines:

- First and foremost, make sure the cover design looks professional, high-quality, and eye-catching. Librarians prefer books with straight-forward titles and attractive covers.
- Plan for a high-quality binding. Spiral bound books are never accepted by libraries.
- Price your book at a reasonable level.
- Choose a unique subject.

"The better the quality with a reasonable price, the better off they are," Capps said. "The best way to communicate with me is to send me a galley or a finished product. Unfortunately that will get more of my attention than the 200 pieces of correspondence I get a month. If I have something in my hand that I can look at, it will get higher priority."

Generally, library distributors do not require exclusivity (if they do, find someone else), they sell on consignment, and they pay the publisher 40-45 percent of retail price. The sales rep will show the librarian any new titles, older titles that have resurged in popularity, and any other books in subject areas that the library is lacking.

The distributor puts a data slip inside the cover of each book, which lists the publisher, author, ISBN, color information, the CIP, an index, and a summary of what the book is about. Distributors ship and bill the libraries on behalf of the publisher. They typically order in quantities of 50 to 75 books from the publisher.

The distributor's sales rep may meet with the librarian for up to four hours in a once- or twice-yearly meeting. They can present literally hundreds, even thousands of covers, in a single meeting, which is why cover design is so important, said Jim Hicks, Quality Books' director of vendor relations.

"The mind will absorb only that which the fanny will endure. After you've gone over three or four thousand titles, sometimes one second will be a long time to look at the cover," Hicks said. "The more striking you can make your cover, the better."

Before signing on with a distributor, do your homework. Research a distributor's reputation by calling other publishers whose title(s) they represent. The number one consideration is if the distributor pays on time; the second is clout. Is the distributor well-known and well-respected in the industry? A general rule of thumb is that bigger is better unless the distributor specializes in niche subject areas.

If a distributor rejects your book, don't hesitate to call and ask why. Perhaps it's a negotiable item: your price might be high or you may need a jazzier cover design.

ESTABLISHING A WHOLESALER

Wholesalers are integral to library sales. No matter how librarians choose which book to buy, they will order the book from a wholesaler three times out of four. Statistics bear this out, For adult and children's trade books, wholesalers accounted for 72 percent of sales to libraries in 1994, with only 28 percent of sales made directly to the publisher, according to the Book Industry Study Group.

After reading a favorable review, a librarian is most likely to place an order for the book with Baker & Taylor in Bridgewater, New Jersey. It's the country's largest warehouser catering to libraries.

How do you register your title with Baker & Taylor? You do so inadvertently when you apply for a Library of Congress number due to the fact that Baker & Taylor receives notice of all new books from the Library of Congress.

Your best bet, however, is to contact B&T while the book is still in galley form. Write to: Baker & Taylor, Publisher Contact Section, P.O. Box 6920, Bridgewater, NJ 08807-0400; (Fax: (908) 218-3980; Phone: (908) 218-3803/(908) 218-0400. Ask for a copy of "Information Outline for Publishers," which explains all of the programs available. Complete and mail the forms they send to you.

Once your book is produced, send one to Publisher Services in Bridgewater for evaluation by the Academic Approval Program and processing for the libraries' cataloging card sets.

Baker & Taylor will pay you 45 percent of the book's suggested retail price and requires that you pick up the tab for freight. They also charge a one-time $100 set-up fee for new vendors.

You'll also want your book on stock with Ingram Book Company, the country's largest wholesaler to independent bookstores. Typically, Ingram will want to work through your distributor, although a few independent publishers have succeeded in approaching Ingram directly.

Some publishers find it difficult to get a wholesaler to carry them. The best strategy, in this case, is to generate demand at the bookstores. If enough people keep asking for your book, the wholesalers will be forced to stock it.

PERSONAL VISITS

Because librarians love to talk to each other about the greatest book they've just read or purchased, it makes more sense than you may think to personally visit a library and donate a book. If a librarian loves your book and likes you, he or she may become one of your most loyal champions. Be sure that you contact the library director as opposed to a busy clerk, who is more likely to give you a ho-hum reception.

Another strategy is to approach the head of the Friends of the Library (FOL) group, said *Midwest Book Review's* James Cox.

In general, FOL members are some of the most active and respected people in the community whose word-of-mouth endorsements count for a lot. Contact the FOL president and request permission to be placed on the agenda for the group's next meeting for the purpose of introducing yourself and making a donation to their library via the Friends, Cox said.

"When a publisher wants to donate a book to a city or a county library, they should first call up that library and ask for the name of the person who is president of that library's 'Friends of the Library' organization," Cox said.

Announce your appearance beforehand in the newspaper, radio, TV, and all the upcoming calendars of events, emphasizing local ties or relevance to the community. Some publishers go as far as running short classified ads.

Bring along to the meeting a camera and a stack of press releases. Talk about your book and give a colorful behind-the-scenes glimpse of what went into writing it. Segue to praise of the role of libraries and their FOLs groups as the "cornerstone of civilization as we know it," Cox suggested.

Wrap up the speech, saying you have copies of the book in your trunk at a special discount for FOL members. As you hand the book to the FOL president, have someone take a picture with your camera. Afterwards, pass out your press release which contains all the pertinent data about your book. Then go home and write a letter to the editor of the community paper, praising the FOL and their wonderful reception of you and your book (enclosing the photo of yourself); write a letter of appreciation to the FOL president and what a wonderful time you had, Cox said.

"Contact the next library system in your county and then the other regional systems and libraries within your state and repeat the process until you run out of libraries, FOLs, books, or time," Cox said.

When asking to get put on the library's agenda, take any positive feedback from the ceremony (a mention in the FOL's newsletter, a thank-you note from the FOL president, a mention in the newspaper), and use it as proof of your credibility.

To make contact with university librarians, first contact the alumnus support group (similar to Friends of the Library groups), Cox said.

The key, he said, is to call the office of the head librarian and ask for the name of the alumnus organization's liaison person for the university library system. If that particular university or college's alumnus organization isn't a library supporter, then ask to be included in the university library's monthly staff meeting to make your presentation and then follow all the steps you would for the regular community newspaper, Cox advised.

Another way to reach librarians is via the library newsletter published in your state. To understand the newsletter in its context, think of the library system as a ladder, Cox said. The first rung is your local library. The second rung is the state regional division to which your local library belongs. The third rung is the state library office.

Your state's library newsletter may not accept press releases or ads for your book, but it might review your book or print a letter to the editor if you can frame it with a "human interest" angle of what's happening at the local library level, Cox said. Embed in your letter the ISBN, price, and 800 number for your book.

To find a contact name and address for the state library newsletter, ask your local librarian to let you see a copy.

SELLING TO COLLEGE LIBRARIES

There are more than 3,500 college libraries, which seek to serve the research needs of students and staff. They will accept specialized books that appeal to higher level graduate courses—particularly if the publisher is already marketing the book for college-course adoptions, said John McHugh, a renowned academic publishing consultant.

There are two ways to reach academic libraries: either through the handful of wholesalers who specialize in libraries, including the Academic Book Center, Yankee Book Peddlers and Midwest Library Services, or via direct mail.

Dan Halloran, president of the Academic Book Center, said a wholesaler will not consider a book from an unknown publisher unless the book receives a "really great" review in *Choice*. Also, the book must be submitted for consideration prior to publication. Typically, libraries provide library wholesalers with a profile of subject areas and a list of eligible publishers. Using the list as an order form of sorts, wholesalers ship anywhere from five to 100 copies with a return rate of five to 10 percent.

Direct mail is another option. For a mailing list of academic libraries, McHugh recommends the *CMG Mailing List Catalog* (800) 677-7959. From among the catalog selections, focus on the list of "collection development specialists," who are in charge of building library collections, McHugh said.

In your letter of introduction, whether it's directed to the wholesaler or librarian, be aware that credentials count heavily. Describe the author's education, experience and relevant track record immediately after describing the book and title. Quote reviews or include copies of the entire review, particularly if the review was published in *Choice*.

PUBLIC SCHOOL K-12 LIBRARIES

Unlike community librarians, public school librarians do not depend on reviews in *Library Journal, Kirkus Reviews, Choice,* etc., for choosing books. Nor do they pay much attention to their biggest patrons—students. Instead, they depend on jobber-supplied promotional material and teacher input, said Jim Cox of *Midwest Book Review*.

Because jobbers rarely deal with micro-publishers, a direct mail appeal to the appropriate teacher is a small publisher's most economical bet, especially if it's a thematic teacher-mailing appropriate to the book, Cox said.

"And don't forget about the professional teacher organizations," Cox said. "They have organizations built on the subject matter of instruction. They have newsletters that go out to their teacher memberships as well."

To find the names of these organizations, call up the local school and ask to talk to the instructor(s) who teach the appropriate subject and ask them the name of the professional groups that exist for music teachers, gym teachers, etc., Cox said.

Cox noted there are several other differences between community and K-12 libraries:

- Community libraries operate on a calendar year; school libraries operate on a fiscal year, usually July 1-June 30.

- Community libraries typically divide their acquisition budget into monthly allotments so they won't get caught short in the last three months of the year and the peak of the annual publishing cycle. School libraries allocate the bulk of their acquisition money between July 1 and September 1, holding back only a small portion of their budget to spend during the school year.

- Community libraries do not require special bindings for durability. Conversely, school libraries often require special bindings to hold up under rough handling by numerous children. The upside in the shorter shelf life of a book at a public school, especially at the elementary level, is that a popular title will be replaced again and again.

- Community libraries have FOL organizations, while school libraries have PTA/PTO organizations. Both have professional organizations and publications for their librarians.

"There are enough differences between community libraries and K-12 libraries to require a specifically shaped marketing plan for each," Cox said.

SELLING VIA DIRECT MAIL

The effectiveness of a direct-mail campaign to libraries has long been debated. Large, heavily stratified libraries, as a rule, tend to throw away the direct-mail appeals for one or two books that they receive from micro-publishers. Many don't even look at mailings from the professional direct mail companies. The busy acquisition director relies on reviews in the library journals and *Publishers Weekly.*

But niche and small libraries may give the flyer a look, especially if your book is unique and directly relates to the library's purpose. For example, a book on do-it-yourself divorces may find interest among women's resource center libraries.

To save on mailing costs, many small publishers try to coordinate mailings with other publishers. Companies that specialize in direct-mail flyers include the Publishers Marketing Association (PMA).

PMA sends packages of flyers to public libraries that have annual acquisition budgets of $25,000 or more. They also offer programs targeted at K-12 libraries, and college and university libraries. Their list does not include specialty libraries.

Using a co-op service is fairly inexpensive (write to each PMA for details of price and flyer design requirement; the addresses are listed at the end of this chapter). You may also want to directly contact other publishers and arrange your own mailing. In that case, you can buy a one-time list. Library list providers are listed at the end of this chapter.

The flyer's design is pivotal: include a well-written book description, quotes from professionals in the book's subject field, quotes from media book reviews, review excerpts from library journals (include dates), a picture of the cover, and a replica of the table of contents. List the ISBN, price, number of pages, copyright, publication date, and CIP. Ask the company for a flyer used in the past that enjoyed excellent results.

Librarians want information, not flash, said Jan Nathan, PMA's executive director. In fact, some are so offended by neon-colored paper, they'll throw the flyer away before reading the content.

The most common mistake people make when designing their direct mail PMA flyers is offering discounts, Nathan said.

"If you offer libraries a 65-percent discount, you're wasting your time. You're absolutely wasting your time," she said, "since librarians normally do not order direct; they order through wholesalers using a purchase order whose discount schedules they work under. I also see people designing a consumer flyer. I see this mistake over and over and over again."

When is the best time to mail? Libraries are most eager to spend just after their budget year begins or just as it ends (the "use it or lose it" mentality).

The fiscal year for many libraries begins on July 1; a smaller fraction runs January 1-December 31. Unfortunately, it's not consistent. The year may run from April to March or October to September; it all depends on whether the library is run by the city, county, state, etc.

After the mailing goes out, you should notice an increase in orders from library jobbers and distributors like Baker & Taylor or Quality Books. Begin by testing a particular market with at least 4,000 flyers. If the response pays for the full expense of the mailing, then continue periodically until the numbers drop off.

HOW AUTHOR TOURS BOOST LIBRARY SALES

Once your book is published, the author's job is to go on a publicity tour, which, of course, should include libraries along the way.

Publicity tours are selling points; you'll need to keep in close contact with your library distributor rep, telling him or her exactly where you'll be on what date, as far in advance as possible. The sales representative will use the author's media appearances and local/national reviews in his or her sales spiel.

EXHIBIT AT LIBRARY TRADE SHOWS

Many small-press publishers exhibit their books at library trade shows. It's a low-key affair—librarians do not like being told what to order. Generally, publishers hand out their catalogs, posters, and any updated information about the book. For comparison purposes, it's nothing like the BookExpo America show.

Few small presses can afford the time or money to individually exhibit at library shows and will jointly exhibit with other publishers. One such company that's arranged these cooperative exhibits (since 1933) is Combined Book Exhibit in Buchanan, New York, according to President Jon

Malinowski. Essentially the books are displayed the way the librarians prefer: by subject area (using the Dewey Decimal system, of course) in bookcases for librarians to peruse. Catalogs of the collection for each show are organized the same way. CBE has a website that shows what the exhibits look like and also includes a survey that offers insight into librarians' ordering preferences. The address is www.combined book.com. For more information, call (914) 739-7500.

Visit library trade shows, particularly the American Library Association and the Public Library Association. And while these shows are critical to attend, state library association shows typically attract the librarians in charge of recommending and/or making purchases.

"You never know who'll be walking through there," said PMA's Jan Nathan. "The California library system is huge, so are the Texas (with both school and public librarians) and New York library associations."

These state library associations have some nice extras to offer. They can tell you about specific awards—the California Young Reader Award or Texas Blue Bonnet Award for children's books, for example.

And don't forget reading conferences geared toward school book purchases, such as the National Council Teachers of English in November or the Michigan Reading Association, usually held in March.

For a listing of state and regional library association addresses and conference dates, write or call the ALA and ask for the "State and Regional Library Associations Directory of Officers, Executives, and Conferences" and a more general conference calendar, "The Calendar: A Listing of Library Association Conferences."

Finally, be sure to include libraries on your book tour. You can often obtain a mailing list of public libraries from your state library association—an invaluable resource when charting your book tour. Be sure to ask if the library has book groups or writers' clubs, and arrange an appearance. Author visits have become a staple of book tours for good reason. They sell books! And so do, for that matter, libraries.

LIBRARY DISTRIBUTORS

All the companies below carry nonfiction and children's titles; none carry adult fiction.

Bill Lange, Selections Office
Best Books
5 Tree Bark Circle
Horsham, PA 19044
(215) 675-7588

Carolyn Olsen, Representative for Vendor Relations
Quality Books
1003 W. Pines Rd.
Oregon, IL 61061
(800) 323-4241

Richard Capps, Product Manager
Unique Books
4230 Grove Ave.
Gurnee, IL 60031
(708) 623-9171
(800) 553-5446

ASSOCIATIONS & COMPANIES SELLING LIBRARY LISTS

American Library Association
50 East Huron Street
Chicago, IL 60611
312-944-6780
Fax: 312-944-8741
The ALA sells lists of libraries by type of library. They can also send or fax you a pamphlet, Marketing to Libraries, which includes names and addresses of mailing list companies.

Cahners Direct Marketing Services
245 W. 17th St.
New York, NY 10011
(800) 337-7184
Offers lists of major U.S. public libraries, as well as libraries with special collections (engineering, law, religion, performing arts, etc.) Prices vary by list.

R.R. Bowker Company
121 Chanlon Road
P.O. Box 31
New Providence, NJ 07974-9903
(908) 665-2818
(800) 521-8110
Offers the *American Library Directory*, a two-volume set that includes names of U.S. libraries and contact information. Cost is $249.95 plus a 7 percent surcharge plus state sales tax.

Gale Research Company
(moving soon)
835 Penobscot Building
Detroit, MI 48226-4094
(313) 961-2242, ext. 1
(800) 877-4253, ext. 1
Offers the *Directory of Special Libraries and Information Centers*, Volume 1 of a three-volume set. Volume 1 ($515) includes names of 22,400 special libraries and information centers. Volume 2 ($430) is a supplementary geographical and personnel index. Volume 3 ($420) includes all the new libraries that are not listed in Volume 1.

The Jenkins Group
121 E. Front St.
Traverse City, MI 49684
(616) 933-0445
(800) 706-4636
Offers customized lists of major U.S. public libraries by region or by zip code. Call for a quote.

COMPANIES THAT COORDINATE CO-OP MAILINGS

Publishers Marketing Association
Contact name: Jan Nathan
627 Aviation Way
Manhattan Beach, Calif. 90266
(310) 372-2732 (phone)
(310) 374-3342 (fax)
E-mail: pmaonline@aol.com

LIBRARY REVIEW JOURNALS

Call for specific submission guidelines. In almost all cases, a cover sheet/publicity release is required and the galley must be bound.

American Bookseller
Dan Cullen, Editor
American Booksellers Assoc.
828 South Broadway
Tarrytown, NY 10591
(914) 591-2665, ext. 250
Prefer to see only press release prior to book publication. If interested, will request a copy of the book or galley.

Booklist
American Library Association
Bonnie Smothers, Adult Books Editor
or
Sally Estes, Books for Young Adults
50 East Huron Street
Chicago, IL 60611
(312) 944-6780
Prefer to see galley (and cover photo, if available) at least 15 weeks prior to publication date. Will accept copied pages.

Horn Book Guide
Jennifer Brabander
11 Beacon Street
Boston, MA 02108
(617) 227-1555
Reviews exclusively children's literature, but screens out publishers who aren't listed in Literary Marketplace (must publish at least three books a year to be listed). Prefers prepublication galleys (2), but will review a published book.

Hungry Mind Review
Bart Schenider, Editor (adult books)
Martha Davisback (children's books)
1648 Grand Avenue
St. Paul, MN 55105-1896
(612) 699-2610
Likes to see galley or finished book. Reviews large and small press, plus university press selections. Call for their themes throughout the year.

Kirkus Reviews
Sarah Gold (nonfiction)
Anne Larsen (fiction)
Kimberly Olson Sakih (children's)
200 Park Avenue South
17th Street, 11th Floor
New York, NY 10003
(212)-777-4554, ext. 16 (for general inquiries)
Requires two galleys about 15 weeks prior to publication. Follow up with a finished book.

Library Journal
Barbara Hoffert, Managing Editor
245 West 17th Street
New York, NY 10011
(212) 463-6816
Requires one galley about three months prior to publication and likes to see the finished book.

Library Talk
Carolyn Hamilton, Editor
Linworth Publishing Company
480 E. Wilson Bridge Road #L
Worthington, OH 43085
(614) 436-7107
Send galley and follow up with finished book.

Midwest Book Review
278 Orchard Dr.
Oregon, WI 53575
(608) 835-7937
Finished books only; no galleys or prepublication manuscripts.

Publishers Weekly
Attention: Forecasts
249 West 17th Street
New York, NY 10011
(212) 463-6781
A publication written for the book industry; would like to receive either galley or finished book three months in advance of official publication date.

School Library Journal
Lillian N. Gerhardt (Children's)
Luanne Toth (all others)
249 West 17th Street
New York, NY 10011-5301
(212) 463-6759
Reviews books they consider appropriate for school libraries. Mail two finished copies.

Small Press Magazine
Mardi Link, Editor
The Jenkins Group
121 E. Front St.
Traverse City, MI 49684
(616) 933-0445
Reviews exclusively small press nonfiction and fiction. Send bound galley or one finished copy. Post-publication is fine.

PRESTIGIOUS NEWSPAPERS/ CONSUMER JOURNALS

These publications typically publish reviews of general interest books just prior to publication or at the time of publication. Send galleys three months prior to publication and follow up with finished books prior to official publication date.

The Bloomsbury Review
Patricia J. Wagner, Editor
1762 Emerson St.
Denver, CO 80218-1012
(303) 863-0406

BookPage
Ann Shayne, Editor
2501 21st Ave. South, Ste. 5
Nashville, TN 37212
(615) 292-8926

Chicago Tribune Books
Elizabeth Taylor, Book Review Editor
435 N. Michigan Ave., Room 40
Chicago, IL 66011-4022
(312) 222-4125

New York Newsday
Jack Schwartz, Book Review Editor
2 Park Avenue
New York, NY 10011
(212) 696-0487

New York Review of Books
Charles McGrath, Book Editor
229 West 43rd St.
New York, NY 10036
(212) 556-1234

**San Francisco Chronicle Book
Review**
Patricia Holt, Book Review Editor
275 Fifth St.
San Francisco, CA
(415) 777-7042

San Francisco Review
126 Park Ave.
San Francisco, CA 94107
(415) 543-7372

INTERNET RESOURCE

Want to get into the heads of acquisition librarians? Check out:
www.library.vanderbilt.edu/law/
acqs/acqs.html.

12.

A SERIOUS STUDY OF SELLING TO THE ACADEMIC MARKET

Education is not the filling of a pail,
but the lighting of a fire.
WILLIAM BUTLER YEATS

DO YOU HAVE A BOOK THAT WILL INDEED LIGHT A FIRE IN SCHOOLS and colleges? Then consider the academic market, which provides a lucrative territory for the right kind of book.

The buyers in this market are picky—books authored by authors lacking credentials need not apply—yet independent publishers offering books that enlighten or educate can and do sell to the academic market. A book on hair braiding, for example, may start out in life in bead shops and end up in cosmetology schools. A fictional account of spouse abuse may get interest from instructors of women's studies. At the very minimum, a publisher can teach a class in a range of settings—community colleges, small business development centers, private or public adult-ed schools, community education classes, or leisure learning classes—and make his or her book a required text.

172

Beyond sales strictly geared to classroom studies, college bookstore sales can represent enormous sales potential. There are many esoteric fields of study that are ignored by the major houses because the sales potential is too small, yet represent lucrative profits for a small press. Many trade books, with little to no revision, can also sell well in the college bookstores.

"Some of the bookstores in the bigger cities have extraordinary collections, and in some communities, they are major trade bookstores," said John "Jack" McHugh, a Glendale, Wisconsin-based publishing consultant, who wrote *The College Publishing Market*, an 84-page booklet. "They move a lot of books over and above the academic need to the community at large."

There are two distinct academic markets totaling more than $4 billion in sales annually. The first is the college market; the second is what's called el-hi, short for elementary and high school. There is, perhaps, a third sub-category of el-hi and that's extended education and vocational schools. We mention the latter because they teach subjects that are more likely to require trade books—computer programming, cosmetology, business, etc.

There are publishers who design and write books exclusively for the academic market. It's a specialized market in which editors must have a real sense of what's happening in the university's classrooms and research labs. Textbooks must meet the exacting demands of professors and are typically accompanied by supplementary workbooks and teacher's manuals.

"I was hired this fall to write a textbook and discovered just how hard it is," said Shel Horowitz, author of *Marketing Without Megabucks: How to Sell Anything on a Shoestring*. "After about seven drafts of the first chapter, the publisher and I agreed to void the contract, with a mutual sigh of relief."

For the above reasons, this chapter is targeted *not* at independent publishers interested solely in academic publishing, but for the publisher who has written a trade book that has a potential demand in this country's classrooms either in the book's current form or with minimum revision. These books aren't intended as primary textbooks, but as *stand-alone supplementary* reading or collateral material.

The potential for crossover from trade to academic is greatest in the soft, contemporary areas of study such as Hispanic, African American,

American Indian and Women's Studies. All of these areas seek a diversity of voices. Extended education programs at community colleges are often open to specialized topics since they offer courses on subjects ranging from customer service to learning word processing.

Tip: A wonderful window into the academic world is through the periodical, *Lingua Franca*, which has a local academic following (many publishers advertise in it). To order a sample copy, call (212) 302-0336.

The academic market is an attractive one because sales are reliable, steady and high-margin. You may receive orders anywhere from 50 to 250 books from just one customer. The college bookstores are willing to order directly from the publisher and typically pay a "flat net price" which equates to a 20- to 25-percent discount compared to a trade bookstore's discount rate of 40 percent. As a note, this situation is in flux. In late 1996, the National Association of College Stores took steps to investigate this dual discount structure to determine whether to file suit. NACS has asked its 3,000 member stores to examine their invoices to determine if they were charged a discriminatory discount based on where the books were to be sold. NACS claims the dual discount based on the books' intended use violates federal antitrust law.

On the downside of college book sales, the return rate can be high, averaging about 23 percent, according to McHugh. Selling and promotional expenses can also run high and must be built into your book price. One Association of American Publishers (AAP) study found the marketing expense for all college publishers ranges from 14.2 percent to 19.2 percent of net sales (sales revenues after returns). An additional 6 percent to 10.3 percent is required for promotional expenses, the study found.

McHugh cautions to keep your expectations realistic: a publisher can augment sales by a few thousand copies over a few years, but academic sales alone are not enough to support a small house.

"It's a quick way to make a slow buck," he said. "It might be two years after your book is launched before you ever see an adoption. I know of a publisher who went out of business, and a year later they got adoptions. Instructors are never in a hurry."

Yet the right book can find an enduring market in academic classrooms and libraries.

- Strunk & White's *The Elements of Style* began life as a trade book, but it's enjoyed widespread adoption by writing and English departments across the country. Over time, it has taken on characteristics of a textbook.

- The American Library Association routinely offers library science books for adoptions.

- Calibre Publishing of Northbrook, Illinois, found its books on self-defensive tactics were well-suited for criminal justice departments.

- High Mountain Press of Santa Fe, New Mexico, calculated correctly that their software support books for computerized map-making would make great instruction manuals for computer science departments.

- Meriwether Publishing in Colorado Springs books on contemporary drama have been adopted by several universities.

Along with these success stories, we offer caveats. Even if a book is chosen for adoption, a publisher may never sell a single book to the university. The students might decide to buy used copies of your book, if available, or the course might get canceled or postponed because of low enrollment.

Also, traditional marketing strategies are expensive. Some publishers send a huge number of samples as review copies to faculty. If they project sales of 4,000 copies, they plan to give away up to 1,500 copies, McHugh said.

We suggest, however, that small publishers cannot afford to provide free copies. We believe the simplest and most affordable alternative is to offer the instructor a sample copy at a 20-percent discount. Doubly reimburse the purchase price if the instructor orders a minimum of 15 copies. Request payment with the order of the examination copy to reduce billing paperwork.

📖   📖   📖

Vernon Avila, a biology professor at San Diego State University, has experienced both the highs and lows of academic publishing. His first $40 (net price to the bookstores) introductory textbook, *Biology: A Human*

Endeavor, sold 20,000 copies. His second edition, *Biology: Investigating Life on Earth*, at the time of publication, sold an additional 10,000 copies.

Avila was originally prompted to independently publish a textbook after suffering through with the politics of academic book publishing. Sales and marketing, he said, too often drove the final product. The publishing firm, at times, prioritized aesthetics above accuracy when it came to illustrations.

"I love books. I cherish the written word," Avila said. "But to these publishing companies, a book is just a product and they could care less. Editors, marketing departments and CPAs care only about the bottom line. With their corporate mentality, you might as well be selling tires," he said.

Avila formed Bookmark Publishing and invested $500,000 over time to print his easily understood biology text that captured an award for its cover and overall production quality. He marketed it on a shoestring, writing personal letters to professors—many of whom he knew. He hired a telemarketing firm, Axiom Marketing Communications, to close sales with those professors who had asked for an examination copy.

"One of the things that made the phone campaign successful is that if a potential adopter had significant scientific questions, the rep would say the author will give you a call and explain why he took that particular approach."

Avila sold 8,000 books through direct mail and another 12,000 at scientific conferences attended by his peers. He found that his presence at the exhibit table proved a valuable selling point.

"It's rare that the author is also the publisher and present to talk face-to-face with colleagues. If they gave me an objection or asked about emphasis or content, I could say, 'Here's why I did it this way,'" he said.

Once a book was adopted by a specific university, the book would usually be re-adopted for about three semesters. An initial book order for 400 typically "rolled over" into sales of 700.

Despite the financial success of the book, Avila was dismayed by how long it took to receive payment from many of the college bookstores, especially those owned by mega-corporations. Some bookstores still owe him thousands of dollars. Other bookstores attempted to return damaged books or returned two books only to order five more. His advice: be absolutely firm and clear about your return policy and enclose the policy in every shipment. Avila will not accept damaged books; the time limit to return books is six months.

Avila also spoke of how the used book market eats into sales.

"It can really hurt your cash flow, especially for the small publisher," he said. "When I got one of my first adoptions in upstate New York for 400 books, I was really excited. I'm thinking, 'This is great!' But when I got the order in, it was for 50 books. I called the bookstore back and told them there had to be a mistake. The class size was 400, and the book order was for only 50. The clerk said, 'Oh no, we already have 350 books and we only need 50 more.' I discovered that these were some of the 3,000 examination copies that I had given out to my colleagues all over the nation. There are book buyers who roam the halls who buy sample copies from my colleagues for five or ten dollars. They sell them to a big warehouse, which turns around and sells them for $25/$30 to bookstores that sell them for $35 to $50 as new or used. It's damning. What really disturbed me was to find out that some of my unethical colleagues order books just to sell to these companies, essentially robbing authors of royalties for their years and years of toiling."

Now Avila is very selective to whom he sends a complimentary copy.

"I follow up on a request and keep my computer files very accurate to make sure I haven't sent five books to the same person. I had some that would request six, eight, 10 books."

To prevent the sample-selling practice, some publishers, Avila said, stamp their book covers, "Professional Review Copy. Not for sale."

For his second edition, Avila decided to copublish with the publishing firm, Jones & Bartlett, which taught him still more lessons about publishing. "Whenever you go into a joint venture, get in writing the exact nature of the venture: who's going to be responsible for what. If they tell you, 'We have a sales and marketing plan,' they might send out a one-postcard mailing . . . Detail the direct marketing plan, number of salesmen, everything."

After five years in the publishing business, Avila takes stock of his experience. He achieved what he wanted: he published a highly acclaimed biology book that proved quality need not be sacrificed for marketing considerations. On the other hand, he's witnessed the greed of colleagues and the politics of committee selections (wining and dining by sales reps counts for a lot).

"I've been very lucky. It's rewarding. Right now someone walking across Boston Commons is reading my book. A student walking in the snows of Indiana or in the sun of a Puerto Rican sky is reading my book. My message is being conveyed."

📖   📖   📖

If you lack professional and academic credentials like Avila, can you still sell books in the college market?

"There *is* a lot of old boy stuff in academe," said publisher Mary Walker. "My husband is a professor. If he were to write a book, he'd get his friends to review it and try to tailor it for their course needs. If a professor makes a text required for a course, you are guaranteed sales. If you want to sell to the college market, you should cozy up to the movers and shakers."

In general, textbooks are written by professors, but those in academia will consider books that aren't written by a peer, Avila said.

"If the author really knows the pedagogy and has a novel way of getting material across, I think they'd consider it," he said. "One of the problems with peer-written books is they forget what it's like when you first start learning the material and they're written in a manner designed for the professor who adopts them rather than the students."

The market is most easily penetrated by small publishers whose book fits at least one of these criteria:

- Offers a voice of diversity.
- The only one of its kind covering an esoteric or technical subject.
- Is authoritative.

Long-term, you'll greatly increase your chances of success by clustering your books around a given subject.

📖　　　📖　　　📖

Linda Grobman has found a natural market for her book, *Days in the Lives of Social Workers*, in which 41 professionals tell real-life stories from their practice.

"I did the book with the idea that individual students or new social workers would be interested in it as a way of looking at different career possibilities."

Adoptions are coming quickly, she said, partly because of the book excerpts and advertisements which she has published through her well-established magazine, *The New Social Worker.*

"I know that at least one adoption has come about as a direct result of a professor reading these excerpts," she said. "I am in a unique position, in that I publish a magazine that gives me a ready-made venue in which to publish excerpts."

She also attended a conference for professional social workers, through which she received adoptions. Exhibiting her book at academic conferences is next, along with a second and more extensive direct mail appeal using mailing lists from such organizations as the Council of Social Work Education.

"It's been adopted by several professors already who teach introductory social work courses, and I anticipate that it will be adopted by more," she said. "I think name recognition really helps. Having professional credentials is important, too."

Grobman sends examination copies on a 60-day approval basis. If the professor does not adopt the book within 60 days, he or she either pays for the book or returns it.

Finally, Grobman actively participates on several Internet mailing lists geared toward social workers, social work students and social work educators, as well as maintaining a website for her magazine and book.

"I don't post commercial messages or information on these mailing lists—prices and ordering information are 'taboo' in Netiquette—but it is acceptable to post announcements of new publications, so I have done that.

"I participate actively in the discussions of professional issues on these lists and have interacted with many of the list members."

📖   📖   📖

GETTING INTO THE EL-HI/COLLEGE MARKET

The el-hi and college market are two distinct markets, yet the approaches to both are very similar: direct marketing appeals, samples, personal visits, and exhibiting books at conventions and association meetings. Some publishers also advertise in journals most likely to be read by their target audience.

The demand for your book will come directly from the instructors, who at the college level, essentially force the students to spend their money at bookstores. The bookstores, in turn, order directly from the publisher.

So how do you persuade an instructor to choose your book? Much of the following advice comes from John McHugh's 86-page manual titled, *The College Publishing Market*, as well as his special reports. To order, call (414) 351-3056. He suggests the following:

- Send direct mail advertising.
- Exhibit at academic conferences.
- Advertise in academic journals.
- Personally sell the book.
- Get your book reviewed in academic journals.
- Find an independent representative who specializes in academic markets or sign up with a telemarketing firm (very difficult for a micropublisher unless the book carries very obvious appeal).

At the el-hi level, some publishers (particularly larger ones) have contracted with school supply companies to sell their books.

Direct-mail campaigns are expensive, so be sure your book is adoptable before conducting a full-blown campaign. Adoption simply means an instructor intends to require your book for a course.

"Before selecting a mailing list for your book, you must answer the question: 'Does a market exist for my books in the college adoption marketplace?' A market exists *if you can identify a college course to match up with the subject matter of your book* or is identical to the title of the book," wrote McHugh in his *How to Sell to the College Market* report.

TESTING THE WATERS

You can get an idea of whether your book appeals to academia by checking your bookstore orders. If college bookstores are ordering copies in multiples of 10 or more, you may have a collegiate book on your hands, McHugh said.

Another way to determine if your book has appeal is to call and then personally visit a handful of college campuses.

"If you wrote a book on date rape and live in a metropolitan area, I'd talk to instructors in women's studies and check to see what's in the bookstore," McHugh said. "Talk to book buyers. Leave some books and get an opinion if it's adoptable."

EFFECTIVE SELLING THROUGH DIRECT MAIL

The traditional and still most successful way to reach instructors at the el-hi and college level is via direct mail and a follow-up phone call. Increasingly, publishers are faxing one-page letters because they seem to convey a greater urgency.

Your direct mail letter should describe the benefits of the book and some kind of reply mechanism that makes it easy for the professor to request a sample copy of the book, whether by postcards or phone call.

Your letter should answer these two questions: Why should an instructor use this specific book for his or her course? Why is the book uniquely suited for the course or program of study?

Some publishers, such as Avila, believe personal letters are more powerful than brochures and vice versa. Whichever you use, the material should include:

- The book's distinguishing characteristics.

- A table of contents.

- Any ancillary instructional materials such as an instructor's manual, solutions manual, test material, etc.

- The author's educational credentials and career accomplishments.

- Excerpts of reviews and testimonials by experts in the field.

- The number of institutions which have adopted the book and names of the more prestigious ones, when applicable.

- A perforated, return, prepaid, business reply card with a fax number (so that the instructor can either fax or mail the reply card). The card should ask for name, address, phone number, enrollment, course name, book currently adopted, course start date, and date when adoption decisions are made. These questions are to screen out "book grabbers." Also ask for the journal/magazine the instructor likes to read in his given specialty to give you an idea where you should spend advertising money.

Mail the letter when it's most effective. General adoption cycles for the fall semester run between mid-January and mid-May. Adoption cycles for winter term are from September to late November.

For names of professors, their disciplines and courses they teach, McHugh recommends contacting mailing broker, CMG Information Services, Inc, 187 Ballardvale Street, Suite B110, Wilmington, MA 01887, (800) 677-7959.

Another source that offers similar lists but varies in specific courses listed is: Market Data Retrieval, 16 Progress Dr., Shelton, CT 06484-1117.

Before investing in the entire mailing of a list, start first with a limited mailing. (Refer to Chapter 19 for specifics on direct-mail campaigns).

Although all of this seems fairly straightforward, you may find it difficult to pinpoint exactly which of the department's instructors will require your book.

"Because the traditional structure of courses has been abandoned in many universities for more creative course designations, it's difficult to promote to professors today," said John S. Sanders, owner of J.S. Sanders & Co. in Nashville, Tennesse, who publishes reprints of older, but valuable books in Southern literature.

"Whereas universities used to teach ninteenth Century English, now there might be a course called, 'Literature and the Law.' It used to be easy to identify your title as appropriate or not appropriate. I have sold books for courses which I would never have dreamed the books would be appropriate for. There's no way I can know."

Simply sending the book to the department and hoping that it will get routed to the right instructor is also risky: "You can't trust the routing. That's an old problem, not a new one," Sanders said.

But that's exactly how books are dispensed at the high-school level, said one vocational school principal. After receiving a flyer or brochure of a book, the school secretary puts it in the mailbox of the appropriate instructor, who looks at the budget, the need for the book, and then decides whether or not to order the book for his or her class.

"I get catalogs all the time with a few books or flyers or pamphlets," said Principal Dean Shipman, who oversees a larger Northern Michigan vocational school. "We have a stack from vendors that is two inches high. Some are huge multibillion dollar companies and some are tiny. "

Although direct mail has its drawbacks, it remains the most effective way of reaching an instructor, Sanders believes. To beat the odds, he typically faxes a letter and follows up by phone.

To write an effective letter, state your business in the first paragraph in a surprising, engaging manner and don't allow the letter to exceed one page. Follow Sanders' advice: "Brevity is the soul of wit. Don't write tedious and lengthy letters. In our contemporary world, we're choked with paper." Write the letter in a respectful tone, yet with the implication you consider yourself on an equal plane with the professor.

Secondly, keep a clean mailing list. As time permits, call departmental secretaries and ask if your material is going to the right person.

Finally, be patient and continue to put your book in front of the instructors as often as possible.

"Send your promotional material on a regular basis," Sanders advised. "For instance, we mailed materials to a University of Alabama professor of English, who taught Southern literature. In the fifth year, he called us and told us, 'I'm so glad to find out you exist.' I thought to myself, 'Why didn't you notice it sooner?' He just didn't. He gets lots of mail like the rest of us."

Do not send samples with the brochure: it's a waste of money. Before sending a free copy, review the information on the reply card or screen your caller's request. If a math professor wants your biography on Malcolm X, for example, politely deny the request. "After a while, you will well know these book grabbers and you will simply ignore their request," McHugh advised.

AIM FOR REVIEWS IN ACADEMIC JOURNALS

The best way to convince an instructor that your book is worthy of purchase is to get a review in an academic journal. Not only is the initial publicity helpful, you can use quotes from the review in your promotional material. Familiarize yourself with the academic journals before submitting your book for review. This way, you can more easily formulate your cover letter.

A cover letter to an academic journal should explain why the readership would be interested in the book, a description of its contents, and the author's credentials. As with any submission, it should include key purchasing information: author, title, copyright date, number of pages, price, ISBN number, publisher, etc. (often summarized on a sticker on the inside front cover).

Even if a book isn't strictly academic in tone, you may still want to consider sending it for submission. Read the journals to get a feel if your book would "fit." If your book is controversial, however, beware of editors who oppose your stance and will pan the book.

If the academic review journals responds to your book with silence, make a follow-up phone call or write a letter. While on the phone, ask the editor's opinion on whether the book is appropriate for adoption.

           📖   📖   📖

Besides direct mail and journal reviews, there's always the classic word-of-mouth approach. Linda Donelson, author/publisher of *Out of Isak Dinesen in Africa: The Untold Story*, which presents a new and controversial view of the subject, has discovered that her book is on the reading list at the University of Washington, the University of Minnesota and has been acquired by several college libraries.

Contrary to John McHugh's advice, Donelson believes that direct marketing her book would *hurt* her image.

"I have the sense you cannot market a book like mine to academia; you have to let them discover it. If you market, you will be taken as suspect. That is why reviews are so important.

"The best way to break into the academic market is to get your book reviewed in *Choice* magazine (reviews academic books for college libraries). I didn't know this and did not submit my book.

"To get in the academic market, you must have academic credentials. It helps if you are a professor at Harvard, which I'm not, but it has been useful to me to be an M.D. In the book, I propose that Isak Dinesen's symptoms weren't due to syphilis—as has been widely written—but from the arsenic used to treat her syphilis."

Donelson said she was lucky that a Danish physician came forward with the same conclusion as she did in an article published shortly after her book. "This article, in an American medical journal, added weight to the theory in my book," she said.

Donelson said her book has been sold on the merit of recommendations. An article about her book in the *Des Moines Register* in August turned up on the bulletin board of a college bookstore in Kirksville, Missouri. Two professors at the University of Illinois at Carbondale were later overheard discussing the book. The University of Washington professor found the book on the Internet; the University of

Minnesota professor met her at a signing in St. Paul. "Moral?" said Donelson. "Network in the academic community!"

📖   📖   📖

INTRODUCE YOUR BOOK AT ACADEMIC CONFERENCES

Another way to get your book into the hands of instructors is to set up an exhibit at a relevant conference or association meeting.

These associations gather into one place many of the instructors in a given discipline: math, literature, physics, etc. When choosing a conference, research carefully to make sure it aligns with the topic of your book. Publishers do find they often get requests, however, for copies of their book. At some associations, the common practice is to sell books; at others, publishers give samples away for emergency reviews or take orders, requiring the professor to fill out a form (again, to screen out the book grabbers).

Typically, these conventions offer breakout sessions where educators discuss specific topics. Jump in and take the opportunity to introduce your book and what it offers on a topic.

If you can't afford the time or expense of attending a convention, considering having a company exhibit your book for you. Once such company is Academia Book Exhibit of Fairfax, Virginia, which specializes in technical and scientific books. To reach them, call (703) 716-5537 or e-mail: at acadbkexbs@aol.com. Another is Association Book Exhibits in Alexandria, Virginia, which exhibits a wide range of books. Call them at (703) 519-3909.

FINDING ASSISTANCE

Many publishers would love to hire an independent representative to sell their books for them. Yet independent reps rarely succeed in the college market, although many have tried. The reason: it's simply hard to make money at it because of the limited number of copies sold in the upper-level adoptions, McHugh said.

"Typically, the adoptions are for upper-division and graduate courses with modest enrollments of 50 to 60 students a year," McHugh said.

Additionally, cash flow is terrible. A book might be adopted in February, shipped in August, and paid for in October. Further, sales may never materialize or might be far less than the enrollment might suggest (if the students decide to share an expensive textbook).

What should you expect to pay an independent rep? Typically, they charge a commission of 10 percent to 15 percent of net sales and pay their own travel costs. The publisher provides the free exam copies and pays for promotion and fulfillment. In most instances, the rep doesn't physically call on the account, but sends what's called a blind sample or review copy to an instructor. A "blind sampled" book means the independent rep makes no follow-up sales call.

"Ask yourself if it is worth it to incur a cost of 10 percent to 15 percent to have someone put together a list of instructors to receive a review copy of your book?" McHugh said.

There are options, however. Axiom Marketing Communications, Inc., telemarkets books for publishers selling to the academic market. In fact, at this writing, it was the only company of its kind in the country. Generally, Axiom doesn't accept overly specialized books from micro-publishers because the payoff is too low and the frustration level too high, said company President Philip Curson.

"It's tough for sales reps who like to be successful to be shot down a lot," he said. "I'm always careful that I give my reps books that have enough going for them."

That doesn't mean he'll necessarily reject a one-book publisher. He successfully sold Avila's biology book, for example.

"We've worked for some very small publishers, sometimes on a fee basis. You can't get out the door for less than $5,000 and that's kind of a test. That's sometimes all people need."

Curson points out there are options for small publishers who want to enter the academic market. Let's say you've published a book on presidents who have served second terms. You could propose the book to Congressional Quarterly, which may agree to repackage the book to fit in with its line of academic offerings.

How to sell a general-appeal book

If you've written a popular trade book that would appeal to students—choosing a career, honing good study habits, building vocabulary—college bookstores might be interested in buying your book. Also, if an instructor lists your book as suggested reading, the college bookstore will very likely be interested in ordering your book.

So how do you get a nonadopted text in a bookstore?

- Many publishers mail their catalogs directly to the chains, the biggest of which is Follett College Stores. Mail your catalog to Follett College Stores, Director of Trade Books, 400 W. Grand Avenue, P.O. Box 288, Elmhurst, IL 60126, or phone (708) 279-2330.

- Consider attending the Campus Market Expo convention, held every April for college book buyers (hint: members of the press are allowed to attend). It is sponsored by the National Association of College Stores. For more information, call (800) 622-7498.

A word on college store distributors

Ask your trade distributor if they regularly call on college stores. If not, it might be worth your while to consider a distributor who does. The *Literary MarketPlace* provides a listing of distributors and sales reps who specialize in the academic market or consider stocking your books with the Oberlin, Ohio-based NACSCORP, a for-profit distributor owned by the National Association of College Stores (a college store trade association). Call NACS at (800) 622-7498 or use the free NACS FAX INFOCENTER at (216) 774-8709 for a listing of documents it offers.

Like trade bookstore distributors, a college store distributor handles nearly every aspect of business, from selling to invoicing to collecting on tardy accounts. The price for these services is steep—they generally take discounts comparable to trade distributors—around 62 percent to 68 percent. They also present the same problem of book returns, which plays havoc with cash flow—books sold to bookstores, which didn't sell to students. Instead of getting a check from a bookstore, you'll get a pile of books.

Before deciding on a distributor, seriously look at the cash flow implications and determine if you have enough capital to sustain you through returns and slow payments. We believe that any discounts exceeding the high 60s simply make doing business with college bookstores unaffordable. Yet if you can find the right distributor (check references!) who'll work hard for you and give you a fair discount, college bookstore revenue can significantly boost your sales.

Personal selling

If you've published a $15 trade book, you'll find it's much more cost-efficient to sell your book via fax and phone call than to personally visit instructors at schools and colleges. On the other hand, it's worth it for a publisher with $40 textbooks. In any case, personal visits can be enormously helpful just to get feedback on your book.

When you call to set up an interview, be sure to mention your credentials and the book's credentials—positive reviews, where the book has been adopted, etc. The main purpose of your visit is to find out whether your book makes the grade for the instructor's course.

"Find out why or why not. Listen and learn!" McHugh advised. "I would recommend a structured visit in which you have a turnkey list of questions. Typical questions can cover: Which courses taught? Enrollment? Book in use? Likes? Dislikes? Purpose of course? Supplements used? Approaches? New trends? Technology? etc.

"During your visit, also perform market research. 'Who else in the department would be interested in adopting this book?' 'Anyone else at other campuses interested in this book?'"

Be sure to visit the bookstore and talk to the owner, who can sometimes share individual instructor behavior and the "inside" story on departmental politics, McHugh suggested.

And, by checking the shelves, you can actually see what books are in use, get a sense of pricing, production, and covers, and see the mix of used and new books, McHugh said.

Selling directly to college bookstore buyers

The company, Campus Direct 2000, sells lists of college bookstore buyers and college media. Contact them at: 91 Longfellow Dr., Centerville, MA 02632, (508) 771-8013; E-mail: coliver@capecod.net.

Also, the company president, Charles Oliver, is helping publishers sell directly to college bookstore buyers via the Internet.

ADVERTISE IN COLLEGE PUBLICATIONS

There are several magazines geared to college students, many of them regional. Check them out at your local college bookstore to see if there might be a good vehicle for advertising. College newspapers also offer great opportunities for advertising, some of them offering ad space at bargain rates.

SELLING ACADEMIC BOOKS ON THE INTERNET

As with any marketing audience, publishers should check out the Internet. PubText, for example, allows publishers to list their books for free. The book is categorized by discipline and educational level, said PubText creator Philip Curson (also president of Axiom Marketing Communications, Inc. in San Diego, California).

For each lead generated, the publisher pays five dollars per valid lead. This may or may not be a good deal, depending on the price of the book and the percentage of leads that result in sales. Publishers can also read comments on their books.

Also, check out the various sites hosted by public schools and colleges, especially those that have set up listings of educational books. Savvy educational book publishers request links to their own site. At the site of the Los Angeles Unified School District (http://lausd.k12.ca.us), for example, many publishers have set up such links.

THE EL-HI MARKET

Most schools have a budget for supplementary books as opposed to what's called basal textbooks. In general, when a teacher wants a stand-alone supplementary text, he or she will fill out a requisition and the school will purchase the book directly from the publisher. This is why publishers rely heavily on mail promotion, telemarketing, exhibiting at teacher conferences, and on-approval sampling and ordering.

Selling books to schools is easier in some states than others. In some Southeast, Southwest and Western states, instructional material must be ordered by schools through state-approved "depositories," which are slowly being phased out. Other states maintain an official adoption list or require that publishers register with them and/or meet specific requirements. For specific requirements, you'll need to write to the state department of education. To make life easier—especially initially—you'll need to concentrate on what are called "open territory" states, which have no such depositories.

The good news in the el-hi market is that with the trend of "whole reading," there's greater demand for stand-alone fiction and nonfiction. Small publishers have secured state adoptions by publishing regionally oriented books.

Here are some other tips for reaching the young reader set:

- Make presentations at the school on subjects related to your book. Tim Smith and Mark Herrick, author and illustrator respectively of *Buck Wilder's Small Fry Fishing Guide*, have booked appearances at schools throughout Michigan, speaking on how to succeed in the fields of writing and illustrating. They typically sell 25 books on the day of their visit plus another 30 afterward.

- Sell your book as a fund-raiser. Carol Noel, the author of *Get It, Got It, Good,* hands out her book on consignment to school groups trying to raise money for clubs or causes.

- Work through sales organizations, book clubs, and catalogs which sell similar or compatible products to your target market. To find out what they are, call the instructors and ask about their favorite catalogs or educational supplier.

- *Paperbacks for Educators* publishes several catalogs that offer books on student counseling, parenting, career planning and placement, and special teens and adults. Call (314) 239-1999 for more information.

- The publishing firm of Gryphon House in Beltsville, Maryland, has a catalog specializing in educational books for preschools, daycares, and early education classrooms. Call (800) 638-0928 for a copy.

• Seek out publicity in the *Creative Classroom* teachers' magazine. With a circulation of 200,000, it is published by the Children's Television Workshop. Try getting publicity for your book in the magazine's section called "Great Stuff," which lists brief information about new books, curricula, programs, etc. Send your promotional materials to: Chrystal Ingram, Creative Classroom, Children's Television Workshop Magazine Group, 1 Lincoln Plaza, New York, NY 10023. Telephone: (212) 595-3456; Fax: (212) 875-6101.

• Contact the specialty book clubs of Scholastic Book Services in New York City (212) 343-6100 or the Weekly Reader Book Clubs (203) 638-2400.

SELLING TO SCHOOL SUPPLY STORES

Another conduit to school sales is the 1,200 and growing school supply/teacher stores that serve them.

How does a book find entry into school supply/teacher stores? In a variety of ways. Store buyers select from distributors, publisher's direct mail and telemarketing efforts, publisher's catalogs, and/or commissioned reps.

To find out more about how these stores operate, start asking questions at your local school/teacher supply store. "Many of the owners of these stores are ex-teachers and very outgoing," said Consortium House's Gene Schwartz, a Bearsville, New York-based publishing consultant. "They are very intimate with the content of the books and love to share information."

Another way to familiarize yourself with this marketing channel is to read the trade journal, *Educational Dealer*. A one-year subscription is $15. Call (315) 789-0458.

Commissioned reps: To find names of commissioned reps who might carry your book, look under the category of "commissioned reps" who service school supply or educational stores in *Literary MarketPlace*.

Direct mail: Interested in conducting a direct-mail campaign to school supply stores? A mailing list of about 900 school supply stores is available from the Educational Dealers & Suppliers Association for $50. Contact the group at 711 West 17th St., Suite J-5, Costa Mesa, CA 92627, (800) 654-7099. Or go to any mailing list catalog and look under the categories of "Educational Bookstores," "Supply Retailers," and Educational Materials Stores," Schwartz said.

Publishers' catalogs: There are a number of publishers specializing in educational books who are willing to carry other publishers' books. To find the names of these publishers, Schwartz suggests scanning the ads in the magazines: *Educational Dealer, Teacher Magazine* and *Creative Classroom*.

Conventions: The Educational Dealers & Suppliers Association holds a convention each April. Call (800) 654-7099. Also, the National School Supply and Equipment Association holds an annual November convention for dealers. The address is: 2020 N. 14th Street, #400 P.O. Box 17005, Arlington, VA 22216. Call (800) 395-5550 for more information.

Distributors: Here are three firms that sell books to the academic market. Call for specific submission guidelines.

- Educational Book Distributors, Bob or Dolly Thoms, P.O. Box 551, San Mateo, CA 94401 or P.O. Box 2510 Novato, CA 94948, (415) 344-8458.
- The Booksource, Attention: Buying Department., 1230 Macklind Ave., St. Louis, MO 63110, (314) 647-0600.
- Social Studies Service, Irwin Levin, President, 10200 Jefferson Blvd., Culver City, CA 90232.

SUMMARY

A well-targeted promotion of your book can reap sales of several thousand copies with generous profit margins. Compared to other types of markets, the cost of promotion is relatively low. It's also great, in general, to work with instructors who are friendly and helpful.

Balance these with the drawbacks of the growing momentum of used book sales, a higher rate of returns, and the "credential hurdle."

Whatever you choose to do, the $4 billion-plus market is huge and it may pay off to take a small bite of it.

13

SELLING TO FOREIGN MARKETS

The world is all gates, all opportunities,
strings of tension waiting to be struck.
RALPH WALDO EMERSON

SELLING YOUR BOOKS OVERSEAS WON'T MAKE YOU RICH, BUT AS ONE Canadian publisher said: "It's like getting money from air." Foreign rights payments can range from pocket change to tens of thousands of dollars, depending on the popularity of the book in the United States and the potential size of the foreign market. Publishers say foreign sales have increased their revenues from 10 percent to 20 percent.

Scholarly and scientific texts, in particular, enjoy a strong overseas market because of the United States' reputation for excellence in research and technology. Certain trade books also sell well because of the popularity of U.S. pop culture.

Aside from money, there's the satisfaction of sharing an author's work overseas, whether the book helps a Third World country improve its irrigation systems or helps prevent communicable diseases. Some independent publishers, relatively unknown in the U.S., have become best-selling authors abroad.

Veltisezar Bautista calls himself a "super best-selling author" in the Philippines, his native country. His Filipino publisher, Paulines Publishing House, has sold 21,600 copies of his book, *Improve Your Grades*, and plans to reprint 20,000 more copies. This is truly success in a country where sales of 2,000 copies earns a book the title of best seller.

Cynthia and Sang Kim, owners of Turtle Press, also saw great success with the release of Sang's most recent book on martial arts.

"Sang is so excited because he is now getting star billing in the biggest newspapers in Korea and the book is debuting in bookstores all over the country as well as in Korean language bookstores in the U.S.," said Cynthia Kim. "After more than 10 years of living here, he has become a major-league author—in his home country. Ironic, isn't it? How did he get such a sweet translation deal? He called up Hundai Media and asked. Serendipity, I guess."

The number-one advantage of selling the rights of a book to a foreign market is that your book doesn't have to be newly published. Even a book that's been around for 15 years can still do well internationally, said Wendy Keller, a book agent and president of ForthWrite Literary Agency in Pasadena, California.

To give you an idea of how many books are exported from this country each year, consider these statistics: American publishers shipped out nearly 900,000 books in 1995 valued at $1.2 billion. The top buying countries included: Australia ($122 million), Canada ($755 million), Japan ($126 million), and the United Kingdom ($201 million), according to the U.S. Department of Commerce.

These statistics don't even include the amount of money publishers and authors have pulled in from foreign rights sales and royalties, said William Lofquist, publishing specialist with the U.S. Department of Commerce.

The most popular categories of export books are: technical, scientific, and professional claiming 30 percent of the market, and adult and juvenile trade books (fiction and nonfiction) with 33 percent of the export market. College textbooks made up 16.5 percent of the market, Lofquist said.

Most publishers either sell translation rights to their books or negotiate a deal with a foreign publisher or distributor. Only a small percentage of publishers sell their books directly to foreign consumers owing to the language barrier, postage hassles, and the prohibitive cost. Generally speaking, business or technically oriented books are most successful for direct-mail appeals. Ads in consumer magazines can also succeed.

For direct sales of trade books, the Internet is becoming an increasingly popular way to get books directly into foreign customers' hands, although this method is still in its infancy.

Can *your* book succeed in the foreign market? If it has sold well in the United States, if it isn't ethnocentric, and if it can strike a chord with a foreign population, the answer is yes.

Not every book that's published in the United States will "travel well" to all foreign countries. Self-help books, for example, do very poorly in England. A foreign sale is usually triggered by a book's initial success in the United States, said book agent Wendy Keller.

Jan Nathan, executive director of the Publishers Marketing Association, offers this excellent advice for any publisher who wants to enter the foreign rights market:

- Books should not contain too many references to either products or groups in the U.S.

- The book's graphics (pictures, illustrations, etc.) should not be too American-looking; cartoon-like drawings are not appreciated by many countries outside of the U.S.

- The book's title should be easily understood in other countries. Avoid idioms that are only relevant in the U.S.

- Your authors should be easily recognized experts.

Can fiction books sell? Not unless they were written by well-known authors; only unknown authors specializing in the new age and gay/lesbian area seem to prosper. A general fiction publisher must be able to quote tens of thousands of sales in the U.S. in a short time period or be authored by a recognizable name before any overseas fiction house will look at it, Nathan said.

"Business books, health books (especially holisitic health), management books, some 'esoterica' (metaphysical books), and self-help books were the most requested in 1996 by publishers from around the world with whom we met," Nathan said.

The foreign market is complex with an infinitely shifting blend of social mores, laws, languages, and currencies. There are new terms to learn, cultural barriers to hurdle, and several different configurations of deals. Some countries simply lack a system of book distribution altogether. But once you find trustworthy partners, you'll be well on your way to getting "income from air" and conveying your book's message worldwide.

SELLING RIGHTS TO OVERSEAS MARKETS

When it comes to the ownership of foreign rights, the author and publisher typically split the advance and royalties. High-powered authors, however, usually receive full proceeds from foreign-rights sales.

In the more common scenario of splitting rights, the author receives these fees outright. In a minority of contracts, the publisher bases the split on the net amount received after the cost of doing overseas business, fees, and commissions paid to the licensing agents.

There are three ways foreign rights to a book can be licensed.

The first is when a publishing company buys translation rights: the foreign publisher pays a fee for the right to translate the book. The publisher may then market the book in any country where that language is spoken. Often it is much easier to market a book in translation rather than in the original English version. Under this agreement, the foreign publisher first pays the translator a royalty directly; the royalty paid to the American publisher is less the royalty paid to the translator.

Secondly, an American publisher may license the reprint of the book in the English language to be sold in a specific country or territory.

The third form of a foreign deal is when the American publisher sells the very same book that's sold in the United States to a foreign publisher or distributor.

ROYALTY FEES

Advances, typically ranging from $2,000 to $5,000, are applied against a royalty rate between 8 percent and 10 percent of the retail price or cover price in the market.

Keller advises to secure an advance in any book deal because the chances of seeing royalty payments are "really unlikely."

"You're better to get cash with an excellent reversion clause so that you can sell the title again in 10 years or whatever you can negotiate."

WHAT CAN AN AGENT DO FOR YOU?

To sell your rights, you can a) negotiate a contract directly with a foreign publisher or with an agent who represents a foreign publisher, or b) appoint a literary agent, either here in the United States or overseas, to represent you in the deal.

An agent will usually set up a deal and take 10 percent to 20 percent of the total fee paid for foreign rights. Fees vary widely depending on the country. Rights may go for as little as $500 to Yugoslavia to as high as $50,000 to England.

Most small publishers feel the agent's fee is justified considering the time and effort that would be required for them to learn about the overseas market—reading foreign publishers' catalogs, reviewing overseas bestseller lists, and making periodic overseas visits.

"Agents can be very useful because of their knowledge of the local publishing industry, its foibles, capacities, and preferences to say nothing of their ability to handle the foreign-exchange aspects of the transaction," wrote Frederick Praeger in *The Business of Book Publishing.*

"The final contract, whether concluded by the publisher or an agent, is often the product of an intricate series of proposals, counter proposals, negotiations, letters, cables, fax messages, and phone calls. Publishers and agents frequently need the assistance of people who understand both the book's original and target languages."

The agent's job is to:

- Collect the money and ensure royalty payments are made on time. A small publisher is typically in no position to do either.

- Understand the intricacies of contracts in each country and explain them to you.

- Settle disputes.

- Understand libel laws and know, in advance, if there's anything in your book that may violate them.

- Know which publishers are deadbeats and caution you to stay away from them.

Agents know the turf and can often negotiate a much higher price than you can. Agents will cultivate a network of foreign agents, publishers, and distributors through regular business dealings and by attending the Frankfurt Book Fair (an international book trade show—more on it later).

"I know who's doing what, who does technology, who does self-help from America," Keller said. "I give everybody a chance to consider a certain work. If they're interested, I'll send a hard copy and the publisher's entire catalog."

Your job as publisher is to support the agent by sending her book reviews, media appearance videos, articles, promotional material, and notice of any new publications.

The best way—besides networking—to find the names of agents or scouts is to reference the *International Literary MarketPlace*.

If you opt to bypass an agent or want to assist your agent in locating a foreign publisher, you'll need to make a list of publishers who sell books similar to your book line.

How do you find such a list? The short answer is networking. Call U.S. publishers who sell books similar to your line and ask them which publishers they use. You can also query the publishers who participate on the Publishers Marketing Association Forum on the Internet. Publishers on the forum are usually happy to help.

Once you've identified your desired publisher, send your catalog and a letter to introduce yourself, your company, and the specific books you think would work in their line and why. Talk about the past sales success of your book and enclose reviews. Follow up with a phone call and make an appointment to meet at the Frankfurt Book Fair, a mammoth international trade show that takes place in early October. Be sure to include your e-mail address and fax number since that's the common way to communicate internationally.

A foreign publisher, in turn, should provide you with its catalog, company overview, and sales statistics. Call the American publishers that it serves and ask about the publisher's performance and integrity.

A WORD ABOUT TRANSLATIONS

If you know a language very well and want to avoid the expense of translation, consider the "Professional Power Translator," a computer program. It gives you a rough translation, but your document will still need a lot of tweaking.

Also, be aware that a book written in the kind of Spanish intended for the country of Spain won't work in Mexico or in America's Spanish-speaking communities. You must publish separate versions for each.

FINDING A DISTRIBUTOR

Instead of selling foreign rights, you may want to have a foreign distributor or publisher buy, promote, and distribute your books. These distributors or publishers are also known as agents.

Using a foreign distributor or publisher is most commonly done in English-speaking countries such as Canada, England, and Australia. Foreign distributors are similar to American distributors in that they will promote your book and handle all billings and collections. Their terms, however, are more favorable. They pay 45 to 55 percent of the retail price and *keep* all the books they buy. Foreign distributors are willing to stock their books in their own country unlike a U.S. export sales agency (more on export agencies below). Agreements differ with each foreign publisher or distributor; sometimes the distributor will pay for all the books on receipt, other times he or she accepts the books only on consignment.

Your agreement should spell out exactly what marketing services the distributor will perform: amount of advertising (and in which journals), exhibiting at conferences and book fairs, door-to-door sales, mailing promotions, etc.

How do you find a trustworthy foreign distributor?

Check out the various export offices of the Department of Commerce. So says publisher Lou Aarons, who writes books on an innovative technique for learning foreign languages. He paid $125 for the department to conduct a search of book distributors in Spain. He received 50 names, one of which he ultimately used. Aarons also suggested looking up the National Trade Data Base, available in most large-city libraries. It lists names of key importers in foreign countries. Using this list for Japan, he found a key contact.

The other route is networking. Start by calling American publishers who publish books similar to yours and ask who they use, said John Brings, president of CASTI Publishing, Inc., which specializes in engineering books.

"It's remarkable how one lead will turn into three other leads that will turn into two other leads and so on," he said. "The best advice I can give is don't be shy to ask as many people as you know in the business."

Illustrating his point, Brings said he had just traded information about his Australian distributor with a publisher friend for names of a Japanese and an Indian distributor.

"It's like trading baseball cards when we were kids," Brings said.

Until a mutual trust can be built with the distributor, he said, his firm requires 100 percent payment up front in U.S. dollars. "No money, no books, that simple. Language and culture are the two largest barriers in building this trust.

"For example, it did not take us very long to understand the capability of our European distributor, which is based in England. Language and culture were not a problem. To date, they are our only distributor that we offer consignment and allow payment on a quarterly basis. But they are aggressive direct-mail marketers and produce promotional literature for our books at their cost. Our quarterly check is usually about $10,000."

One way to build trust, Brings suggested, is to meet with all of your distributors face-to-face.

Another option: Employ the services of a U.S. export sales agency. These agencies represent the titles of anywhere from 10 to 100 publishers and use a cadre of sales representatives in the countries they serve. Like a foreign distributor, they will handle everything from promotion to distribution to collections.

An export sales agency typically takes a 40- to 45-percent discount, plus it will take a 15-percent commission on each sale. It will place orders with the publishing firm as it receives them, and usually pays quickly with U.S. checks.

SELLING TO OVERSEAS CUSTOMERS ON THE INTERNET

Internet booksellers report that a large share of their book orders arrive from the far-flung corners of the world.

Publisher Cynthia Kim of Turtle Press lists these advantages to a web page:

1. Saves on postage (especially air mail) by directing customers to the Turtle Press website instead of sending them a catalog by mail.

2. Saves on telephone bills by taking orders, follow-up questions, and providing service by e-mail. This also saves overseas customers money because they don't have to phone, mail, or fax (all of which costs money on a per/use basis).

3. Reaches new markets. Most of the current orders to Turtle Press are generated by direct-mail pieces or magazine ads. The web page has brought Turtle Press an entirely new group of customers.

If you do decide to market your book on the Web to a French, German, Italian, or Spanish-speaking public, make sure the order form and book description are in a foreign language, said Linda Thalman of WebFrance International, a French firm that offers books and online services.

Let's say you have a French customer who wants a guide book to Florida for their summer holidays. They'll be able to read enough English to use the book, but a short summary in French about the book and a well-translated order form just might encourage them to buy it on the Web, Thalman said.

Internet sales are discussed in great depth in Chapter 20.

GETTING PAYMENT FROM DIRECT SALES

Whether you sell books directly to consumers via the Internet, direct mail, or magazine ads, Visa and Mastercard are the easiest forms of payment, Kim said. Some publishers ask foreign publishers to deposit money directly into their credit accounts.

It's much easier for the customer to use their credit cards than to obtain checks or postal money orders in U.S. dollars. Credit cards can be called in by phone, cleared, and finalized in just a few minutes. If there's a misunderstanding, a fax or a phone call to the credit-card company will clear it up quickly.

A WORD ON SHIPPING

Many book publishers ship books by surface mail via the U.S. Postal Service, but some publishers advise checking out shipping brokers and freight companies.

Said John Brings, president of CATI Publishing, Inc., "If there is a problem with foreign distribution, it is shipping. Shipping overseas can be a nightmare. Our first big shipment to England (300 books in 1993) was sent first-class air mail and arrived damaged. Boxes were split open, dented, holes, everything imaginable. Fortunately our distributor was kind enough to clean up as many books as possible; about 150 were salvaged. The post office couldn't care less even though the shipment was insured."

Brings turned to a shipping broker that literally contacts all available shipping companies and gets quotes for each overseas shipment.

"We then pass on this quote to our foreign distributor and let them make the decision regarding the shipping means and company. This way the distributor becomes responsible for the shipment, although we assist them as much as possible, particularly to get the best price and delivery time. The lowest price is not always the best means."

THE BENEFITS OF CO-PUBLISHING

If you plan on marketing a book that has yet to be printed, consider co-publishing with a foreign publisher. That is, sharing the cost of acquiring and producing a book. What are the advantages? Let's say you want to publish a new book, which you plan to eventually take out of the United States. If you can produce the book at a significantly lower cost for 15,000 copies than 5,000, it makes sense to jointly produce the book with two or three other foreign publishers, who are willing to share the cost of production.

There are many different advantages and permutations to co-publishing: share the cost of a large print run; send camera-ready copy to the other publisher who then prints the book in a foreign country; or share marketing resources (such as the fruits of public relations—book reviews, articles, etc.) in the respective countries, particularly if it's English-speaking.

SURVIVING THE FRANKFURT BOOK FAIR

There are several international book fairs held annually, but the biggest by far is the Frankfurt Book Fair. With up to 20 miles of aisles, 8,000 exhibits, 200,000 participants, and publishers from 110 different countries, the Frankfurt Book Fair makes the sprawling BookExpo America Convention look like a summer warm-up. It's hard to believe that it began as a two-room affair in 1947 at the German National Library with fewer than 1,000 books displayed.

In the *Business of Book Publishing*, Frederick Praeger writes that the fair "defies description."

"It is a place where east and west, north and south, can meet, where representatives of the long-established firms encounter the book world's newest entrants. Although there is a good deal of cross-fertilization and stimulation, the frenetic atmosphere and shortage of time create considerable pressure. The atmosphere is also charged with hope, camaraderie, and the sense of belonging to an international institution devoted to communication and knowledge."

Frankfurt can be intimidating, yet if you're genuinely interested in selling your books overseas, it offers no easier entry into the international world of book-selling.

Publisher Larry Rood of Gryphon House, Inc. (a publisher of books aimed at parents and teachers), describes his first year at Frankfurt as "insanity."

"It is so huge and so monstrous. The task you have is one of defining an incredible amount of fine detail," he said. "In most countries, there will be some little publishing house or some big publishing house with a division that does what you do. But finding those people in each country is an exceedingly time-consuming process. We spent hours and hours saying, 'Here are the books we do. Do you publish books like this?' You keep asking and asking. They told us, 'You're close. Go check out so and so.' Basically it took five years before Frankfurt started to pay off."

Prior to embarking on a trip to Frankfurt, said Bill Hanna, vice president of Stoddart Publishing Co., Ltd. of Canada, be sure to sketch out specific goals. Some publishers go to Frankfurt to find ways of exporting their books. They'll meet booksellers, publishers, agents, and distributors. They may sell foreign rights to their books. Others go to Frankfurt to buy translation rights to books that are written outside of the United States in order to enlarge and enhance their lists.

Finally, a publisher may want to find a foreign publisher for a co-edition of a future book.

If you already have an agent trying to sell rights to a foreign publisher, it's useful to back up the agent by talking to publishers directly and then asking your agent to follow up.

Preparation is the order of the day. If you plan to exhibit, you need to send in an application form in March. Begin setting up meetings in early July or even earlier. Write letters and send catalogs to potential publishers, distributors, or agents with whom you'd like to meet. Use the *International Literary MarketPlace* for names and addresses. Information about your book should include the target audience, sales history, reviews, an author biography, a description of the book, and the rights available.

"By the first week of September, my dance card will be full for a fair that lasts five-and-a-half days," Hanna said. "We add two to three days to the front of it. We'll see a horrendous number of people. The usual norm is one meeting every half an hour, from 8:30 a.m. to when the fair finishes at 6:30 p.m."

If you are too small to exhibit by yourself, consider joining forces with another small publisher, Independent Publishers Services, or the Publishers Marketing Association. A standard, all-equipped booth runs about $1,100, Hanna said.

Rood said his firm "thrived in the supportive environment in the PMA stand at Frankfurt, working as part of a group with them and making contacts."

SELLING DIRECTLY TO FOREIGN CONSUMERS

In many Third World countries, direct mail is your only hope of reaching your desired customers because these countries typically lack a book distribution infrastructure. To develop a mailing list of research institutes and government agencies, consult *The World of Learning* (published by Gale Research Co. in Detroit and Europa Publishers in London). For academic and commercial lists, contact the appropriate embassies in Washington, D.C.

Before deciding on a direct marketing strategy, be aware that it's costly. So costly, in fact, that selling a book or package of books at less than $100—the bare minimum—is usually not profitable.

That's the opinion of Alfred Goodloe, president of Direct International, which publishes an international newsletter on the international direct-mail market, Publisher's Multinational Direct.

"A trade book, a novel, or a book that sells for $20 or $25, is not going to work in direct marketing," Goodloe said. "It doesn't mean it can't be sold. It just means it will go the bookstore or library market."

In general, business and technical books do best in direct-mail sales. Goodloe says books packaged as manuals in a standard notebook binder work best and he lists these criteria:

- The manual should be practical, organized in a straightforward way, and easy to comprehend. It should be able to serve as a working document with work sheets that a business can effectively use.

- The manual must promise a clear and generous benefit to the bottom line. It must go beyond an inspirational document and offer concrete instructions. If people can see a direct connection between the report and the bottom line, they won't hesitate to invest several hundred dollars. Topics might include: How to reorganize your sales force and triple sales within 90 days. How to recruit the world's finest salesmen. How to develop a strategic plan that will double profits within a year.

- If your book will appeal beyond executive management to middle management, it might be worth the expense of translating the work into the local language.

- For a mailing list, consider the international readership of the *Harvard Business Review, Business Week, The Economist,* and the *International Airlines Passengers Association.*

- If you have published a special report other than English and can market it in the country's own language, rent a list from the country's leading business magazines.

- Another publishing venture to consider: publish a newsletter in your area of specialty at $150 to $300 a year.

One last idea: If you have several titles in a related area, combine the titles in a set: "Let's say you have *The Sales Management Set* and each book covers a different aspect. You put them together with the same covers, Volume 1, 2, 3, 4, 5, and they all have to work together and build on one another," Goodloe said.

14.

BOOK CLUBS: THEY DON'T PAY MUCH, BUT CONSIDER THEM ANYWAY

God gives us opportunities;
success depends upon the use made of them.
ELLEN G. WHITE

SOME BOOK CLUB DEALS PROVIDE A PILE OF EASY CASH TO A PUB-lisher while other book club deals are no deals at all. You have to carefully analyze each offer before signing on.

In many cases the monetary reward is marginal, yet it's important to consider some of the other advantages of signing up with a book club. First and foremost, publishers can capitalize on the prestige of getting their books accepted into a club, particularly if chosen by a major club—Book-of-the-Month Club or Literary Guild (the flagship club of Doubleday Book Clubs) or one of their specialty clubs. Publishers often tout this when pitch-ing their book to libraries, distributors, foreign publishers, etc.

"The money is not that great," agreed book marketing consultant Kate Bandos. "You shouldn't expect to make much or any money. You're doing it for the exposure and the status. Even with lesser known clubs, people are always hesitant to stick their neck out and say, 'This is a great book.' If someone else has supposedly looked through thousands of cookbooks or the 'How to Make a Sweater Book,' and picked this one, it's a stamp of approval. It's already been taken out of the slush pile and put in the spotlight."

Another plus to signing up with a book club is that a book club order can potentially reduce your overall printing costs. If the club piggybacks its order onto your print run, the increased quantity can reduce the printing bill by about 10 percent.

Third, you don't have to worry about returns. A book club keeps all the books they buy. They are buying a subsidiary right—the right to produce and publish the books themselves (sometimes they buy the books directly from your inventory at cost, which saves them the trouble of printing books themselves).

A final positive: book clubs reach buyers you may not be able to reach otherwise. By advertising your book through a book club, you are increasing the universe of your book sales.

A small publisher's book usually finds interest in the smaller clubs or specialized clubs of the majors. Under the umbrella of Book-of-the-Month, for example, are the History Book Club, Money Book Club, Fortune International Book Club, The Good Cook, Crafter's Choice, Country Homes and Gardens, One Spirit and Children's Book-of-the-Month Club. With Doubleday Book Club, there is the Children's Book Club, Fireside Theatre, Military Book Club, Mystery Guild and the Science Fiction Book Club.

John Major, a senior editor at Book-of-the-Month Club, said that the History Club is the biggest user of small-press selections. Books that are primarily regional, academic, technical or otherwise highly specialized are generally not considered for acceptance, he said.

The Literary MarketPlace lists 141 book clubs ranging from the American Artist Book Club to the *Writer's Digest* Book Club. The key to marketing your book to a club is finding the specific club whose audience matches the targeted audience of your book.

A book club is typically defined as offering members a selection(s), which each month is fully described in a brochure. If the member fails to send back a response card that no book or another book is desired, the selection is automatically shipped. (Some catalogs call themselves a book club when, in fact, they are simply offering books for purchase.)

The typical book club will offer royalties of up to 10 percent based on the club's retail price, generally 70 percent to 80 percent of the book's original price. When a book club buys rights to a book, it can offer the book however it chooses, including offering it as a premium (books offered as an incentive to get someone to join or as a reward for heavy book orders—"Buy four books, and get one free." Royalties on premium books are very low at about 4 percent. Generally, the author and publisher split all royalty money.

Each book club deal is different, although essentially the book club pays the publisher for the right to offer a book to its members for a specific time, usually two to five years. Some clubs will manufacture their own books and pay royalties. Some will piggyback onto the publisher's print run paying $X a book plus royalties. Some book clubs purchase books outright from the publisher's existing stock. Because book clubs often pay a standard dollar amount for books (which they assume is cost), book deal profits often depend on how savvy the publisher is at getting a low manufacturing cost, Bandos said.

What should you expect as an advance? Typically, book clubs pay half of what they expect to earn based on their first order. Advances for a book purchased by a major club can reach as high as $100,000 and even more, but far less for unpredictable sellers—in the hundreds of dollars versus thousands of dollars.

One more note: book club purchases are nonreturnable, however, some contracts will include a clause that gives the book club the right to remainder books if the publisher doesn't want to buy them back at the original cost. The potential danger, of course, is the club may flood the market with cheap, remaindered books at a time when you're trying to sell them at full price. These contracts *are* negotiable; try to get this clause stricken.

HOW TO GET YOUR BOOK CONSIDERED

Large book clubs like to see your book while it's still in manuscript form, six to nine months in advance of publication. Smaller book clubs prefer galleys, but are willing to consider books even after they're published.

Cover letters should reflect that you clearly understand the club members' preference for books. Mention titles that are similar to yours, which have proven popular in the club. If the club has never listed a similar title, give some good reasons why your tile would indeed appeal to its members. You'll also need to include the estimated publication date, estimated number of pages, a brief description of the book and summary of its content, and the number and type of illustrations. Also very helpful are photocopies of sample illustrations and brief biographical material about the author, noting any previous books, if any, Major said.

Add force to the letter by mentioning plans for a media tour or the fact that the author has been mentored by a famous author who is going to put his or her weight behind the book or that the U.S. Surgeon General wrote a testimonial on the back cover.

"You can send us a galley, then send us a finished book with reviews and that's fine," said Judy Estrine, acquisition editor for Doubleday Book Club. "It helps if we see something more than once. It's what the big houses do. They send us an advanced galley, then an uncorrected copy, then the finished book. These things establish a relationship. Don't give up and get depressed. It's really the name of the game to be in our face."

Follow up your first query with news to encourage acceptance of the book, i.e., the book has gone into a second printing, quotes from advance book reviews, news of an audio rights or movie rights sale, etc. In the case of books chosen as a major selection or alternate selection, the book clubs often go into a bidding war of sorts.

Although the larger book clubs prefer to see manuscripts, they will buy books after they're published, particularly the specialized clubs. Jane Perkins, editorial assistant for Quality Paperback Books, said she combs small-press catalogs for books.

"Now we're looking for books with lesbian content," she said. "It's pretty much open. I like unique, interesting, vampire type stuff, especially humor. If I think it's going to be big, normally I want the book. It's always helpful to get promotional literature, but reviews are best, awards they've won, and sales reports. I want to know if it's gone into a second printing."

Book-of-the Month Club and the Literary Guild usually demand exclusivity while the smaller book clubs do not.

At the same time you submit your manuscript to the book clubs, you should also send a copy to *Reader's Digest Condensed Books* (not to be confused with the magazine), which pays in the tens of thousands of dollars for condensed-book use plus royalties. The editors condense each book to a length consistent with its content and with the author's style and purpose. The line-editing takes many months.

Over the years, the success of Condensed Books has given birth to additional book series, including *Today's Best Nonfiction* and *The Best of the West*, an anthology of Western novels and nonfiction, according to a report issued by the company's corporate communications department.

What do the editors look for? Books that entertain and inform, books that have strong central characters—whether heroes or villains—and an engaging narrative. Editors focus, in particular, on stories that focus on issues behind the headlines. The 25th volume in 1993, for example, contained a biography, a true crime book, a business story, and a personal family memoir, the report said.

While true that *Reader's Digest* chooses books that often end up on the *New York Times* Best Seller list, the editors are dedicated to seeking out lesser-known books. Such titles include *Still Missing* by Beth Gutcheon, *Payment in Full* by Henry Denker, and *Home Mountain* by Jeanne Williams, the report said.

What are your chances? Out of 3,500 manuscripts a year, the editors choose only a handful to feature in "Today's Best Nonfiction." The books are chosen *many months* before the originals are published.

📖　　📖　　📖

When publisher Lynne Van Der Kar of the Van Der Kar Press, received an offer from Book-of-the-Month Club's division, One Spirit, she didn't think it would be worth a lot of money. The offer for *Kombucha . . How-to and What It's All About* amounted to a $750 advance, 8-percent royalties, and a 4-percent royalty for books sold as premiums or giveaways.

"I called my friend and said, 'There's no money here. Why would I want to do this?' And he said, 'Prestige. You just started your business, this is your first book, and it's been chosen by Book-of-the-Month Club. You don't get that?' I realized that not everything in this business is for money. Being able to put 'Book-of-the-Month Club Selection' on all my materials immediately made the book credible. Every time I mention that it's in Book-of-the-Month Club, everybody is always impressed."

Prestige aside, Van der Kar took the proffered Book-of-the-Month contract to a lawyer friend and insisted on changes in the four-page contract.

"The biggest red flag was they wanted exclusive book-club rights for five years, but the right to remainder the book after a year. We agreed the term was for five years, but if they remainder the book, the term is over.

"They wanted me to return all monies earned if 'in their judgment' any of my representations and warranties were false or breached. I told them that was draconian and it was eliminated from the contract. If I'm guilty, they can cancel me, but I owe them no money."

She wanted 30 days, not 15, to decide if she wanted to buy books in the case they were remaindered. She rewrote the "Interpretation and Arbitration" clause to a more standard format. And she added a clause saying any amendment to the contract had to be in writing and signed by both parties. Finally, Van der Kar persuaded the club to pay for shipping and duplicating materials costs.

"In my opinion, they gave me all of the above. There were a couple of other points that couldn't be changed and I could live with them so that was it."

📖   📖   📖

BOOKCLUBS

Antiques & Collectibles Book Club
Jennifer M. Clark, Dir.
Newbridge Book Clubs
333 E 38th St.
New York NY 10016-2772
(212) 455-5072
Fax: (212) 573-6327
Features books on antiques and collectibles.

The Architects' Book Club
Bill Walker, Mgr.
McGraw-Hill/Tab Book Clubs
148 Princeton Rd.
Hightstown NJ 08520
(609) 426-5000
Features both technical and nontechnical nonfiction and fiction books on a broad range of architectural topics, including biographical, for the professional and nonprofessional.

Architecture & Designers Book Club
Charles Decker, Dir.
Newbridge Book Clubs
333 E. 38th St.
New York NY 10016-2772
(212) 455-5014
Fax: (212) 573-6327
Features books on architecture, design and house and home.

Arrow Book Club
Ms. Pat Brigandi, Editor
Scholastic Inc.
555 Broadway
New York NY 10012-3919
(212) 343-6100
Fax: (212) 343-6928
Features books for children grades 4 through 6.

Astronomy Book Club
Joe Craig, Dir.
Newbridge Book Clubs
333 E. 38th St.
New York NY 10016-2772
(212) 455-5053
Fax: (212) 573-6327
Features books on astronomy.

Audio Book Club
Marc Sinensky, Exec VP
2295 Corporate Blvd NW, #222
Boca Raton FL 33431
(407) 241-1426
Fax: (407) 241-9887
Features audio versions of business, relationships, new age, spirituality, and psychology as well as other non-fiction and fiction materials.

Audiobooks Direct
Christine Zall, Editor
Doubleday Book Clubs
1540 Broadway
New York NY 10036-4039
(212) 782-7200
Fax: (212) 782-7205
Features audio versions of general-interest genres.

Audio-Tech Business Book Summary
Fred Rogers, President
Suite 701, 566 W. Adams
Chicago IL 60661
(312) 345-1910
Fax: (312) 345-1913
Features business-related technical books, including marketing and management manuals.

Aviators' Guild
Carlo Devito, Mgr.
McGraw-Hill/Tab Book Clubs
148 Princeton Rd.
Hightstown NJ 08520
(609) 426-5000
Features nonfiction books aimed at the amateur and professional.

Behavioral Science Book Service
Marge Lurie, Dir.
Newbridge Book Clubs
333 E. 38th St.
New York NY 10016-2772
(212) 455-5097
Fax: (212) 573-6327
Features books relating to behavior and psychology.

Bob's Book Club
Bob Cox, President
6209 SW 3rd St.
Des Moines IA 50315-5740
(515) 285-7377
Features all genres of fiction and non-fiction.

Books of Light
Leslie Swanson, Ariel Press
289 S. Main St., Ste. 205
Alpharetta GA 30201
(770) 664-4886
Features books relating to alternative health and medicine and other new age and spirituality genres as well as science fiction and fantasy leaning toward new age-type genres.

Carnival Book Club
Linda Ferreira, Editorial Director
Scholastic Inc.
555 Broadway
New York NY 10012-3919
(212) 343-6100
Fax: (212) 343-6928
Features books for children grades K through 6.

Cassette-of-the-Month Club
Janice Yates, Audio Forum
96 Broad St.
Guilford CT 06437
(203) 453-9794
Features audio versions of fiction and non-fiction for the general audience.

Catholic Book Club
Barbara Coto, Mgr.
The America Press
106 W. 56th St.
New York NY 10019-3893
(212) 581-4640
Fax: (212) 399-3596
Features only Catholic-related material.

Catholic Digest Book Club
Jean Altman, Book Club Mgr.
Ste. 1268, 475 Riverside Dr.
New York NY 10015
(212) 870-2552
Features Christian-related materials as well as other genres with religious content.

Chemical Engineers Book Club
Bill Walker, Mgr.
McGraw-Hill/Tab Book Clubs
148 Princeton Rd.
Hightstown NJ 08520
(609) 426-5000
Features nonfiction books and textbooks for the chemical engineering industry.

Chemists' Book Club
Bill Walker, Mgr.
McGraw-Hill/Tab Book Clubs
148 Princeton Rd.
Hightstown NJ 08520
(609) 426-5000
Features nonfiction books and textbooks on chemistry for the amateur and professional.

Children's Book-of-the-Month-Club
David Allender, Dir.
BOMC/Time-Life Bldg
1271 Ave of the Americas
New York NY, 10020-1300
(212) 522-4200
Fax: (212) 522-0303
Features children's stories/literature and educational materials.

Christian Family Book Club
Marian Kromberg, Editor
Eagle Book Clubs
33 Oakland Avenue
Harrison NY 10528
(800) 879-3270
Features Christian-related materials as well as other genres of interest to today's Christian families.

Cinema Book Society
D. Richard Baer, President
Hollywood Film Archive
8394 Beverly Blvd.
Los Angeles CA 90048
(213) 933-3345
Featuring books on movies and the movie and television industry.

Civil Engineers' Book Club
Bill Walker, Mgr.
McGraw-Hill/Tab Book Clubs
148 Princeton Rd.
Hightstown NJ 08520
(609) 426-5000
Featuring nonfiction books and textbooks on civil engineering.

Columbia House Audio Books
Gordon Henry, 19th Floor
1221 Ave of the Americas
New York NY 10020-1001
(212) 596-2680
Fax: (212) 596-2213
Features audio versions of general-interest genres.

The Computer Book Club
Carlo Devito, Mgr.
McGraw-Hill/Tab Book Clubs
148 Princeton Rd.
Hightstown NJ 08520
(609) 426-5000
Features computer information aimed at the everyday computer user.

Computer Professionals' Books Society
Carlo Devito, Mgr.
McGraw-Hill/Tab Book Clubs
148 Princeton Rd.
Hightstown NJ 08520
(609) 426-5000
Features nonfiction technical books and textbooks on mainframe and networks for the computer professional.

Conservative Book Club
Marian Kromberg, Editor
Eagle Book Clubs
33 Oakland Ave
Harrison NY 10528-3739
(914) 835-0900
Fax: (914) 835-2708
Features conservative-interest books in subjects such as business, political, government and religion.

Crafter's Choice Book Club
B J Berti, Editor
BOMC/Time-Life Bldg.
1271 Ave. of the Americas
New York NY 10020-1300
(212) 522-4200
Fax: (212) 522-0303
Features crafts and hobbies materials.

Creative Needlecrafts Book Club
Renee James, Special Sales Mgr
Rodale Press, 400 S. 10th St.
Emmaus PA 18049-3622
(610) 967-5171
Fax: (610) 967-8962
Features books on needlecraft.

Crossings Book Club
Michelle Rapkin, Editor-in-chief
Doubleday Book Clubs
1540 Broadway
New York NY 10036-4039
(212) 782-7200
Fax: (212) 782-7205
Features books for today's Christian family.

Crossings for Kids
Ellen Borges, Senior Editor
Doubleday Book Clubs
1540 Broadway
New York NY 10036-4039
(212) 782-7200
Fax: (212) 782-7205
Features books for children of all ages.

Dance Book Club
Constance Woodford, Dir
Princeton Book Co.
P.O. Box 57
Pennington NJ 08534
(609) 737-8178
Features books on dance.

Decorative Artists Book Club
Ms. Mert Ransdell, Dir.
F & W Publishing
1507 Dana Ave.
Cincinnati OH 45207-1056
(513) 531-2222
Fax: (513) 531-4744
Features home-decorating crafts and ideas books.

Deseret Book Club
Acquisitions Department
P.O. Box 30178
Salt Lake City UT 84130
(801) 534-1515
Fax: (801) 578-3392
Features all areas of fiction and nonfiction for the Mormon audience.

Doubleday Book Club
Sharon Fantera, Editor
Doubleday Book Clubs
1540 Broadway
New York NY 10036-4039
(212) 782-7200
Fax: (212) 782-7205
Features general-interest genres.

Early Childhood Teachers' Club
Deborah Lehman, Dir.
Newbridge Book Clubs
333 E. 38th St.,
New York NY 10016-2772
(212) 455-5140
Fax: (212) 573-6327
Features books for pre-kindergarten-age children.

Ecological Book Club
Roger Corbin
Devin-Adair Publishing
6 N Water St.
Greenwich CT 06830-5817
(203) 531-7755
Features nonfiction books on environmental and ecological issues as well as practical advice/how-to for the organic gardener/landscaper.

Electronics Book Club
Lisa Shrager, Mgr.
McGraw-Hill/Tab Book Clubs
148 Princeton Rd.
Hightstown NJ 08520
(609) 426-5000
Features informational books on electronics for the home hobbyist.

Electronics Engineers' Book Club
Lisa Shrager, Mgr.
McGraw-Hill/Tab Book Clubs
148 Princeton Rd.
Hightstown NJ 08520
(609) 426-5000
Features nonfiction technical books and textbooks aimed at the electrical engineering professional.

Enjoy-A-Book Club
Karen Richter, Acq. Editor
555 Chestnut St.
Cedarhurst, NY 11516-2223
(516) 569-0324
Features children's literature with Jewish content only.

Evangelical Book Club
Joyce Bohn, Gen Mgr
Mott Media
1000 E Huron St
Milford MI 48381-2422
(810) 685-8773
Features books covering all genres with Christian and/or moral content.

Executive Program
Charles Decker, Dir.
Newbridge Book Clubs
333 E. 38th St.
New York NY 10016-2772
(212) 455-5014
Fax: (212) 573-6327
Features books relating to all aspects of business.

Firefly Book Club
Steve Metzger, Editor
Scholastic Inc.
555 Broadway
New York NY 10012-3919
(212) 343-6100
Fax: (212) 343-6928
Features books for pre-kindergarten children.

Garden Book Club
Josh Samton, Dir.
Newbridge Book Clubs
333 E 38th St.
New York NY 10016-2772
(212) 455-5142
Fax: (212) 573-6327
Features books on gardening.

Golden Book Club
Rachel Smith, Acq. Editor
Troll Communications
100 Corporate Dr.
Mahwah, NJ 07430
(800) 526-5289
Fax: (201) 529-9347
Features books geared toward children grades K-3.

The Good Cook
Pat Adrian, Editor
BOMC/Time-Life Bldg
1271 Ave. of the Americas
New York NY 10020-1300
(212) 522-4200
Fax: (212) 522-0303
Features cooking-related material.

Graphic Artist's Book Club
Ms. Mert Ransdell, Dir.
F & W Publishing,1507 Dana Ave.
Cincinnati OH 45207-1056
(513) 531-2222
Fax: (513) 531-4744
Features graphics and commercial arts books.

Guild America Books
Barbara Greenman, Editor
Doubleday Book Clubs
1540 Broadway
New York NY 10036-4039
(212) 782-7200
Fax: (212) 782-7205
Features general-interest genres.

History Book Club
Kathleen McDermott, Editor
BOMC/Time-Life Bldg.
1271 Ave. of the Americas
New York NY 10020-1300
(212) 522-4200
Features historical nonfiction including military, political and current news and events.

Home Schooling Book Club
Joyce Bohn, Gen Mgr., Mott Media
1000 E Huron St.
Milford MI 48381-2422
(810) 685-8773
Features school-age books and textbooks
with Christian and/or moral content.

I Can Read Book Club
Kristine L. Frankel
Collier-Newfield Publications
919 Third Ave.
New York NY 10022
(212) 508-6142
Features books for early readers.

Intermediate & Middle School Book Club
Susan DerKazarian, Dir
Newbridge Book Clubs
333 E 38th St.
New York NY 10016-2772
(212) 455-5063
Fax: (212) 573-6327
Features books for grades 4-8.

The International Marine Book Society
Joyce Hunsucker, Mgr.
McGraw-Hill/Tab Book Clubs
148 Princeton Rd.
Hightstown NJ 08520
(609) 426-5000
Features fiction and nonfiction nautical
books for both the professional and nonprofessional.

Irish-American Book Society
Roger Lourie, Editor
Devin-Adair Publishing
P.O. Box A
Old Greenwich CT 06870-0601
(203) 531-7807
Features fiction and nonfiction books and
textbooks related to Irish history, govern-
ment, linguistics, arts and literature.

The Jewish Book Club
Pam Roth, Mg. Editor
Jason Aronson Publishers Inc.
230 Livingston St.
Northvale NJ 07647
(201) 767-4093
Fax: (201) 767-4330
Features Jewish-related materials as well
as other genres of interest to today's Jew-
ish families.

Library of Computer & Information Sciences
Rich O'Hanley, Dir.
Newbridge Book Clubs
333 E 38th St.
New York NY 10016-2772
(212) 455-5013
Fax: (212) 573-6327
Features technical books and textbooks for
the professional high-end user.

Library of Science
Lynn Duffy, Asst.
Newbridge Book Clubs
333 E 38th St.
New York NY 10016-2772
(212) 455-5108
Fax: (212) 573-6327
Features books relating to all aspects of
the sciences, i.e., health and medicine, psychology, technology, natural sciences and
physical sciences.

Library of Speech-Language Pathology
Deborah Lehman, Dir.
Newbridge Book Clubs
333 E 38th St.
New York NY 10016-2772
(212) 455-5140
Fax: (212) 573-6327
Features books in areas of developmental
language, linguistics and psychology aimed
at the professional reader.

Laissez Faire Books
Andrea Millen Rich, Publ.
Ctr For Independent Thought
73 Spring St #507
New York NY 10012-5802
(212) 925-8992
Fax: (212) 219-1581
Features nonfiction books relating to economics, consumer issues, education, history, political policy and philosophy.

Large Print Home Library
Andrew Wheeler, Editor
Doubleday Book Clubs
1540 Broadway
New York NY 10036-4039
(212) 782-7200
Fax: (212) 782-7205
Features all genres of books offered in large print.

Limited Editions Club
Sidney Shiff, Pres.
980 Madison Ave.
New York NY 10021-1848
(212) 737-7600
Fax: (212) 249-3939
Features illustrated books.

Literary Guild of America
Karen Daly, Editor-in-Chief
Doubleday Book Clubs
1540 Broadway
New York NY 10036-4039
(212) 782-7253
Fax: (212) 782-7205
Features best-selling fiction and some nonfiction.

Lucky Book Club
Alex Fischer
Scholastic Inc.
555 Broadway
New York NY 10012-3919
(212) 343-6100
Fax: (212) 343-6928
Features books for children grades 2-3.

Mac Professional's Book Club
Rich O'Hanley, Dir.
Newbridge Book Clubs
333 E 38th St.
New York NY, 10016-2772
(212) 455-5013
Fax: (212) 573-6327
Features books for the Macintosh user.

Mechanical Engineers' Book Club
Bill Walker, Mgr.
McGraw-Hill/Tab Book Clubs
148 Princeton Rd.
Hightstown NJ 08520
(609) 426-5000
Features technical books and textbooks for the mechanical engineering professional.

Men's Health Book Service
Renee James, Sp Sales Mgr.
Rodale Press, 400 S. 10th St.
Emmaus PA 18098-0001
(215) 967-5171
Fax: (215) 967-8962
Features books related to men's issues such as sports, lifestyle, health, medicine and sexual issues.

Military Book Club
Michael Stephenson, Editor
Doubleday Book Clubs
1540 Broadway
New York NY 10036-4039
(212) 782-7200
Fax: (212) 782-7205
Features military and historical military books and textbooks.

Money Book Club
Laurie Calkhoven, Editor,
BOMC/Time-Life Bldg
1271 Ave of the Americas
New York NY 10020-1300
(212) 522-4200
Fax: (212) 522-0303
Features investment-related materials.

Movie Entertainment Book Club
Marian Kromberg, Editor
Eagle Book Clubs
33 Oakland Avenue
Harrison NY 10528
(800) 879-3270
Features books on celebrities, Hollywood
and the film industry.

Mystery Guild
Beth Goehring, Senior Editor
Doubleday Book Clubs
1540 Broadway
New York NY 10036-4039
(212) 782-7200
Fax: (212) 782-7205
Features mysteries.

Natural Science Book Club
Joe Craig, Dir,
Newbridge Book Clubs
333 E 38th St.
New York NY 10016-2772
(212) 455-5053
Fax: (212) 573-6327
Features books on natural science.

Nature Book Society
Holly Lavieri, Book Acq.
Rodale Press
400 S 10th St.
Emmaus PA 18049-3622
(610) 967-5171
Fax: (610) 967-8962
Features books on nature.

Newbridge Multimedia Club
Rich O'Hanley, Dir,
Newbridge Book Clubs
333 E 38th St.
New York, NY 10016-2772
(212) 455-5141
Fax: (212) 573-6327
Features books on the technology and
trends of the information and multimedia
industries.

North Light Book Club
Ms. Mert Ransdell, Dir.
F & W Publishing
1507 Dana Ave.
Cincinnati OH 45207-1056
(513) 531-2222
Fax: (513) 531-4744
Features books covering the fine arts.

Nurse's Book Society
Kristen Miller, Dir.
Newbridge Book Clubs
333 E 38th St
New York NY 10016-2772
(212) 455-5728
Fax: (212) 573-6327
Features books related to the nursing pro-
fession.

One-Spirit Book Club
Robert Welsh, Dir.
BOMC/Time-Life Bldg
1271 Ave of the Americas
New York NY 10020-1300
(212)522-4200
Fax: (212) 522-0303
Features new age, metaphysical, spiritual-
ity and alternative books.

Organic Gardening Book Club
Holly Lavieri, Book Aqs.
Rodale Press
400 S 10th St.
Emmaus PA, 18049-3622
(610) 967-5171
Fax: (610) 967-8962
Features books on organic gardening.

Prevention Book Club
Renee James, Special Sales Mgr
Rodale Press
400 S 10th St.
Emmaus PA 18049-3622
(610) 967-5171
Fax: (610)967-8962
Features books on preventative health and
medicine.

Primary Teachers' Book Club
Susan DerKazarian, Dir
Newbridge Book Clubs
333 E 38th St.
New York NY 10016-2772
(212) 455-5063
Fax: (212) 573-6327
Features books for grades 1-3.

Provident Book Store Reader's Club
Jack C Scott, Dir.
Mennonite Publ. Hse.
616 Walnut Ave
Scottdale PA 15683-1992
(412) 887-8500
Fax: (412) 887-3111
Features fiction and nonfiction relating to Christianity, family life, peace and social issues; some aspects of the Mennonite lifestyle and religion.

Psychotherapy Book Club
Juliann Popp, Mg Editor
Jason Aronson Publishers Inc.
230 Livingston St.
Northvale, NJ 07647
(201) 767-4093
Fax: (201) 767-4330
Features psychology and self-help books.

Quality Paperback Book Club
David Rosen, Sr. Editor
BOMC/Time-Life Bldg
1271 Ave of the Americas
New York NY 10020-1300
(212) 522-4200
Fax: (212) 522-0303
Features all genres of quality fiction and literature.

TheReader's Subscription
Josh Samton, Dir.
Newbridge Book Clubs
333 E 38th St.
New York NY 10016-2772
(212) 455-5142
Fax: (212) 573-6327
Features only academic books in areas such as the humanities, literature, poetry and drama.

Science Fiction Book Club
Ellen Asher, Editor
Doubleday Book Clubs
1540 Broadway
New York NY 10036-4039
(212) 782-7200
Fax: (212) 782-7205
Features science fiction-genre books.

See-Saw Book Club
Emily McBurney
Scholastic Inc.
555 Broadway
New York NY 10012-3919
(212) 343-6100
(212) 343-6928
Features books for children grades K-1.

Small Computer Book Club
Rich O'Hanley, Dir
Newbridge Book Clubs
333 E 38th St.
New York NY 10016-2772
(212) 455-5013
(212) 573-6327
Features technical and non-technical books for users and programmers.

Spiritual Book Associates
Robert Hamma, Editor
Ave Maria Press Bldg
Notre Dame IN 46556
(219) 287-2838
Features fiction and nonfiction spirituality and religious books.

TAB Club
Greg Holch, Editor
Scholastic Inc.
555 Broadway
New York NY 10012-3919
(212) 343-6100
Fax: (212) 343-6928
Features books for pre-teens grades 7 through 9.

Thomas More Book Club
Todd Brennan, Editor
205 W Monroe 6th Fl
Chicago IL 60606-5013
(312) 609-8880
Fax: (312) 609-8891
Features primarily Roman Catholic theology and some general Christian books.

Troll Book Club
Rachel Smith, Acq. Editor
Troll Communications
100 Corporate Dr
Mahwah, NJ 07430
(800) 526-5289
Fax: (201) 529-9347
Features books geared toward children grades 6-9.

Trumpet Book Club
Eva Seave, Editorial Director
Scholastic Inc.
555 Broadway
New York NY 10012-3919
(212) 343-6100
Fax: (212) 343-6928
Features books for children grades pre-K through 4.

Weekly Reader Children's Books
Kristine L. Frankel
Collier-Newfield Publications
919 Third Ave
New York NY 10022
(212) 508-6142
Features fiction and nonfiction for children of all ages.

Woodworking Book Club
Ms. Mert Ransdell, Dir
F & W Publishing
1507 Dana Ave.
Cincinnati OH 45207-1056
(513) 531-2222
Fax: (513) 531-4744
Features books relating to the crafts, hobbies and house and home aspects of woodworking.

Writer's Digest Book Club
Ms. Mert Ransdell, Dir.
F & W Publishing
1507 Dana Ave.
Cincinnati OH 45207-1056
(513) 531-2222
Fax: (513) 531-4744
Features how-to and other reference books for writers.

Young Readers' Book Club
Chip Lovett, Exec. Editor
Grolier Enterprises
90 Sherman Turnpike
Danbury CT 06816
(203) 797-3500
Fax: (203) 797-3197
Features fiction and nonfiction geared toward young readers ages 4-14.

CONDENSED BOOKS

Submit books or manuscripts for consideration by *Reader's Digest Condensed Books* and *Today's Best Nonfiction* editors to:
Christine Crisci, Editorial Assistant
Condensed Books/Today's Best Nonfiction
The Reader's Digest Association, Inc.
Reader's Digest Road
Pleasantville, NY 10570

15.

BUCKS "R" US: HOW TO SELL TO WAREHOUSES AND MASS MERCHANDISING CLUBS

Who bravely dares must sometimes risk a fall.
TOBIAS SMOLLETT

HERE'S A TRIVIA QUESTION: WHAT WAS THE LARGEST OUTLET FOR children's book sales in 1994?

Answer: Discount stores like Kmart, Walmart and Target have captured a full 30 percent of all children's book sales. Granted, the survey includes coloring book sales, but it's still impressive.

Book clubs came in at a distant second (17 percent), and chain bookstores at 10 percent. Independent bookstores captured only 5 percent behind food/drug stores (9 percent) and mail order (6 percent). Warehouse price clubs captured 3 percent, according to a 1994 Consumer Research Study on Book Purchasing conducted by the NPD Group.

What about overall book sales? Warehouse clubs and discount stores combined sold 14 percent of all consumer books (warehouse clubs, 6 percent; discount stores, 8 percent), according to the same study.

These outlets represent enormous sales potential—a single best-seller book order can call for 40,000 copies, even more. Plus you may reach an

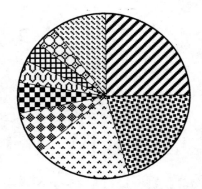

▨	Chain Bookstores	25%
▨	Independent Book stores	21%
▨	Book Clubs	18%
▨	Discount Stores	8%
▨	Warehouse Clubs	6%
▨	Mail Order	4%
▤	Used Bookstores	4%
▨	Food/Drug Stores	4%
▨	All Others	10%

Source: 1995 Consumer Research Study on Book Publishing; Published by the Book Industry Study Group

audience who might never see your book otherwise. Yet this is one of the most difficult of all channels. For your book to succeed, they must not only move off the shelf, they've got to *fly* into consumers' hands.

If they don't, it is *not* advantageous for a small press to work with a discount store or mass merchandiser. In general, these huge corporations typically take 90 days to pay and usually don't pay in full, retaining a certain fraction of the payment for potential returns. Also, these outlets are generally unwilling to negotiate a "no returns" policy with new or small publishers.

On average, publishers sell books to warehouse club distributors at a wholesale discount—generally, 55 percent to 60 percent. That compares favorably to national book distributors who generally take a 63-percent discount or higher.

Although warehouse club sales are quite risky for one- to two-book publishers, there are ways of minimizing the chance of losses; for small publishers and unproven books, the publisher and warehouse club may agree to "test market" a book by placing small quantities in 10 or 20 regional stores. If a book does extremely well, the club will roll out the book nationally and order much higher quantities. If it doesn't, a couple thousand copies of the book have found a home and everybody is happy.

This is an outlet publishers shouldn't attempt until their book(s) has been proven a winner in terms of sales and publicity. There's simply too much to lose. Besides, these corporations usually "qualify" publishers in terms of how many books they publish, their credit history, and past sales success. Yet if your book has shown that it has angel wings and *can* fly off the shelves, go for it. Small presses—like Crossing Press in Freedom, California (publishes cookbooks and health books), and Papier Maché (published the best-selling *When I Am An Old Woman I Shall Wear Purple* and *If I Had My Life to Live Over, I Would Pick More Daisies*) have done very well in these outlets, but both had excellent sales track records.

So how do you go about getting your book into these stores?

The buying process among these outlets works like this: warehouse clubs and mass merchandising stores buy their goods from distributors and rarely from publishers because of the handling costs involved.

Therefore, a lot of times a warehouse club buyer decides to buy a book on the recommendation of its distributor's rep. Other times, a publisher's rep has visited the warehouse club buyer and successfully persuaded him or her to buy a title (small publishers, however, don't have enough clout to get in to see a warehouse club buyer; it's even hard for Simon & Schuster). Finally, buyers of certain clubs will determine themselves that a given book would be a great buy after reading a great review, hearing about it from numerous friends, seeing it in a book trade show, or reading or hearing an author interview. If they want the book, they'll ask their distributor to get it for them.

As a publisher, you need to tackle these stores from both sides of the stream—the warehouse club or mass merchandiser's book buying department and the distributor which serves them.

When ordering quantities, the book buyer determines if they want to offer the book as a "single skew" or as an assortment. A "single skew" simply means the book stands by itself. These books are typically the bestseller types. Small publisher's book are typically offered in an assortment display, meaning it's offered alongside books of similar size, price, and subject matter. Therefore, it behooves a publisher to do the homework and suggest a specific assortment with all the respective publishers' names and contact numbers. Your book will get presented much faster, said the marketing director of a major distributor. For example, if you have published a regional cookbook, look up publishers of other regional cookbooks and ask if they'd be willing to sell their book at Sam's Club or Target or whatever.

Some publishers balk at the thought of getting displayed side-by-side with their competition, believing it would drain sales away from their own book. In reality, the publisher may never get these sales in the first place since many warehouse club shoppers don't patronize bookstores.

Before trying to pitch your book to a distributor, wholesale club or mass merchandising store, be sure to make a few visits to the particular store to get an idea of what they offer. Generally, these stores carry best sellers, but in terms of fiction from small publishers, they'll carry children's books (well-illustrated books with a cute story do best) or young adult selections. You might also find regional-interest books and calendars on the shelves.

A store visit not only allows you to determine if the book fits in with the current book inventory; you can also check on whether there's a fit between your book and a given department. Tim Smith, for example, was able to get Meijer Inc., a midwest chain of "one-stop shopping" centers to stock his book, *Buck Wilder's Small Fry Fishing Guide*, in its outdoor department.

If you are convinced after your visit that your book could do well in a given store or warehouse club, call the store's corporate office and ask for the name of the appropriate book buyer. Next, call the buyer and be ready to discuss in a few words the book and its past sales successes in particular outlets. If the buyer seems interested, mail a book, cover letter, and hard evidence that the book will perform like a winner: sales performance in other outlets that would suggest success in a warehouse club, media appearances (past and future), book reviews, and a summation of your overall publicity campaign.

Selling to chain stores can be a terrific challenge. Jim Denardo, president of the Michigan sales firm, Adventure Marketing, describes trying to sell Tim Smith's *Buck Wilder's Small Fry Fishing Guide* to Meijer Inc.

"Chains are not that easy. Meijer once told me they wanted the *Buck Wilder* book, but that they couldn't buy it directly from me. I did a flip on that one," he said. "I had to sell it to another company, Faber Brothers, because it's the fishing distributor for Meijer's outdoor section. It's a tangled web. The whole industry is that way."

Denardo has learned that it takes persistence to get into major chains. After he makes contact with the right book buyer, he has to make at least a dozen calls and send several review copies.

BUCKS "R" US

Wade and Cheryl Hudson, owners of Just Us Books, found persistence paid off when it came to getting into Toys "R" Us. The publishers of Afrocentric children's books, Wade first contacted the corporate office and asked for the name of the children's book buyer. He then sent five copies of previously published books with a cover letter. He made five or six calls just to rise above the noise of all the other titles the buyer received! He made four subsequent shipments of the five books, he said, just to get the company's attention. Finally, Toys "R" Us placed its first order for $36,000 worth of books.

To establish the company's credibility, the Hudsons placed a full-page ad in *Publishers's Weekly* and also ran ads in the *School Library Journal*, the *New York Times Book Review*, and other publications. The ads were expensive, but they familiarized the buyers with the Just Us Books name, making it easier for the company to get into the door.

The Hudsons eventually signed up with a distributor, which will help the firm get its books into other chains, too.

Is a warehouse club or mass merchandiser for you? If the fit is right, absolutely—the profit potential is enormous, but tread carefully.

Here is a list of several wholesale clubs, mass merchandisers, distributors and wholesalers.

- Advanced Marketing Services, Tammie Johnson, Purchasing Assistant, 5880 Oberlin Drive, #400, San Diego CA 92121; (619) 457-2500; Fax: (619) 450-3581. A wholesaler for mass merchandisers and warehouse buying clubs. They also have a division that serves office products warehouses.

- Barnes & Noble Distributorship (formerly Supermarket Book Distributors), 100 Middlesex Center Blvd., Jamesburg, NJ 08831; (908)

656-2000; Fax: (908) 656-2680. A book distributor to warehouse clubs.

- B.J.'s Wholesale Club, Inc., Lynne Gariepy (children's books), Todd Lilienfield (all others), 1 Mercer Rd., Natick, MA 01760, (508) 651-7400. Fax (508) 651-6251. Operates 81 clubs along the coast from Maine to Florida.

- Kmart Stores, Doug Miller, Book Buyer, 3100 West Big Beaver, Troy, MI 48084, (810) 643-1000. A mass merchandiser with 2,073 Kmart stores nationally and 92 Super Ks. Buys books through Handleman National Book Distributors.

- Levy Home Entertainment, 4201 Raymond Dr., Hillside, IL 60162-1786; (708) 547-4400; Fax: (708) 547-4503. The company employs five buyers—call to check the appropriate buyer's name. Levy is one of the country's largest distributors; it services discount stores, including Kmart, Target, Venture, Payless, Thrifty and grocery store chains.

- Handleman National Book Distributors, Betsy Politi, Sales & Marketing Director or Mary Schuetz, Book Buyer, 500 Kirts Boulevard, Troy, MI 48084. (810) 362-4400; fax: (810) 362-5160. One of the top 10 book wholesalers in the country. Clients include: Meijer, Kmart and Sam's Club (off and on).

- Price Costco, Pennie Clark Ianniciello, Book Buyer, 999 Lake Drive, Issaquah, WA 98027-5367, (206) 313-8100; Fax: (206) 313-6718. E-mail: Pricos@halcyon.com. Price Costco also publishes a magazine, *The Price Costco Connection* (some publishers feel if you can break into the magazine with a book-related article, chances of getting into the warehouse club are greater). Anita Thompson is managing editor (206) 313-6442; David W. Fuller is editor, (206) 313-8510.

- Target Stores, Susan Masko, Book Buyer, P.O. 1392, Minneapolis, MN 55440; (612) 304-6073, ext. 6180; Fax: (612) 335-5175. With

736 discount stores, this mass merchandising chain features young adult and children's books, promotional books, paperbacks, and regional calendars.

- Toys "R" Us, Baird Little, Book Buyer, 461 From Rd., Paramus, NJ 07652; (201) 262-7800. With 680 stores, buys soft- and hard-cover children's books.

- XYZ Distributors, Amy Tuttle Mascillino, 12221 West Feerick St., Wauwatosa, WI 53222; (414) 466-6900, ext. 40, Fax: (414) 466-6855. This company is a distributor to many major warehouse clubs.

16

SCORING BIG PROFITS WITH SALES TO GIFT AND SPECIALTY STORES

Things don't turn in this world
until somebody turns them up.
JAMES A. GARFIELD

THE GIFT AND SPECIALTY STORE MARKET IS A WONDERFUL PLACE TO sell books that allows your creativity to run wild. And hopefully sales, too! Yet it's a complicated market to get into, and requires a snappy, vibrant cover and attention-grabbing title to succeed.

But guess what? Retail stores, in general, keep the books they buy, and they usually pay within thirty days. That's far better than bookstores, which can take up to three months to pay and can return all books without impunity. You also receive a 50-percent discount on the books they sell.

Consider also that there are 200,000 non-bookstore outlets in the country, ten times the number of bookstores and they sell about half a billion dollars worth of books every year.

There are other advantages to selling in non-book retail stores: Your books don't have to compete with thousands of titles as they must in a bookstore. Retailers are also willing to put out appealing counter displays or floor racks, or may display your books with other items to inspire gift packages.

Gift book sales are also a lot less reliant on your promotional abilities. They are almost invariably an impulse buy. People don't go into retail stores looking specifically for a book, said retail distributor Jim Denardo, "But once they see the book, the life that's in it, they grab it! They know! The key is getting it into stores and getting it in front of them."

Finally, retailers are less snobby about small publishers than are bookstores. If they see a cover and title that will sell, they'll choose the book over a more staid selection from a bigger house.

PREPARING YOUR BOOK

Before you attempt the specialty market, be sure your book has what it takes. This market, *more than any other*, requires an eye-catching cover, particularly for gift stores. We're talking four-color, a title in bold, colorful print, and a professional-looking illustration, graphic, or photograph. (Photographs usually work best for cookbooks, although not always.) Remember, the monster publishers like Time Life invest heavily in the cover and layout of the book's interior; these books will sit side-by-side with your books so don't lose out on the first impression.

Secondly, you'll need an irresistible come-hither title and subtitle, particularly for gift stores. Here are some you might have heard: *Nice Guys Don't Get Laid, P.S., I Love You, Random Acts of Kindness, 1,001 Ways to Be Romantic,* and *365 Days of Creative Play.*

But a great title doesn't promise an easy road. After Marcus Melton, author of *Nice Guys Don't Get Laid,* decided that the Spencer Gifts chain stores would be a perfect market for his book, he realized that persistence took on a new definition.

"I sent it to the buyer they had, and got no answer," he said. "I sent it again. I received a turn down. I kept making calls, twice, maybe three times. I did with other chains, too, but they were the ones who finally picked me up."

Chain stores like Spencer Gifts, however, do have a downside. They pay only 25 percent to 30 percent of the retail price. For its 5,000-book buy, Spencer's also asked Melton to provide 500 point-of-purchase displays (P.O.P.s), which cost $2 apiece. The margin of profit was slim, Melton admitted, "But I shipped it, it was gone, I got a check, and it was over. There were no returns," Melton said.

Melton also sold the book to a distributor, Pipe Dream, which specializes in distributing off-color products to joke shops and the like.

Sometimes the books in your line may be perfect for the gift market if only it had a makeover with a new cover, title, package—or all three. Consider the possibilities. A children's book on birds could come packaged with eggs that hatch when immersed in water. A children's camping guide with a jackknife would make a perfect gift for a favorite niece or nephew.

The "Do It" series became a retail marketing hit partly due to the books' easily portable nature, reported a 1995 *Inc.* article. The gardening book, for example, is bound together by a single rivet much like paint-sample cards. Published by Chronicle Books, it was picked up by Crate & Barrel stores, numerous gift stores, and bookstores. Fueling the good publicity were two design awards and a mention in *U.S. News & World Report.* Company sales climbed to nearly $800,000, according to the *Inc.* article.

WHAT IS A SPECIALTY STORE?

Specialty stores reflect the huge range of human interests and endeavors. Besides the 150,000 gift stores in the country, there are tens of thousands of specialty retail stores: gourmet shops, restaurants, museum shops, nature stores, hospital shops, video stores, grocery stores, drugstores, toy stores, department stores, camera stores, fishing stores, sports shops, bike stores, gyms, stationery stores, lodges, fruit markets, T-shirt shops, pottery shops, home improvement stores, hardware stores, pet stores, record stores, tattoo parlors, even athletic shoe stores. And that's just the beginning.

This huge range means that you must think carefully of how to match your book's audience with a store's clientele.

As you think of the specialty-store market, first analyze your audience. What kind of money do they make? Are they male or female, professional or blue collar, where do they go to shop for products that are related to your book?

After you pinpoint the kind of stores they would visit, go visit the stores yourself. Would your book fit in? Look at the prices and the character of books in the store? Which ones sell, which ones fail? Does your book fit the "feel" of the store. You'll notice gift stores, in particular, have a definite attitude. Romantic, whimsical, outrageous, Bohemian, sexual, etc. Would your book fit in? Look at the prices and the character of books in the store.

Strike up a conversation with the owner—maybe even set up a lunch appointment to ask questions. Who do they buy their books from? How do they choose which books to carry? What kind of point-of-purchase displays work best? What are the worst kind of book covers/displays? How long do they keep a book around? Which sales reps/wholesalers/distributors do they use most often as it relates to books or products that complement your books? Are there any to avoid? What discount do they pay for books? Which books succeed and which fail? What price should a book never exceed? Are there any pricing strategies that they'd recommend (like slapping a 20-percent discount sticker on each book)? Is there a demand for your kind of book. What kind of books sell best?

Show retailers your book if it's been produced or, if not, a rough sketch of the book cover, title, and table of contents. What do they think about it? If you feel there's a lot of excitement about your book, proceed to the next step: researching the market.

RESEARCH, RESEARCH, RESEARCH

After identifying your market, your next job is to familiarize yourself with how the market works. To do this, read both trade magazines and consumer magazines.

In the gift-store market, for example, trade magazines *Giftware News* and *Jewelry & Gem Business* will tell you how the distribution works in the market, how the retailers learn about new products, what discounts they pay, new trends, and details on upcoming trade shows.

Consumer magazines are the kind that you'll find in bookstores or drugstores. These magazines will tip you off to trends and teach you the buzzwords of each market.

Both trade and consumer magazines will give you a feel for what's hot in a given retail area and what's yesterday's news. To find out the names of magazines, check out the *Gale Directory of Publications* or the *Standard Directory of Publications*. They both list magazines by subject interest, including the magazine's address and phone number. You can usually order a sample magazine for a couple of dollars.

DISTRIBUTION

Many specialty book distributors will provide distribution to a given non-bookstore retail outlet. Dot Gibson Distributors, for example, distributes cookbooks to cooking stores, gift stores and gourmet shops. Sourcebooks (a division of LPC Group) services gift stores.

As in other industries, you will find that you must work within the existing distribution system. Major non-book distributors and wholesalers, for example, serve the toy and drugstore market. You can find out exactly how the distribution works by going to trade shows, reading trade magazines, and asking the store personnel.

HOW SALES REPS WORK

Before describing a sales representative's function, be aware that a gift sales rep likes to write big orders and *usually* won't take on just one or two books from a given publisher. If you can persuade a rep, however, that the fit is exceptionally good between your book and the rep's line or that you plan on marketing the book heavily in the rep's territory, the sales rep may make an exception.

Sales reps visit stores within a given territory and often maintain a permanent booth at a state or regional gift showroom. A sales rep presents a line of products to a given store and takes the order; you, as the publisher, are responsible for warehousing, shipping, and invoicing. Many publishers will contract with a fulfillment house for this service rather than trying to do it on their own.

A sales rep's standard commission is 10 percent to 20 percent of net for retailers (independent sales reps take less; reps belonging to a national group take the high end). For a given book, for example, a retailer will pay a 50-percent discount (referred to as keystone) of the retail price. Let's say your book costs $10. The retailer will pay you $5 for each book. The sales rep will charge you $1 (20 percent of $5) for each book sold. That leaves you with $4 per book, or 40 percent of the retail price.

Reps expect to get paid within 30 to 90 days of the close of the month of when in which books are shipped. They also require exclusivity. That means, if a book is sold in their agreed-upon territory—even if it's sold by you—they will still get a commission.

Sales reps generally choose books that complement the rest of their line of gifts. Sales rep Pam Ellstrom, who services the state of Michigan, said she will carry only books that fit in with her existing lines of gourmet foods, fragrances, and lighthouse gift items (in fact, she carries six different lighthouse books).

"I get the book lines because the publishers know I'm in the stores everywhere. That's how I sell cookbooks. I have a better chance of getting in the door if I have other items to sell than just cookbooks," she said.

If you choose sales reps to distribute your book, there are two ways to go: either with a network of independent sales reps or with a regional or national organization of sales reps.

Which is best for you?

If your book has national appeal, consider going with a national organization of reps. The obvious advantage is you won't have to patch together a national sales force yourself. You'll have one central point for sales information and you'll write only one commission check each month. The drawback is a) you can't talk to the individual reps and b) you lose significant control. There's nothing you can do if they have weak reps in specific territories because of the exclusivity agreement under which they operate.

Finding and contracting with independent sales reps is obviously messier, but it gives you much greater control.

Yet how do you put together an effective sales force? You can find a good sales rep by calling or visiting the stores you've targeted. Ask the owner for the name of the rep who sells their best-selling gift books in the price range of your book. Even better, ask for the sales rep's name who sells merchandise related to your book. Query as to the sales rep's reputation. When you keep hearing the same name pop up for a specific geographic area, you'll have your candidate.

To get the names of stores to call in a given geographic area, call up the marketing office of a trade show and ask for their mailing list of the most recent show (these lists are often divided by size, location, and type of shop), suggests publisher Diane Pfeifer in her PMA Newsletter column, *Gift Rap*.

You could also ask other publishers who have published gift-market type books, tactfully of course, for their list of sales reps. This is a big favor, so you'll want to establish a relationship first, Pfeifer suggests.

Another common way to find a sales rep is to place an ad in trade gift magazines describing your book and its potential market. Also, look for ads subtitled, "Lines Wanted."

When you're ready to sign up a sales rep, ask them about the territory they reach, the discounts they pay, the trade magazines they read, and what criteria they use for books. Ask to see their catalog, how often they publish it, what are their order quantities, the hottest times for book sales, and their lead times for catalog listings and distribution. Also, ask about the publisher's responsibilities.

Once you decide on a rep, make sure you sign an agreement that specifies their responsibilities, territory, commission, and markets.

How distributors work

Book distributors typically use a contingent of sales reps across the country to sell your books. They not only write orders for your book, but handle all shipping, billing, and collections.

Typically, distributors send out seasonal catalogs to retail buyers. They may display their wares at major gift shows, a permanent showroom, use road reps and/or promote your book to the media. Each distributor's terms vary—there really is no industry standard. Research carefully the different terms each offers (ask about more favorable discounts depending on volume). Discounts may vary from 55 percent to 68 percent. A distributor may also charge for freight and various fees, such as putting your book in their catalog.

How do you find a distributor that is right for you? Look at the books in their catalogs that best match your line. Sourcebooks, for example, chooses books that "lighten up lives," whether it's humor, inspirational, or spiritual, according to Michael Ritter, sales manager.

"We don't want a collection of quotes or sayings, but books that have a little more meat to them, where you can spend a lot of time reading them, but you don't have to read them cover to cover," said Ritter, adding that the firm rejects about 90 percent of the book pitches it receives.

Dot Gibson, president of Dot Gibson Distributors, looks for books with an excellent cover, name, layout, quality of printing, and, of course, good recipes.

Gibson said her firm generally buys about 100 books at a time and immediately pays the publisher. Other gift book distributors don't pay the publisher until after the books are sold. Your contract should spell out the timing of payment, shipping turnaround times, discounts, book return credits, etc.

A distributor or sales rep may ask for a point-of-purchase display to enhance sales. Many publishers have found that a sturdy, highly visual display is a good investment and will pay off in sales. If possible, put four books on a display instead of one because you'll get four times the opportunity to make a sale.

DISTRIBUTOR OR SALES REP? WHICH SHOULD YOU USE?

If you are a one- or two-book publisher, a national distributor may be your only choice because sales reps typically won't take you on.

The advantage of a national distributor is simplicity. A distributor's services are comprehensive. When you sell a distributor a batch of books, you're done with it. When a sales rep takes the orders, you still have to deal with shipping, billing, and collections for multiple locations.

Publishers like Diane Pfeifer of Strawberry Patch strongly prefer sales reps because these reps pick and choose their product line, as opposed to distributor reps, who have products "imposed" upon them.

Ultimately, circumstances may dictate your decision. Your targeted specialty stores may only use a particular distributor or may rely entirely on sales reps. Go with it. Design your displays to fit with whatever the sales rep or distributor wants.

TRADE SHOWS

There is no better place to get acquainted with the movers and shakers of the industry than trade shows. You'll meet people from every area of involvement: media, suppliers, distributors, manufacturers, and those hard-to-get-to buyers. Ask for business cards (to use later as a mailing list) and solicit comments about your books. You may want to get feedback from distributors about book ideas (they may offer to take it on!).

You'll make a zillion contacts in the space of a few hours—contacts to immediately pursue when you return home. Seminars at the trade shows can also be of immense help. You'll get free advice and sometimes direct help with a given problem.

A trade show is a spectacular place to check out the lines of sales rep groups or distributors to find a good fit between your books and their products. Or they may check out your book line and approach you! This is also a good place to talk to store owners and ask for their recommendations for a rep.

If your books are regional or niche, consider displaying your books at smaller trade shows. If your line has national appeal, choose the larger shows.

In general, winter and summer shows are best. In winter, shops are looking for resort, souvenir and catalog products. In summer they're shopping for the holidays. You'll get weaker results in fall and spring shows.

Before committing to a display booth, call the show office and ask for the names and phone numbers of previous exhibitors. Call a few of them and ask for their results, and for any tips for a successful day.

OTHER POINTERS

Pfeifer and other publishers suggest these tried-and-true strategies:

- Send a direct mail piece to wholesale gift shops. A good mailing list is pivotal; you may want to get together with other publishers to share names. The best list would include only names of vendors who have consistently responded to mailings.

- When you design the display that will hold the books (six to 12 are good numbers), make sure you print on the back of the display the following: "To re-order NAME OF BOOK, call (800) XXX-XXXX."

- If you want to test out a countertop display in specific stores without investing in a permanent book display, Traverse Bay Display Co. sells white corrugated countertop displays for books. They'll send you a sample display and shipping carton for the cost of freight, around $4.50. Call (800) 240-9802. (Special order styles and custom designs are also available.)

• Think about how your book could tie in with an existing product. Have you published a book on potty training? Call up a potty chair manufacturer and propose pairing your products. Your idea will be far better accepted if you present prototype art for the packaging.

• Strongly consider joining trade or professional associations, such as the Hobby Industry Association or the Southwestern Craft & Hobby Association. These associations are clearinghouses for news on seminars, trade shows, meetings, and networking meetings. They sometimes offer services, too, such as market research and marketing.

• If your book line is too small to get entrance into a trade show, offer to rep a friend's gift line.

FOR DATES OF MAJOR GIFT SHOWS, CALL:

Atlanta: (404) 220-3000
Chicago: (312) 527-4141
Dallas: (214) 655-6100
Los Angeles: (213) 749-7911
New York: (212) 686-1203
San Francisco: (415) 861-7733

GIFT BOOK DISTRIBUTORS

BestSeller Gift Books
4952 N. Dixie Highway
Ft. Lauderdale, FL
(800) 227-6420
(general gift)

Cogan Books (wholesaler, also)
15020 Desman Road
La Mirada, CA 90638
(800) 733-3630
(cookbooks, childrens' books, and decorating books)

Dot Gibson Distributors
161 Knight Avenue Circle
Waycross, GA 31502
(912) 285-2848
(cookbooks, some childrens' books)

Royal Publications
790 W. Tennessee Ave.
Denver, CO 80223
(303) 778-8383
(sells to health food stores, sporting goods shops, and pharmacies)

Southwest Cookbooks
P.O. Box 707
Bonham, TX 75418
(903) 583-8898
(cookbooks, journals, and blank recipe books)

Sourcebooks
121 North Washington
Naperville, IL 60540
(708) 961-3900
(gift books, business and trade books)
Source: *Gift Rap* by Diane Pfeifer, used with her permission.

GIFT MAGAZINES

Gift Basket Review
1205 W. Forsyth Street
Jacksonville, FL 32204
(904) 634-1902

Giftware News
112 Androssan Court
Deptford, NJ 08096
(609) 227-0798

Gift & Stationery Business
51 Madison Avenue
New York, NY 10010
(212) 714-1300

Gift & Decorative Accessories
51 Madison Avenue
New York, NY 10010
(212) 689-4411

17.

THE ART OF GETTING YOUR BOOKS INTO CATALOGS

Boldness in business is the first, second, and third thing.
THOMAS FULLER

MOST PUBLISHERS ORIGINALLY DECIDE TO PURSUE CATALOG SALES NOT only to tap a new market, but to sell books without the bookstore-type headaches of heavy returns and long, drawn-out payments.

Catalog sales offer big advantages over retail sales. Most catalogs pay within 30 days of receiving your invoice, and almost always buy on a non-returnable basis. And independent publishers have just as much chance of breaking into the catalog market as do the New York publishing firms.

Most publishers discover there are a couple of fall-out benefits. First, a book receives wonderful exposure in catalogs, particularly prestigious catalogs like Crate & Barrel. That exposure most often leads to additional sales in other outlets, such as gift store or bookstore chains, according to John Storey, founder of Storey Communications in Pownal, Vermont.

"When Crate & Barrel picks you up, it gives the book unbelievable publicity," he said. "It's like a rising tide that other outlets want to get on."

Second, catalog sales allow you to glean valuable marketing data for free. If a particular book does well in a catalog, you can learn exactly what kind of people will buy your book. (Conversely, if it does poorly, you'll know what kind of people won't buy your book.)

"Basically, the catalog will tell you precisely the audience that it mails to and helps you pinpoint your own audience," Storey said. "This information is just as important as the sales you'll get."

So how to get your book into the pages of a catalog? Your strategy will require a mix of marketing savvy and hard work. The two keys: extensive research at the front-end and highly persuasive and persistent query letters.

GET IN ON THE GROWING MARKET

Before we get into the specifics of selling to catalogs, here are some facts that ought to help in your market planning (Source: Direct Marketing Association).

- Businesses make up a surprising portion of catalog sales. In 1995, 38 percent of catalog sales were to businesses, while the rest—62 percent—were to consumers.

- If you fear that most people throw away their catalogs, you might be surprised to learn that more than 83 percent of Americans open, read, look at, or set aside for later reading the catalogs received in the mail.

- An estimated 13.2 billion catalogs were mailed to consumers and businesses in 1995.

- The average household receives 1.7 catalogs per week and 1.7 direct-mail pieces per day of delivery. Active mail order buyers, however, might receive more than three times this amount.

- Catalog sales have shown consistent, healthy gains each year since 1983 and continue to do so. From 1994 to 1995, the revenue of catalog companies grew by 7 percent, from $65.3 billion to $69.9 billion.

- Clothing accounts for the greatest proportion of merchandise purchased from home. Books rank third, with 28.8 million Americans ordering books by mail.

◆ According to a survey from the research firm of Deloitte & Touche, most catalog shoppers are married women, college-educated, homeowners in a dual-income household, with one or two children, earning salaries of $30,000 to $99,000, and they shop more often than other traditional retail shoppers.

SUCCESS STORIES

Getting into the right catalog at the right time can translate into thousands of book sales, even for a book that you might consider a has-been. If a catalog does well with your book, it will probably keep placing orders year after year.

John Storey tells of the book, *Let it Rot*, a book on composting that was published about 15 years ago with satisfactory sales of about 35,000.

"The book did well, but back then it appealed mostly to the hardcore country crowd," Storey said. "Since then, landfills have closed and the people in Birmingham, Michigan, don't know what to do with their grass clippings. The book wasn't doing much—selling about 50 a month—so we pitched it to *Plow and Hearth* and *Garden Supply Co.* We've sold 100,000 copies since then. It gained a whole new life."

To convince the two catalogs that composting was indeed a new trend among suburbanites, Storey enclosed a *New York Times Sunday Magazine* feature on composting.

In one unusual success story, a catalog was responsible for the creation of a book. A June 23, 1996, *Parade Magazine* article reported on a mail-order company, Sounds True, that specializes in personal and spiritual development audiotapes.

One of its early audiotapes was recorded by Claris Pinkola Estes. After the tape came out, a publisher asked Estes to write her ideas in book form. The result? The best-selling *Women Who Run with the Wolves*.

Here's an example of how a creative entrepreneur used catalogs to achieve her dual mission of selling books and encouraging girls to read. Pleasant T. Rowland founded her own mail-order company, Pleasant Company, to sell the American Girls Collection of books, dolls, and accessories. Each historically accurate doll comes with a book that traces the life of a 9-year-old heroine. Each of the five series of books depicts a different era in American history; the books end with a nonfiction account of what life was really like.

Mrs. Rowland believes that direct marketing has been the best way to achieve her goal of fostering a love for reading while saving money on mass-media advertising.

TAKING AIM AT YOUR MARKET

The first thing every publisher must do is to study catalogs and determine which ones best fit a specific book. This isn't as easy as it sounds. There are about 10,000 catalogs in this country and that doesn't even include the Internet.

There are catalogs specializing in honey, aquariums, cats, supplies for nurses, weird scientific inventions, ethnic crafts and time-saving books especially for women. There's even a catalog for single women that offers eligible bachelors!

Catalogs take specialization to the ultimate degree. That means you need to figure out exactly what kind of people would buy your book. Draw up a profile: How much money do they earn, what is their lifestyle, interests? Where do they live? What kind of catalogs do they favor? Say your book is on financial scholarships for mature students. Your job is to find a catalog for older adults who are seeking a career change, live in a college town, and have purchased by mail in the last six months.

If you decide to take the plunge and publish your own catalog, call a list broker. A firm called Resi-Data Marketing, Inc., in Hillsdale, New Jersey, for example, can sell you names that fit an ultra-specific profile, drawing on its database of more than 100 million names sorted by age, income, new births, even types of mortgages they've taken out.

When choosing a catalog, look not only for a product fit, but also an image fit: Does it use color? One-color catalogs look chintzy. Other criteria: Does the catalog have a toll-free 800 number, enough phone lines to handle orders, and the ability to accept credit cards? Does its overall image match your book?

Sometimes you must agree to an exclusive distribution agreement meaning that you won't be allowed to advertise your product in any other catalog for a set period of time, such as two years. Avoid these kind of agreements, if possible, unless the catalog can guarantee a purchase of at least 5,000 books.

Publisher Claire Kirch of the publishing firm Spinsters Ink., in San Francisco, likens finding the right catalog for the book to finding a job.

"If you fit the job description, you're hired! I always look at the catalog to make sure our books are right for it," she said, adding that the book, *Mother Journeys*—a collection of essays—has done very well in women's catalogs.

Once you've found the right catalog, you'll need to contact the person who chooses the merchandise and write to them. You can usually get the contact name, title, and catalog address by simply calling the catalog's 800 number and asking, said Rebecca Austin, co-owner of Austin and Nelson, book publisher reps.

If you feel that you'd like some support in choosing and contacting the different catalog companies, consultants like Austin are willing to do the legwork.

Explains Austin: "We do basically the same thing a publisher has to do except we have people whom we've been working with for a long time (such as *Signal*, *Wireless* catalog). We know what they're looking for and we can target a book better."

You may also want to invest in one of the following catalog directories:

- *The Catalog of Catalogs*: Woodbine House, 5615 Fishers Lane, Rockville, MD 20852. Price is $22.95. Lists consumer catalogs, address, and phone number. Organized by subject. Phone: (800) 843-7323 or (301) 468-8800.

- *The Directory of Mail Order Catalogs*: Lists about 7,300 catalogs. Price is $135. Gives names of the buyer and executives, the size of catalog, how often it goes out, the number of pages, and the business address and business phone of each catalog. Phone: (203) 435-0868 or (800) 562-2139; Fax: (203) 435-0867.

- *Mail Order Business Directory*: B. Klein Publications, P.O. Box 8503, Coral Springs, FL 33075-8503. Price is $75 plus $3 shipping. Lists

10,000 catalogs and mail order firms. Phone: (305) 752-1708; Fax: (305) 752-2547.

- *National Directory of Catalogs*: Oxbridge Communications, 150 Fifth Avenue, Suite 302, New York, NY 10011-4311. Price is $345. Includes a listing of more than 8,000 U.S. and Canadian catalogs, phone numbers, brief product descriptions, contact names (product buyers and company owners), how much they charge to rent the mailing list, and if they offer advertising in their catalog (not many catalogs do this). Phone: (800) 955-0231 or (212) 741-0231; Fax: (212) 633-2938.

- *The Wholesale by Mail Catalog*: HarperCollins Publishers, 1000 Keystone Industrial Park, Scranton, PA 18512. Price is $17. Five hundred sources of wholesale or discounted products, including many catalogs that feature books.

Don't forget the local library in your research. Order issues of *Catalog Age*, *DM News*, *The Catalog Marketer*, and *Non-Store Marketing Report*. These magazines feature articles on catalog concerns, trends and issues.

Another idea: If you have written a book on a particular subject, then get your name on a mailing list so you can receive the related catalogs. Written a book about children? Subscribe to the parenting-type magazines or buy a children's book by mail and soon catalogs will flood your home.

LEAD TIMES

Just like everything else in the book industry, catalogs have extremely long lead times. Catalog buyers typically begin looking at Christmas products, for example, right after the holidays wrap up and make their decision in February, March and April. Generally, a catalog-buying committee will finalize its product selection about nine to 10 months before the catalog comes out. They may ask you to ship inventory five months before the publication date. Try to find out when the selection committee meets and time your query letter to arrive a few weeks beforehand.

GETTING IN TOUCH

Once you find a catalog that fits your book, you'll need to write a query letter (using the buyer's name and title) that's accompanied by a flyer about your book. The biggest mistake publishers make, Storey said, is simply shipping off their catalog of books with a cover letter and expecting the buyer to thumb through it and pick out a few books. It isn't going to happen. The catalog will get tossed.

Essentially, you, the publisher, need to do the thinking for the buyer. Explain in your letter exactly why your book fits in with their line of merchandise (citing specific examples of products or books in their existing line that relate to your book) and why a consumer needs it. This is where your research comes in. Storey, for example, wanted to place a book in Crate & Barrel's catalog. As part of his research, he visited the Crate & Barrel retail store in Chicago and spent enough time there to get a feel for its style.

"We decided to propose a book called *Picnic*—a simple cookbook nicely done," he said. "When we made our proposal, we gave them a very specific idea that they could plug into: merchandise the book along with a picnic basket."

Crate & Barrel accepted *Picnic*, marketed it as Storey suggested, and sold more than 75,000 copies.

Mention in your letter if your book has any movie interest, audio rights, or foreign rights sales interest—anything that shows other people think it's an invaluable book to own. Include feature stories on the books, great reviews, and any articles, particularly those in special-interest magazines that show the book appeals to the catalog's specific audience.

Along with your query letter, send a flyer with general introductory information: the title, retail price, a picture of the cover, the book size, number of illustrations, number of pages, the ISBN, and wonderful things people have said about your book. Do *not* send a book, at least not initially. It will likely get tossed. If your budget is big, however, send a separate photo of your book or the book cover itself.

Stella Otto, who publishes a series of backyard gardening books, conveys her book information in a clever promotional piece that she gets printed at the same time her books are produced: on one side is the cover, on the other are the table of contents, the date the book was printed, and various promotional and review blurbs. With this, she mails a flyer with comprehensive factual information.

Once you send a query, follow up with a phone call and ask if the buyer has any question or requires additional information. If the catalog buyer shows interest, be prepared to send a book or two plus a fact sheet that includes: title, retail price, shipping weight, your discount schedule, order address, order phone number, and the number of books held in stock. This last piece of information is to reassure them that you'll be able to fill orders. You may want to add a notice that orders in excess of 5,000 books (or whatever) require a four-week notice.

If they reject your book, try again and keep trying. Update your query letters with any new publicity or good news about the book or news clips that show the topic is now hot among the buying public.

DISCOUNTS

For the catalog business, you'll have to make up a discount schedule based on quantity ordered. Legally, you cannot give one catalog a 70-percent discount for 5,000 books and a 50-percent discount to another. You must be consistent based on the quantity ordered.

You can base the schedule on the number of gross books ordered (one gross equals 144) because catalogs typically order that way, or by the number of cartons of books packaged. Most publishers establish a range of a 50-percent discount for a dozen books up to 65 percent for 10,000 books or more.

A word of caution: Make it clear that the higher discount is for one order only—not orders given over six months. Some publishers, to preclude haggling, just establish a standard 50-percent discount with a footnote: for quantities larger than 500, please call.

You'll find that some catalogs try to impose their own terms on the publisher, asking for discounts of up to 80 percent. Don't consider it because you won't make money. If their terms are only slightly different than yours, go with them. Otherwise, stick to your discount schedule. If you give one catalog a 70-percent discount for 10,000 books, you'll have to give it to everybody.

Remember that catalogs are not lured into buying books by an offer of a deep discount, but rather by the idea that the book is a "hidden gem" that will ring up thousands of sales, Storey said.

Still, Storey Communications sometimes offers catalogs financial incentives such as free freight or a special discount for high-volume purchases.

GETTING EXPOSURE AT TRADE SHOWS

A wonderful way to get noticed by catalogs is to attend trade shows that exhibit products related to your book. Each market has its own trade shows and buyers are always looking for new items.

Amerishop, for example, a full-service merchandising company that publishes an in-flight catalog, finds many of its 66,000 products at trade shows.

First, find the catalogs that match the personality of specific books you want to place. Then introduce yourself, your book, give them your business card, a flyer on your book and be ready to explain why you think your specific book is good for that particular catalog. When you return home, call up the people you've met, asking them if they need any more information. And send a query letter.

Here's a listing of trade shows (Source: *1,001 Ways to Market Your Book*, by John Kremer):

- Gift markets: The National Stationery Show (mid-May in New York), the New York International Gift Fair (mid-January and mid-August), the Chicago Gift Show (early February and late July), the Washington Gift Show (mid-July), the Wisconsin Gift Show (late August), the Boston Gift Show (mid-September), the Missouri Gift Show (mid-September).
- Miscellaneous: National Back-To-School Variety Merchandise Show (mid-February), the Mid-Year Variety Merchandise Show (mid-June), and the National Merchandise Show (late September). They all take place in New York.

- Toys: The American International Toy Fair (mid-February in New York) and the Atlanta Spring & Summer Toy Fair (late September).

- Crafts and hobbies: The National Craft and Hobby Expo (late October), the Craft, Model and Hobby Convention (mid-January), and the National Craft Supply Market (mid-March). Plus regional shows.

- If you want to learn more about direct marketing, attend the DMA Annual Conference (late October: the address and phone number are at the end of this chapter), the National Mail Order Merchandise Show (late March in New York), and Mail Expo (mid-September in Washington, D.C.).

- Health food markets: The Natural Foods Expo (in mid-October). Plus regional shows.

- Sporting goods: The World Sports Expo (mid-October), the National Sporting Goods Association Fall Market (mid-September), and the Mid-America Sports Market (late February).

- Housewares: The Houseworld Expo (mid-April in Chicago), the International Housewares Exposition (mid-January in Chicago), and the Mid-America Hardware Show (late February).

SHIPPING TERMS

Catalogs typically buy books in bulk since they are considered a low-end item. Typically, they ask you to ship your books months in advance. Demand with catalogs can be volatile— keep enough stock on hand and make sure your printer can turn an order around within a few weeks.

If your book is quite expensive, the catalog may ask you to drop-ship it. In that case, the catalog will notify you of an order for your book and a cancellation date if your book is not delivered in time. Typically you must fill the order immediately or within an agreed upon period of time, such as four weeks. Obviously, that means you must keep sufficient stock on hand. Expect to abide by the cataloger's shipping methods.

PAYMENT AND RETURNS

Most catalogs pay net 30 days. On the first order, it's wise to ask for a prepayment. If you don't know the catalog's financial reputation, ask them to fill out a credit form. You'll find out quickly if there's a problem.

"People won't come out and say there is a problem with this guy paying on time," said publisher Stella Otto. "But they'll be real slow to respond to you. You have to read between the lines."

It's also wise to insist on a policy of no returns. This policy forces catalogs to make wise purchasing decisions in the first place rather than to over-buy and leave you eating the returns nine months later.

CYBERSPACE CATALOGS

Predictions are that either the cable companies or phone companies (or a partnership of the two) will provide catalog shopping on a 500-channel cable system. Consumers will enjoy interactive shopping that lets them see pictures of the product, ask questions, and order with a mere click of the button.

The computer home appliance hasn't arrived yet, but the Internet and other online services have become increasingly popular places to shop, particularly among international and rural consumers. Here are some ideas on getting started now in cyberspace sales.

- On the Internet, call up one of the many search engines and plug in the words "catalog" plus the subject of your book. Visit the different websites and jot down the name and phone number of the catalog's publisher. Follow up with an e-mail query, a written query letter, and a phone call.

- CompuServe, based out of Columbus, Ohio, offers direct mailers a spot in its Electronic Mall. You can try to get your book into a catalog of your choice, or you can subscribe to CompuServe and offer your books through the service's electronic classified ads.

- You can also check out the electronic malls on your online service to determine if they accept classified ads.

- Check out the specialized online services, such as Bloomberg Financial Markets, a New York City online service that's used by brokers and investment managers around the world. Reportedly, financial books do very well on this service.

OTHER HINTS

Sometimes your book might be priced too low to justify the space it will take up in the catalog, said Charles Leocha, president of World Leisure Corporation. Leocha's books, *Getting to Know You* and *Getting to Know Kids in Your Life*, each sell for $6.95—too low to capture a catalog's interest.

"When a catalog gives space to a book, they'd like to get more money for each book sold," Leocha said. "If they have a choice between my book at $7 or someone else's at $14.95 and they could sell the same number of copies, they'll go with the more expensive book."

Leocha's solution: He intends to bundle together the two *Getting to Know You* books for a combined price of $13.90.

- The Direct Marketing Association, with more than 75 years of experience in direct mail, offers a variety of services to its 3,600 members. Even if you don't want to join, they might be able to point you to a myriad of resources. For more information write to: The Direct Marketing Association, 1120 Avenue of the Americas, New York, NY 10036-6700. Phone: (212) 768-7277.

- Todd Publications publishes a directory of companies that sell products to catalogs. The catalog is sometimes used by major catalogs looking for new products. Send a news release to: Mail Order Product Guide, 18 N. Greenbush Road, West Nyack, NY 10094. Phone: (914) 358-6213.

DIRECT MARKETING MAGAZINES

Check out these magazines for two reasons. First, to familiarize yourself with the catalog market. Secondly, you'll want to mail the magazine a press release about your book.

For a sample issue, call the following numbers or ask for them at your local library. Some of the magazines below offer free subscriptions to qualified subscribers. Be sure to ask about it.

Catalog Age, Harry Chevan, News Editor, 911 Hope Street, Six River Bend Center, P.O. Box 4949, Stamford, CT 06907-0949. Phone: (203) 358-9900; Fax: (203) 357-9014.

Direct Magazine, Dan Harrison, Managing Editor. Address and phone are same as above.

Direct Marketing, Ray Schultz, Editor. Address and phone are same as above.

DM News, Larry Jaffe, Senior Editor, Mill Hollow Corporation, 100 Avenue of the Americas, New York, NY 10013. Phone: (212) 925-7300; Fax: (212) 925-8758.

Target Marketing, Alicia Orr, Managing Editor, North American Publishing, 401 N. Broad Street, Philadelphia, PA 19108-1074. Phone: (215) 238-5300; Fax: (215) 238-5412.

18.

EXCAVATING THE GOLD MINE OF CORPORATE, ASSOCIATION AND GOVERNMENT BOOK SALES

Business? It's quite simple: it's other people's money.
ALEXANDRE DUMAS

WHEN PROCTOR & GAMBLE OFFERED A THREE-BOOK SET OF *CURIOUS George* books to spur sales of LUVS and Pampers diapers, Charmin toilet paper, and Puff's tissues, the campaign was enormously successful both for P&G and the publisher. Customers bought more than 30,000 copies at a cost of $4.99 and proof-of-purchase seals from 90,000 P&G products.

Another popular campaign was conducted by the Wendy's fast-food chain, which gave away the *I Wonder* series of books with every children's meal (*I Wonder Where Butterflies Go in Winter* and *I Wonder What the Rainforest Is*). Indeed, educational books have flourished in corporate sales, said Dick Price, Western Publishing Company's marketing manager.

His firm also customized a Christmas book for Avon; he produced a separate version for white, black, and Hispanic children and added a fold-out diorama and punch-out characters. Avon offered the books as an incentive for buyers to order from its Christmas catalog.

Freixenet USA in Sonoma, California, chose Paul Dickson's book, *Toasts* (a book that suggests celebratory toasts, grouped by occasion), for a two-bottle champagne gift set. The publisher, Random House, agreed to skinny down the 250-page tome to a 64-page soft-cover book, retitle it *The Freixenet Book of Toasts and Graces*, and change the color covers in order to coordinate with the black and gold Freixenet champagne label.

These examples, called out by writer Regina Eisman, in her 1993 article for *Incentive* magazine, prove that the corporate market can be truly lucrative for the aggressive and creative publisher.

"The list of uses for books goes on and on," Eisman wrote. "A fitness-products company can use an exercise book or low-fat cookbook as a premium. A department or specialty store can give away a wedding-planning guide at a bridal fair. A camera sweepstakes can be enhanced with a book on how to take better photographs."

The corporate incentive market is huge—estimates range around $20 billion. Books capture an estimated 6 percent or $1.5 billion of the market. And once a corporation buys your books, it *keeps* your books. For small orders of up to 5,000, corporations generally take a respectable discount of 50-55 percent. As the size of order goes up, the profit per book goes down. For large orders of 20,000 to 25,000, for example, a corporation may take up to a 70-percent discount or pay a dollar or two above printing cost. Yet compared to a national distributor, which has the privilege of returning any or all books without penalty, it's still a good deal. Corporations also pay a lot quicker than book distributors.

The corporate market has untold uses for buying books. A premium, for those unfamiliar with the jargon, is offered as a prize, bonus, award or reward that's given to induce someone to do something, whether it's to buy a product, sell more products, subscribe to a magazine, sign up for a loan, or enter a competition.

Sometimes a corporation gives away gifts for the public relations value. Gifts may go to an employee or a vendor at Christmas time or to celebrate an anniversary or as a thank-you for a loyal client. Every time recipients look at the book, it's hoped, they will think fondly of the company.

Corporations also offer "self-liquidators." That means the company charges the recipients a certain fee, which, in turn, covers their investment.

Cereal companies do this often, offering items for a very low price plus two proof-of-purchase seals.

Corporations have bought a huge range of nonfiction books as premiums, but even fiction titles have enjoyed success. When Paddington Corp. promoted its Amaretto di Saronno liquor in summer, 1992, with a "Summer Midnight Parties" theme, it gave away Sidney Sheldon's *Memories of Midnight* to customers who ordered the drink, Eisman wrote.

The most common use of book incentives right now: tying a travel guide into vacation packages, said *Incentive* editor Jennifer Juergens.

A Mexican cookbook, for example, was used to promote an employee incentive trip to Cancun. The cover detailed the trip's highlights, whetting the employee's appetite not only for Mexican food, but for a delicious vacation.

Books are a chosen premium for many corporations because they're inexpensive to buy, easy to ship, and have a high perceived value because they educate and entertain; a book enriches the life of a person who receives it, making it a much better gift than a T-shirt tucked away in a drawer. People typically keep books around a long time, so they stay as an eternal reminder of a special corporate program, event, competition or trip.

Books are also easy to customize with a new cover, discount coupons in the back of the book, stickers, an inserted letter. They also can be easily packaged to complement the company's product.

Despite these advantages and the market potential, small publishers often fail to even think of selling to corporations or hesitate to do so because it just seems too daunting. Yet selling books to corporations is generally less labor-intensive than selling to schools and libraries.

In all honesty, selling books to corporations does involve a hefty investment of time. A publisher needs to research the various corporations, hound the corporation for a decision, and perhaps travel to the corporate site for negotiations. There have been cases, however, when a sale has taken only one phone call and a follow-up visit.

Research is pivotal when trying to target the corporation. Sometimes its obvious. If you've written a book, *Crock-Pot Recipes to Die For*, you'll want to pitch companies that sell crock pots. Books that involve text on a particular product are the easiest to sell. Some require greater creativity to dream up a connection to a corporation. Have you written a book on a famous basketball player, for example? Contact sporting goods and tennis show companies. A book on saving energy might go to an insulation firm or to an electric company trying to get customers to agree to an energy-saving device. Child-care books are frequent giveaways of parenting magazines.

To be considered by a corporation, send a copy of your book and a letter. Your letter should:

- Stress the relevance of your book to the corporation or product.

- Give proof in your letter that your book is a winner. Use sales statistics, testimonials, book reviews, etc.

- Educate the company as to the advantages of using a book as a premium: the lasting value of a book, how people will appreciate the content, the ease of customizing the book, and the simplicity of shipping.

Some have suggested thinking ahead and listing companies in the book where relevant in order to be more favorably regarded by them for a premium sale. Yet this tactic can sometimes backfire; you may inadvertently mention a loathsome competitor or end up with a chintzy looking book.

After you send your book and letter to the appropriate brand manger, make follow-up phone calls and don't give up. Be prepared to answer their objections.

Diane Pfeifer, for example, spent four years making follow-up phone calls to the brand manager at Quaker Oats about her cookbook, *Gone With the Grits*. Her task was made more difficult because the brand managers kept playing musical chairs. Finally, the effort paid off and Quaker called her with a message: they wanted to put a coupon offer for her book on 4 million boxes of grits! The company placed an order for 15,000 copies, and agreed to pay a 55-percent discount off the retail price of $9.95.

In early December, Pfeifer said that Quaker called her in a panic asking if they could pay her the $68,100 owed to her as soon as possible.

"I've been in business eight years and have *never* heard that before," Pfeifer said in a wry post to the Internet PMA Forum.

It wasn't Pfeifer's first time dealing with a corporation. She had just printed her first book, a popcorn cookbook, and visited the local office of TV Time Popcorn, owned by McCormick Spice.

"The manager there called me as soon as I walked back into my house and offered to pay $4 a book for 5,000 books. Yes, $20,000," Pfeifer said.

"I was, of course, elated, but then thought I better bring in a consultant since I was so naive about this business. As you can probably guess, she blew the whole deal, asking for the sky (spokesperson stuff, etc.). I later discovered he had $20,000 to play with, and I had walked in at the right time."

Lori Marcus of Cadillac Press in Lake Tahoe also had good luck pitching her book, *Bartending Inside-Out*. The company agreed to pay a 50-percent discount for the $14.95 book. A small sale, maybe, but it entirely paid for Marcus' first printing of 2,000 books.

Negotiation is often a big part of corporate sales. Marcus agreed to insert a premium liquor name every time a recipe called for it and to customize the cover. The company, in turn, agreed to pay for the special color and the text changes. Her negotiation illustrates a point: closely work with your printer for estimates when negotiating a deal.

Marcus considers herself a beginner, but admits she did compose a "strong, strong query letter."

"Two of the people called me while they were reading the letter. I wrote that most liquor companies give away T-shirts and gadgets. Why not give away knowledge? And that's what got them."

📖   📖   📖

Here is Lori Marcus' letter to the 10 liquor companies. Four of them responded positively:

Dear _____,

I have been bartending throughout the country for most of the past fifteen years, but have never been able to locate any books on bartending that gave me more than recipes and home bartending tips.

I could find no book that explained how to change a keg, how to cut garnishes, or how to fold a bar towel so that it looked neat on the bar; all basics to the bartending profession.

It's surprising how many bartenders consider themselves professionals, but could not tell you the difference between Scotch and bourbon, or what gives gin its flavor.

As one of those so-called "professionals," I decided to put together a book on bartending geared to novice and seasoned bartenders, bar owners, and managers. This is a book for "profession, profit, and fun"; a book for those interested in taking their service and knowledge to a professional level.

It is concise (about 120 pages, including basic recipes), interesting, and provides easy reading, touching on all aspects of the profession.

Anyone can learn the mechanics of bartending, but with the changing attitudes and laws associated with alcohol service, today's bartender must be versed on many levels of service and knowledge.

Here is a sampling of topics covered in the book:

Learning to bartend and expanding your skills; How to mix, pour, layer and serve cocktails; Cash handling—how to increase tips; Declaring tips; Beer: Types of beer, the difference between bottled and draft beer. . . .

I hope this outline gives you a feel for this book's potential. This will be a welcome addition in any bar. I've included 20 pages of basic drink recipes to insure that the book remains in view and behind the bar, not tucked away in a drawer or closet.

It was suggested that I contact you about placing subtle advertisements for your products throughout my book. Advertising that could include:

- Mention of Hennessy XO where I explain how letters and stars are used by some manufacturers when showing quality levels between products.

- The mention of Dewar's, Johnnie Walker and Cardhu where I explain about single malts and blends.

- The use of Grand Marnier in the recipes located at the back of the book.

Beyond this advertising, I would also like to explore the possibilities of Schieffelin & Somerset using the book as a promotional gift for key accounts.

Promotional items given away by liquor companies seem limited to posters, gadgets, T-shirts and mirrors. Why not give away something in keeping with the integrity of the products that you promote? Why not give them knowledge with a book that teaches about your products and stresses responsible service.

If you are interested, I would be happy to send you a copy of the book. I am presently doing graphics and pulling it together for printing with plans to publish soon.

Thank you for your time. I look forward to hearing from you soon.

📖   📖   📖

Marcus not only captured a book deal, she also was hired by Seagram's to conduct an employee seminar. She is now pitching her book to liquor distributors ("the salespeople want copies so they know what they're talking about"), hotel chains, and restaurant supply firms.

"These sales take a long, long time," Marcus said. "You have to be prepared to wait. There are so many different people they have to go through, and they'll forget about it if you let them. I must have made thousands of phone calls."

TAKING AIM

To locate a specific corporation, we suggest seeing firsthand what's out there. Get in your car and drive to a large store in a metro area to familiarize yourself with the products (you will need this information in customizing your letter to each company). Once you find the company names, you'll need to get the address and phone number. One of the best resources is *Brands and Their Companies, A Gale Trade Names Directory*, published by Gale Research. Other standard references of corporations are *Moody's Indexing Service* and *Standard & Poors*. To find corporations organized by product (liquor, for example), consult the *1997 Directory of Premium, Incentive & Travel BuyersTM*, which lists 12,000 corporations and 19,000 premium and incentive buyers with their contact information. It provides an index that lists companies by the type of product or service they sell. It's available in most libraries. If you're heavy into corporate sales and want your own copy, it costs $259.95; to order, call (800) 521-8110, ext. 1.

Two sources to learn more about companies. Check out the Internet site, http: www.companiesonline.com to search for a specific company (lists 75,000 with basic information). Even better, go to The Thomas Register of American Manufacturers (http://www.thomasregister.com) or check out the book by the same name. After registering your company—a fairly quick process—you can initiate a search by selecting a key word or company name. The Thomas Register, with 155,000 companies, has the most comprehensive database that we could find on the Internet.

As you do your research, seek out specific information on the corporation with the question: Why would my product appeal to this organization? Does the product and your book appeal to the same kind of target audience (upscale, downscale, relevant to the book's subject matter)? Your final step is to call the company to identify the contact name—usually the marketing manager or brand manager. Besides helping you identify exactly who should receive your package, a phone call affords you the opportunity to introduce yourself and your book, and sets up the expectation for its arrival. About seven business days after shipping, make a follow-up call.

TIPS

- Ask for half the payment prior to getting the book printed, and the remainder within 30 days of delivery.
- When a corporation asks for more information, be prepared to make a good impression. Chat with the marketing manager and find out what they might have in mind. Then, professionally prepare a customized mock-up and deliver pronto!
- Visit trade shows and conventions to meet personally with potential corporate buyers. For a directory of trade shows, go to a metro library and consult *Trade Shows Worldwide*, published by Gale Research. If that's impossible, call a few companies and ask the marketing secretary for the major trade shows.
- Speaking of trade shows, go to those which are geared for incentive/premium buyers. The largest, by far, is called the Motivation Show, an annual event attended by about 25,000 people each year. It's held at the McCormick Center in Chicago alternately in September and October. Anyone is welcome and there's no fee for entry if you register ahead of time. For more information, call (630) 850-7779.
- Contact the Incentive Manufacturers Representatives Association (IMRA), Inc. This association is made up of manufacturers and sales

reps in the incentive industry. It's possible that a sales rep (who un-
doubtedly has more contacts than most publishers) may be willing
to pick up your book, and sell it to a corporation for a commission of
5 percent to 10 percent. To find the sales reps' names in your state,
call (630) 369-3466, and IMRA will fax you the names for free. Or
consider buying the IMRA Incentive Manager's Handbook, which
includes names of sales reps in the country and a discussion of all
aspects of incentive sales, such as sales support materials and model
contracts.

• Consider hiring a consultant who specializes in premium/incentive
  sales. The country's best known consultant is Cliff Martin of Interpub.
  His address is 2945 Pearl St., Eugene, OR 97405; Telephone (541)
  342-6901; e-mail: cliffmar@efn.org. Martin has published several how-
  to reports on this topic, including Premium and Special Sales. He
  plans to publish a comprehensive book about corporate sales in 1997.

• One way to sell to corporations is through trainers who speak to
  corporate groups on a regular basis. Many of these trainers sell books
  and tapes related to their topic, including, of course, books they themselves have authored. You can ask a speaker to sell your book on their
  table and split the profits. How do you find such a speaker? Check
  out the National Speakers Association's listing of its 3,800 speakers
  on the Internet—http://www.nsaspeaker.org. You can search names
  by topic, key word, last name, geographical location, or alphabeti-
  cally, Or call the NSA at (602) 968-2552 and order a printed list for
  $25 plus shipping and handling.

INCENTIVE TRADE JOURNALS

If you believe your book is a natural for a company incentive product, consider
advertising in these following magazines aimed at the incentive market:

Potentials in Marketing Magazine
50 South Ninth St.
Minneapolis, MN 55402
(612) 333-0471
Publishes a "New Product" section that features color photos and descriptions of new
incentive product ideas. Products are featured at no charge, but the competition is stiff.
Companies can ask for more product information by filling out a card. The magazine will
send you a computer printout with the names and contact information of the requesters.

Incentive
355 Park Ave. South
New York, NY 10010
(212) 592-6200
Includes a section, "Eye on Merchandise," which features new incentive product ideas (magazine requires a color slide of the product). If your book is selected, there's no charge; the magazine will print a catchy description and include the company's contact phone number.

Promo
11 Riverbend Drive, South
P.O. Box 4949
Stamford, CT 06907-0949
(203) 358-9900

ASSOCIATIONS

You can also make a bundle selling to associations, but the process is not as straightforward. Your first trip must be to the library where you'll find the *Encyclopedia of Associations,* published by Gale Research. Here you'll find a huge range of associations, the membership count, contact information, budget, and whether or not the association publishes a newsletter.

Use this information when trying to figure out your pitch to the association. In your letter, you'll need to detail how your book relates to the association's mission and philosophy. For smaller associations (memberships of less than 100,000), seek out no more than a review. Many publishers run an ad alongside the review to reinforce the review and to provide ordering information.

For advice on querying a large association, which represents a potentially huge sale, we talked to Bev Harris, one of the rare consultants in the country who specializes in these kind of sales.

"Most are nonprofit, so here's your angle: they usually publish a newsletter that they direct mail to members. Propose to them that your book will help fund-raise for them, and propose this deal: They agree to review your book in their members' newsletter, and they also include an order form for the book right in the newsletter itself. You supply the information (and mini-sales pitch) that you want on the order form. (Some publishers provide the actual artwork so they can ensure it will look good). The association gets 50 percent of the retail price (or 40 percent, or 25 percent, depending on how low you think they'll go). You get the rest. The order form charges members full price plus shipping/handling.

"You and the publisher agree which newsletter will contain the review. Usually, for accounting checks and balances, one person takes the money and the other fulfills the order. But I have set up huge deals where the association trusted me to handle both sides, and printed my address and ordering number on the form.

"This is a great way, by the way, to line up cash coming in before your printing bills hit. You can expect a 4-percent to 10-percent response rate, depending on how strong the endorsement is. If you know a person at the association, especially a bigwig, you can sandwich in a powerful endorsement to pump up response rates. One more thing: the 'membership' that many associations claim is often inflated, because the 'membership' that matters to you is the *active membership* that receives the newsletter. Many associations quote one number for 'members' and, privately, a different number for 'active members.' Usually active members are about one-third of the 'members' number.

"Arranging for a book review (and accompanying order form) in the association's membership newsletter does work. The last time I did it, the result was a $120,000 profit within 16 weeks, no cost to us, no risk."

Bev said association negotiations are a delicate art. A woman, for example, sent her this query:

"I started to write a proposal letter, but got the squirmy feeling that asking for a review in exchange for a kickback on the book was kind of unethical. Don't get me wrong, I'll do it in a heartbeat—I am just worried that the associations that I approach may be instantly turned off. Have you run into this? Or are they quite receptive? Have you ever furnished them with a review that they can edit as they see fit?"

Bev responded with the following note:

"When you have a squirmy feeling and you're trying to sell someone on an idea, listen to that squirmy feeling. Keep thinking your approach through until it 'feels' right. Here's how I make it feel right.

"First, I read everything I can get my hands on and talk to someone who's involved, to get a feel for the association. I want to know what *they* are excited about. I want to know their issues and who's who. That's the

'Abe Lincoln approach'— Abe said, 'If I had nine hours to chop down a tree, I'd spend six hours sharpening my axe.' The reason you feel squirmy is because your axe isn't sharp enough. The bigger the tree, the sharper your axe needs to be.

"Here's an example of how I set up a deal with one particular non-profit association. The book I was promoting was one by a popular columnist, and the deal that we ended up with was worth about $100,000 in publisher profits. (It was a really big tree.) First, I did an Internet search and found they had a web page. I printed off about 100 pages. They included their mission statement, the complete archive of their newsletters, and I used a highlighter as I read. Your association doesn't have a web page? Call someone there, make a dandy impression, but don't let them know you're planning a profit-making move. Express interest in the association. Ask them to fax you stuff. Devour it. Highlight all the names.

"Make an appointment with someone who's a decision-maker. If you're a writer, invent a reason to write about them (something that's in their best interests) and actually follow through and do it. That gives you the ideal reason to make an appointment with a biggie. And telephone appointments can work just fine.

"Because this particular nonprofit had 600,000 members, I invested $750 in a visit to Washington D.C., where I met with an official at the organization. I'm sure he wondered why he was spending the time with me. During that meeting I basically just asked him what was important to *him* about his nonprofit, and found out what else he was personally interested in. I said I'd like to help the nonprofit by doing something to encourage people to join, or to help in fund-raising. I asked *him* what types of things they do, because it would help me think of ideas.

"He suggested a bunch of things (that I couldn't help with). I thanked him for so many interesting ideas. I also followed up by finding a way to use the book to help him personally with a project he was working on. The ol' Zig Zigler idea: Help other people get what *they* want and then, they'll help you get what *you* want.

"Still, everything I did was just being helpful. I followed through on the small things I had promised, and three weeks later, this man called me to thank me. Timing is everything. That's when I asked him who I could

talk to about getting a book review for fund-raising. He not only gave me
the name of the president, but he called the man and told him he thought
I had a good idea. Then I called the president and, again, asked him *his*
ideas on how I could help fund-raise. I listened carefully, and then proposed the deal. He didn't ask me to, but I arranged for a slip to be added
to a mailing I was doing, inviting folks to contribute $25 toward a mem-
bership to the nonprofit. Just being genuinely nice. (And thinking, 'Maybe
next summer when we come out in trade paperback, I can repeat this deal.')

"Everything was done in person and on the telephone until the last
step, when I arranged for a simple 'Letter of Agreement' (*not* 'contract').
The result: an enthusiastic endorsement, 10,000 books at $24.95 each,
our cut 50 percent. Note that associations often don't use the bookseller's
lingo 'discount.' You start by telling them the retail price and tell them
they get such-and-such percent for each book sold.

"The idea is, you feel comfortable when you know you are helping
them. Most folks just say, 'Will you do this for me?' You start with finding
out about *them*. In today's high-tech society, we're still the same. We like
people who are nice.

"I'd want to know, before writing any letters, what the mission of the
association is, what their current 'wants' are. Try asking this question: 'If
you could wave a magic wand on behalf of your organization, what would
you ask for?' You'll be surprised at the answer. Are they trying to get more
members? Outlaw cruelty to horses? Set up a successful horse show? Expect a surprise when you ask that question.

"Taking the horse example, suppose your contact is currently stressed
about how to get more people to attend a horse show (a goofy example,
but anyway ...) You think, 'How could I help...' Well, if they'd send you
some flyers you could tuck one in each book and add them into your mailings. Surprise! You could post on some newsgroups to announce the show.
Then tell them that you did that for them.

"While you are doing all these nice things, you will probably realize
that they might be willing to put a stack of your brochures by the door at
the horse show—or even stuff programs with your order forms! By figur-
ing out how to help them, you think of new ways to help yourself! Now
you've got a contact, who turns into a friend, who helps you get that book

review, suggests other places for you to promote your book, even introduces you to contacts at new places!

"If the association is too small to invest time 'just being nice,' find smaller ways to be nice. But take the time to study up on what they're all about *before* you contact anyone, and find a reason for the contact that serves *them* more than you, and you'll find that queasy feeling disappears. All of a sudden, you've got genuine excitement."

SUBSCRIPTION NEWSLETTERS

For-profit subscription newsletters can also help you sell your book. Most of these include a "stuffer" with every issue. They insert a flyer for various products with every newsletter they mail, along with an order form, according to Bev Harris, who frequently sells books through this venue.

"The standard cut for stuffers is 50 percent for the newsletter publisher," Harris said. "As with associations, usually one takes the orders and the other fulfills. You get the best response if you can persuade the publisher to sneak an endorsement for the book into the newsletter. By the way, most major newsletter publishers line up their stuffers at least three months in advance and depend on stuffer income. Some send out two or three different stuffers with every issue. They are always looking for stuffers.

"A drawback for book publishers is the price point. Newsletter publishers like stuffers that sell for $98 or more. If you've got several related titles, consider bundling them together and calling them some sort of a 'kit' so that you can price the set at a higher, more attractive price point.

"When you contact the newsletter, ask for a sample while you're at it. Large newsletters have 50,000 to 100,000 subscribers; there are tons of newsletters with 5,000 to 10,000 subscribers. When I've done stuffers with newsletters, my response rate has been one-half percent for non-endorsed solicitations and marginally related publications, and up to 5 percent for endorsed solicitations with closely related publications.

To contact Bev Harrison directly to find more about association and subscription newsletter sales, you can reach her via e-mail at talion@ix.netcom.com

GOVERNMENT AGENCIES

Just like corporations, the government spends billions of dollars in supplies and services, and they do indeed buy a lot of books. Training guides are particularly hot with the government, said Michael Keating, research manager for the publications *Government Product News* and *Introduction to the Government Market*.

"A major midwest city just spent $60,000 on diversity training and study guides to help city employees work more cooperatively," he said.

Keating said a Santa Fe author who just published a book on how to create and update a web page will probably find government agencies a very lucrative market since many government employees are struggling with this very problem.

"By all means, there are opportunities. Some people say there's more red tape selling to the government, but it's like selling to any large organization, be it General Motors or whatever. And there are advantages, such as 'set-asides' (vendor preferences) for women and minorities."

Keating said that the Internet has become a wonderful place to find what's called "request for quotes": basically a government call for bids for certain products. There are also for-profit services on the Internet that will notify vendors when the government puts out a quote for their specific products. Publishers can find online the newsletter, *Commerce Business Daily*, which announces proposed contracts by federal agencies. With a threshold of purchases $25,000 and over, it doesn't include every proposed purchase, but does include many. Many public libraries also carry *Commerce Business Daily*, Keating said.

Selling to the government *is* challenging. There are 85,000 local, state and federal entities, bizarre jargon and complicated forms to learn. To familiarize yourself with the market, check out these publications:

- *Introduction to the Government Market*, Penton Publishing, 1100 Superior Ave., Cleveland, OH 44114; (800) 736-8660 or (216) 696-7000. This 30-page guide is expensive at $20, but is filled with valuable tips. It includes contacts names, additional sources of information for selling to the government, and detailed guidelines for selling to each level of government.

- *Government Product News*, also Penton Publishing. This magazine is sent to 85,000 local, state and federal administrators.

- *Government Procurement*, also Penton Publishing, goes to 15,000 government purchasing officials who are members of the National Institute of Governmental Purchasing.

- *U.S. Government Manual*: To locate agencies related to your book topic, check out the subject index in this book.

19

FLEXING YOUR ENTREPRENEURIAL MUSCLE: HOW TO SELL DIRECTLY TO READERS

Going into business for yourself, becoming an entrepreneur,
is the modern-day equivalent of pioneering on the old frontier.
PAULA NELSON

THERE ARE MANY PUBLISHERS WHO HAVE MADE A SMALL FORTUNE IN selling directly to consumers in tightly defined markets. The ways are varied: advertising in trade magazines, direct mail, sales through seminars, and simply doing a host of media interviews and giving out an 800 number to listeners. Direct selling is a great way to sell books, although it will challenge all of your entrepreneurial skills—from learning the mechanics and logistics of the various direct sale channels to making pitches with near-surgical precision to the target audience to creating a pitch that's heard above all the others. The payoff, though, is worth it. Each book you sell will capture the full retail price with very few returns.

Selling direct takes hard work, creativity, and capital. But those who succeed think of their work as the ultimate in entrepreneurship and wouldn't do business any other way.

The more tightly targeted your book is to niche markets, the easier it is to sell by direct mail. E & A Publishing in Columbus, Ohio, for example, specializes in books that help teachers prepare students for the proficiency tests given to Ohio students. The books are sold almost wholly by direct mail to Ohio public schools.

Bock Information Group sells mainly police books, but has branched to other pursuits, such as a booklet aimed at property managers, including one on preventing and dealing with drug activity on rental property. "We sell them by the thousands to apartment-owner associations," said President Wally Bock, who is building a small fortune from the business.

"I think of myself as an information entrepreneur. What I do is harvest, process, and sell information," said Bock, adding that his latest endeavors are two newsletters about doing business on the Internet: *Cyberpower Alert* (aimed at independent business professionals) and *Internet Executive Briefing* (aimed at corporate employees).

Mallery Press in Flint, Michigan, sells quilting books through quilt shops and direct sales to quilters in back-of-the-room sales and mail-order campaigns. To date, President Ami Simms has sold more than 180,000 books of the firm's five titles.

Elf Publishing in Somerville, New Jersey, sold more than 4,000 copies of *Pope John Paul II, An American Celebration*, a photo story of the pope's U.S. visit in 1995, directly to readers of Catholic newspapers from mid-October through December.

"The best part was that I traded space in the newspapers for $2.50 per book sold through their ads. I had no upfront expenses other than creating and mailing the ads," said company President Loren Fisher.

DIRECT MAIL

Books are a perfect product for direct mail; they don't spoil, they command a high markup, and they can be mailed at a special third-class bulk rate.

Direct mail usually works very well if the book offer meets three criteria: it satisfies a concrete need, it makes clear the reader can't get the book any other way or can't get it at such a bargain, and it's written with a great headline and copy.

Yet direct mail is expensive. Here's some advice from Bev Harris, a book marketing consultant.

- Because of the high expense involved, direct mail is profitable for items that bring in about $100 per sale, or have strong repeat income (such as getting something four times a year and automatically billing it to their credit card.) For a book, don't consider direct mail unless the price is over $20, and then only with a *very* targeted list, starting with a test mailing of no more than 2,000 pieces at no more than 40 cents per piece. At that, you'll need a 2-percent response just to break even. You can get up to 5-10 percent with an awesome list, but don't count on it. Test first.

- Don't do direct mail on rented lists with a $20 book. Typical response on rented lists is often one-half percent (that's a successful mailing on a rented list) and at a half percent, you'd need per-piece mailing cost at just 10 cents on a $20 book. Which is impossible.

- It's better to bundle books together as a "buy three and get such and such, FREE" to increase the price point on direct mail.

- Despite the volume purchasing advantages, never mail 100,000 pieces unless you've done extensive testing. Despite the economy of scale, zero percent of 100,000 is zero dollars and a whopping financial loss. That disaster does indeed happen if you miss the target or use an ineffective message.

- Test both the mailing list and the message, starting with quantities no smaller than 2,000 and no larger than 5,000. Code all response mechanisms so that you know exactly what the results are.

- Before you 'roll out' with a bigger mailing, 'stair-step' your tests into larger and larger segments of lists that appear to work. Some list brokers 'seed' their lists (they'll deny this) and, when you rent a small quantity for test purposes, they stack it with the best prospects. Direct mailers are having problems lately with 'rollouts' (expanding the test mailing)—and are finding that the rollout usually does not perform as well as the tests. Sometimes it performs *much* worse.

- Test with 2,000-5,000. If it works, test again with 5,000-10,000. If that works test again with 25,000. Only if that works should you roll out. That assumes the list you are renting has that many names. Lists perform incredibly differently; each must be tested separately.

- Even if you get good response on 25,000, an equal response on the rollout is not a sure thing—seasonal factors play heavily, with January being the best time for direct-mail response on publications. At least, that's the conventional wisdom. Harris said she had her best luck with consumer mailings that hit homes the week after Christmas, before New Year's; and January; she's also had good luck in February, August, September and October. Business-to-business marketing is much more variable, since you have to time things to match business needs and cycles.

- You should start getting orders within five days of the mailing hitting the homes. Size of mailing counts, of course. The bigger the mailing, the sooner you should look for replies.

- If you have credit card merchant status and a fax machine, include both a call-in order option and a fax friendly order form with an invitation to fax. Like this: "For fastest delivery of [your book], call 1-800——." Or, "FAX this to our secure, confidential fax fulfillment office at ———." The fax order option does make a difference, as well as any option that allows people to act on impulse.

- Harris tested third class against first class three times; all three times the first-class mailing outperformed third class two-to-one. But even with big-bulk-sort discounts that means 20-some cents just for postage. Price point is critical! It's hard to make a buck if you are selling stuff for under $50-$100 or unless you have ongoing income expectations (such as publications with 45-percent renewal rates.)"

How to Push Down Costs Without Sacrificing Quality

Mailing costs are important to consider. Before you design the mailing, it's well worth your time to visit the post office and ask about regulations and cost. Once a prototype of your mailing is complete, take it to the post office to be weighed. A fraction of an ounce can translate into hundreds of dollars of unnecessary postal expense, which can be averted simply by dropping a page or using lighter-weight paper.

For more information on mailings, write to the Office of Consumer Affairs for several informative and free publications. They're at 474 L'Enfant Plaza West S.W., Washington, D.C. 20260.

To minimize printing and postage expenses, publishers should use a standard-size envelope and paper size. A 4-page letter, reply card, envelope, postage, stuffing, and copying costs in the range of about 90 cents.

Also, seek several printing bids and produce only a modest quantity until you're sure the offer is long-term. But don't skimp on appearance. A cheap-looking package leaves an impression of a fly-by-night firm and turns off prospects.

FINDING A GREAT LIST

Before you embark on a full-blown direct-mail campaign, research your market so that you can describe your audience with precision to a list broker.

Where do you get a good mailing list? There are a lot of list brokers out there willing to sell names to you, ranging in price from 10 cents to 80 cents a name. The more criteria you give for a name—income level, house owner, gender, occupation, etc., the more each name costs, yet the better your "pull" or response will be. The better you've researched your target market, the better list you can ultimately define.

Here are a few mailing list sources to consider:

1. Governmental agencies: Mail to the people who can authorize the purchase. Government agencies possess a wealth of information. They're typically willing to give you the names and addresses of government employees and agencies, but not always the names and addresses of private citizens whom they serve. They include courts, register of deeds, county clerks, state departments of transportation, and federal bankruptcy courts.

E & A Publishing sends flyers to school libraries and school districts, its biggest customers of the Ohio proficiency test preparation book series.

Free copies of the book go to the curriculum director or building principal, but always with a follow-up phone call for an order.

The mailing list was obtained from Ohio's Department of Education, which provided an address of every school, the school's principal, and superintendent.

One tip offered by Cindi Englefield, company president: send all direct mail materials to the person who can authorize payment. "We put together one-piece mailers just loaded with information about the book and what the material covers. The printing isn't expensive. We use a quick print. We even bulk mail it ourselves," Englefield said.

2. Catalog companies and stores: Visualize exactly the kind of customer in every detail imaginable. Now research the catalog companies that are targeting that same customer and ask to rent or buy their list.

If you buy a list, you can use it forever with no penalties. Rented lists can only be used once. Don't try to use a list more than once because list brokers plant tipoff names to catch offenders. However, the names of people who order your books or query for more information or a catalog are yours for the keeping.

Wally Bock sought lists from catalog companies and police-training companies that sold merchandise to police officers. When he called a company, he asked what it would cost to buy the list, as opposed to asking what they'd rent it for.

"Some of these folks are relatively unsophisticated and don't know about renting," he said.

Bock recommends trying to get the best list possible from a reputable list broker, even if you have to pay a premium. Always ask when the list was last cleaned.

"The best of anything costs you money," he said. "If you get a good list broker, you'll get good lists presuming they're to be had. But they won't be cheap."

When you ask for a list from a broker, try to be as specific as you can about the target customer's characteristics. The more you can accurately narrow down your potential buyer, the greater your response. Specify income level, hobbies, gender, age, homeowner, parent or childless, frequent catalog buyer, etc.

3. Libraries: If you're low on money and have tons of time, go to a metro library and cull company names from phone books that cover your targeted geographic area. It pays to make a phone call to get the right name of an individual in each firm as time permits. A mailing with individual names pulls far more strongly.

4. Nonprofit groups: These groups are a wonderful resource for lists, but often you'll have to negotiate for use of the list, i.e., offering their members a special discount, promising not to sell the list to anyone else, etc.

5. Other publishers: If another publisher sells a book to an audience similar in profile to yours, propose sharing names of active respondents. Or consider a co-op mailing with other publishers or manufacturers of complementary products.

Two of the most well-known vendors that put together publishers are Twin Peaks, (800) 637-2256 in Vancouver, Washington, and Publishers Marketing Association, (310) 372-2732) or check out their website, http://www.pma-online.org. Before investing in a mailing, query other publishers as to their success with a particular list.

Writing the direct mail letter

Wally Bock credits the great response to his direct mail offers to these key guidelines:

- In the headline, say specifically what benefit the book offers: "Here's what you need to potty train your child in one day: a doll, a big bag of M&Ms, and my 10-page booklet."

- The copy needs to include a story about somebody who has a problem or anxieties or fears about something that's bothering them. To solve the problem, this person has read the book and received very specific, marvelous benefits. This person should be similar in profile to the person who's reading the letter.

- Support the person's emotional decision with data and other kinds of anecdotal proof.

- Give consequences if the prospect doesn't take action: "If you don't get this book, your child's potty training ordeal may stretch over several months with tears and endless accidents." Get real people and credible organizations to echo your claims of proven results.

- Explain why this is the best deal the market has to offer in terms of price, quality and convenience (and it should be!). Be sure to say the book is not available anywhere else, if that's true. A real disincentive to order by mail is an absurd charge for postage. There's absolutely no incentive to buy a book by mail at full price plus postage fees if the book is available at a bookstore.

- Ask the person to act now. You'll need to give the person a specific reason, whether it's free shipping, a specially discounted price, a $3 coupon on a potty seat, or a free special report on a related subject— "10 easy and ultra-cheap kid projects for a rainy day."

- Offer a guarantee of satisfaction. This gives your prospect more confidence, and, statistically, few people return a product.

- Provide background information about yourself and your firm to lend credibility to the offer. People need to trust you before they send money.

- Repeat the book's benefit on the order form. "Yes, I want to learn exactly how to potty train my toddler in one day."

- Make it easy to order by accepting credit cards, an 800 number to call, and a postage-free envelope.

- Mail to the same list every two to three months. The results of a second and third mailing are often as good as the first mailing. When you fail to make a profit, it's time to find another list.

TEST MARKETING

As Harris suggested, before embarking on an expensive, full-blown campaign, test your list and your copy with 2,000 to 5,000 names. If you get a response of less than 1 percent or excessive "nixies" (wrong addresses), rework your copy or get a new list. Keep careful track of your costs and project your total profit. A revenue ratio of 2.2 times the money you spend should be considered minimum, said Tom and Marilyn Ross in *The Complete Guide to Self-Publishing*.

When asking for a sample, ask the mailing list broker to give every name starting with "S," every Nth name, or every name with the zip code from 40000 to 50000.

Statistics show that half the total responses arrive within two weeks of the date your first order was received.

TIPS FOR A SUCCESSFUL APPEAL

- Hand-addressed letters get opened more frequently than labeled letters. Also, boost your chances of the envelope getting opened by printing on it a statement about the book's benefit, "Open this envelope if you want to learn how to get your finances under control forever."

- The better your list, the better your response. Develop a system to keep the list up-to-date. Make a separate list of those who responded to the offer for development of what's called a "house list" of qualified buyers, which you can then rent to others and use for small-scale, highly targeted mailings. Purge any names that haven't responded within the last year. Make all address changes and corrections immediately.

- Maintain your house list diligently. To keep track of new addresses, make sure each piece of mail goes out with "ADDRESS CORRECTION REQUESTED" below the return address. That way, the post office will place its address correction sticker on it before returning it to you. That allows you to update your database and minimize wasted postage.

- What offers pull the most? A letter sent first class (it gets much better treatment from the post office, yet it costs more), an offer with professional artwork, a reply card with a shaded background, longer letters (to save money, print on both sides of the paper), letters that offer special discounts for a short time, letters that look like real letters, and promotional material that features artwork of the book cover.

- Colored paper offers pizazz without the accompanying higher printing cost for an additional color.

- Make sure people are treated with dignity and warmth when they call with an order.

- Read this excellent book for marketing advice: *Influence: The New Psychology of Modern Persuasion*, by Robert B. Cialdini. For an overall view of direct marketing, read Dan Poynter's *The Self-Publishing Manual* and *The Complete Guide to Self-Publishing* by Tom and Marilyn Ross.

Network your way to a great list

An interesting thread erupted on the Internet PMA Forum during the winter of 1996. A publisher, who had written a book on the subject of cancer, queried if anyone knew how to obtain a mailing list of cancer patients. She had hit roadblocks because patient records are confidential.

The ensuing conversation resulted in an experienced response by Gail Golomb, owner of Four Geez Press and author of *The Kidney Stones Handbook: A Patient's Guide to Hope, Cure and Prevention*. She wrote a long note on how she's able to reach those who need to hear her prevention message.

"You may not be able to get patient mailing lists (and I do say 'may') because of the confidentiality regarding patient privacy," Golomb wrote. "But with time and proper marketing and networking, you will meet the 'right' people in your chosen field who will go out of their way to help you! And yes, some doctors will help you with patient mailings under their own letterheads.

When you give their patients the latest information and it's absolutely 100 percent correct, they are more than glad to help. Why? Because you're helping them educate their own patients."

Golomb subtly promotes and sells her book through an educational newsletter, *The Kidney Stones Network Newsletter*. She shared her experience of funding the newsletter and developing an effective mailing list of not only patients, but also physicians who practice kidney stone prevention (not all do!) and physicians who seek out materials for their patients.

Golomb believed pharmaceutical companies could help distribute her newsletter and found a firm that agreed to purchase copies. Negotiations broke down, however, after the company insisted on reviewing the newsletter's copy before publication.

Shortly afterward, the Ohio Urological Association offered to pay for the first printing without any copy restrictions. Six months went by, and the first pharmaceutical firm reorganized and Golomb received a call from the new marketing staff. They wanted enough copies of the newsletter so that all eight of their sales reps could drop off copies when they visited urologists.

"This pharmaceutical firm now pays me enough to produce and print each and every newsletter. They have put me on their payroll as a 'consultant.' They give out my newsletter to physicians whom I would never have been able to reach," she said.

The pharmaceutical firm helped in other ways. It provided her with names of physicians who practice kidney stone prevention and supplied her with patient pamphlets on metabolic tests, and kidney stone "catchers"—a premium Golomb now offers to newsletter subscribers.

Golomb has also found important names through the Internet, where she has met field researchers who are searching for cures. They have readily provided her with physician names—both in the United States and throughout the world—who practice stone prevention.

Support groups also sell or contribute patient information lists because they understand the importance of education.

"We often talk about the financial rewards of writing books," Golomb wrote. "Sometimes the finances are hidden under a rock. As you become more well-known in your field by connecting with those who are on the front burner in your specific medical fields, it will get easier."

📖   📖   📖

ADVERTISING IN TRADE MAGAZINES

Most publishers already know what kind of magazines their customers read through experience, research, and intuition. Still, it pays to do some definitive research before placing an ad for your book in a magazine. Go to the library and find *Consumer Magazine* and *Agri-Media Rates and Data*. Here you'll find everything you need to know about a magazine publication: rates, editorial focus, and circulation numbers. Audited circulation means the actual number of subscribers. Circulation means estimated number of readers including the recipient plus family and friends. If you've written a book for business professionals, check out the reference book, *Business Publication Rates and Data*.

Order the magazines and examine the classified and display ads to determine whether your advertisement belongs in the magazine.

For the most cost-effective advertising, place your ads in the most tightly niched magazine possible.

Many publishers can't afford to pay full price for a magazine display ad (it wouldn't pay off in sales), and are able to negotiate a 50 percent discount. Ed Hinkelman of World Trade Press, a publishing firm, said he always asks for a discount . . . and gets it.

"We wouldn't be in business today if we had to pay full price," he said. To get the best results for your ad:

- Offer more than one item: Cynthia Kim, publisher of a martial arts books, said advertisements in niche or trade magazines can be extremely effective, but it's necessary to advertise more than one book in order to make a profit. An ad that offers $40 worth of books/videos pays back the ad investment much quicker than an ad offering a $10 book, for example.

  Besides bundling books, she suggests offering an incentive, such as "Order three martial arts books, and receive a free 60-minute video tape."

- If calls are coming to you directly, offer them a related book that you've published at X amount of dollars off. They get a bargain, you've made a sale, plus you save on postage, mailing supplies, and handling.

- Start small: Test out your copy in a small classified ad before jumping to bigger and/or more frequent ads. Headlines make the real difference. Try three or four different ones. To track the ad's success, put a code number in the address to be used when ordering. "SA0196, for example, could mean *Sports Afield*, January of 1996.

- Write short copy and write it convincingly. State the *benefit to the reader* clearly, genuinely, enticingly, and without hyperbole. Use warmth—don't sound like a snake oil salesman. Some publishers make the fatal error of bragging about the author and/or company in the headline. Self-promotion does not sell books.

A *Forbes* magazine article told of this unique direct appeal that was dreamed up by Bloomsbury, a medium-sized publishing house in Britain.

To promote Joanna Trollope's book, *A Spanish Lover*, Bloomsbury printed 1.3 million copies of the book's first chapter in 1993 and negotiated with the *Sunday Times* to insert the chapter in the newspaper, the article said.

"Bloomsbury recouped half of the $100,000 production costs by selling ads in the insert and offered an $8 rebate to any *Times* reader who bought the book in the first three days after publication. The book went straight to number one on the *Sunday Times* Top Ten best-seller list. Since then, all of Joanna Trollope's books have been number one best sellers."

Of course, small publishers don't have $100,000 to throw around, but think of the possibilities! The key is hooking the readers and then providing an incentive to buy quickly. One reason this was an unusual move: most publishers would prefer to have a newspaper *pay* for first serial rights rather than having to dish out the money to publish the chapter as an advertising insert. But reality has a habit of stepping in, and perhaps serial rights aren't forthcoming because the author is an unknown. As a variation on Bloomsbury's strategy, how about getting a local or regional weekly to agree to publish your first chapter for free in exchange for being able to run an offer that any reader who bought the book by a certain date would get an $X rebate? Or asking a newsletter to publish a chapter or large excerpt, and giving the newsletter a share of all ensuing sales of the specially discounted book?

SELLING BOOKS THROUGH AN **800** NUMBER

Before spending a dollar for paid advertising, figure out how to get a story about your book into newspapers or magazines or an interview on radio and television for free. The objective, of course, is to get the listener or reader interested in your book and eager to order via an 800 phone number (try to choose an 800 number that's very easy to remember).

When pitching a story, think of yourself as an expert talking on a specific angle related to your book: Are schools dumbing down the curriculum? How to outmaneuver the IRS before tax day. Ten simple things you can do to become a happier parent. Has gymnastics robbed young girls of healthy bones? Ten no-cost or low-cost ideas for a romantic Valentine's Day.

To get a busy producer's attention, mail or fax a story idea and follow up with a phone call. If your pitch relates to today's front-page news, definitely fax your story idea.

"It's not the how, it's the what you communicate," said Steve Hall, vice president of Bradley Communications, which publishes *Radio/TV Interview Report.*

Radio/TV Interview Report and its recent competitor, *Media Talk*, each go to about 4,000 radio and TV producers around the country. Their sole purpose is to garner interviews for authors. The rates of these magazines are comparable, with a half-page priced at $350. Some publishers have registered with the Internet "www.guestfinder.com" site, which specializes in publicizing notable people for media interviews.

Prepare well for the interview. Anticipate the questions they'll ask. Tease the book by mentioning specific chapters and exactly how the information can benefit the reader. Have a joke or two ready. Tell the audience how to get your book and that if they call today, they'll get something special. An autographed book, perhaps. A special report. Free shipping. A box of Valentine candy. A $5 discount. But give them an incentive to order immediately, Hall said.

For an in-depth treatment on this subject, read Joe Sabah's book: *How to Get on Radio Talk Shows All Across America Without Leaving Your Home or Office.* If you want the book for keeps (it costs $35), call (303) 722-7200 to order.

SEMINARS AND BACK-OF-THE-ROOM SALES

Are you a good speaker? Are you funny? Have you published a book in a specific area of expertise? Consider giving professional seminars. It's a great way to attract the right kind of customers for your book. A lot of authors find that they can draw in customers with a low-cost, even free, seminar and then sell books, videos or audio tapes afterwards in what are called back-of-the-room sales. Others have grown an entire career around the book—using it as an anchor of credibility—and conduct seminars year-round.

How does one get into the business of speaking for money? The avenues are varied and often lead to different destinations. Some speakers specialize in what are called public seminars in which the public-at-large is invited to a public gathering place, such as a hotel. Others hire themselves out for in-house seminars, in which a corporation, church, or nonprofit association fills the seats and pays the speaker a pre-established fee.

If you give public seminars, very specifically target your audience. Don't focus on motorcycle owners, but on Harley-Davidson owners who are having trouble with their Cafe Racer models from 1984 to 1995.

There's another decision to be made; some people use what are called speaker bureaus which act as agents. A bureau essentially finds work for the speaker and takes care of any and all details. All the speaker has to do is show up. The bureau generally takes half the speaking fee in return. A speaker's bureau, however, isn't for everybody. Generally, a bureau represents only people who can command a minimum of $2,000 a day. A maxim in the industry is that when you need an agent, they don't need you. When you no longer need an agent, they'd love to put you on the roster. That's not always true, however. Particularly sexy subjects in a well-delivered speech will grab the attention of an agent. One woman, for example, is giving speeches around the country about her experience posing for *Playboy* magazine. Another avenue: find an organization to co-sponsor a seminar such as a church, chamber of commerce, or Rotary Club. It gives you credibility and helps solve the biggest dilemma of giving a seminar—filling seats.

For example, if your book focuses on a Christian approach to money management, you could ask churches to co-sponsor a seminar on the subject. You deliver the seminar, they publicize it to the congregation. So that begs the question: What percentage of the receipts do you share with the church? If they handle all the details and all you have to do is show up to make the presentation, then you might give them two-thirds of the receipts. If you do all the work—letter writing, sign-ups, registration, making handout copies, room planning, refreshments—then take 90 percent.

Make sure the content of your speech includes both humor and truly useful information. It's the only way to get repeat business.

Going into the seminar business usually requires a very serious investment of time and money. But some people have slipped selling books into their existing lifestyle. Michelle Beaudry, a standup comedian, sells nearly all of her comedy books at her shows.

In less than a year, Beaudry has sold 400 of her *Travellers Laffbook USA* after shows at the full $9.95 list price. The $4,000 in sales paid for all her publishing expenses for the title and she still has 1,300 left to sell.

Here's her advice on pitching a book without offending your crowd: Overselling the availability of titles while on stage is the kiss of death. If your act reads like an infomercial, people get annoyed. They have paid a cover charge, after all. So readers be warned: direct sales have to be handled delicately.

"When I tell the crowd my title's price," Beaudry said, "I use the same joke printed on the back of my books: "'Ten dollars in the USA, a million in Canada.' This joke takes the sting out of the pitch."

Here are some tips to get started:

- Do you feel you could use a little education in the humor department? Read *Comedy Writing Secrets*, by Mel Heiltzer.

- Before going professional, join Toast Masters to sharpen your speaking skills. Also, volunteer to speak for free at local service clubs. Videotape your speech; it's your product and people will want to see it before booking you.

- Try giving speeches for free and request the audience fill out forms afterwards. Ask them to suggest future seminar topics. If you detect a trend, seize it. Develop a new speech and market it; use the addresses from the questionnaires as a mailing list.

- Excerpt the wonderful things people say about you on the questionnaire for your promotional brochure. (Of course, make sure the person checks on the questionnaire that it's okay to quote.)

- Avoid visual aids: very few people can use them effectively, and if you have to provide the equipment, they're a pain to haul around.

- Offer an upsell. For example, if you give a 3-hour seminar, the upsell is a two-day workshop.

- Create a series of professional reports as an option to a book. They're more easily updated, cheaper to produce, and carry lower individual price tags than book.

- At the end of your presentation, walk to the back of the room while your introducer announces you'll be signing books. Ask for a volunteer if you need one, and be prepared to accept credit cards. Use a trusty swipe machine and handle the data transfer later.

- Read Paul Karasik's book, *How to Make it Big in the Seminar Business*, published by McGraw-Hill. It's chock-full of advice and resources (including 160 public seminar companies and 543 of the best seminar sites). He offers detailed advice for those interested in conducting seminars.

- Join the Tempe, Arizona-based National Speakers Association which claims membership of 3,600 people, at least half of whom sell books, tapes, videos, or all three. For more information, call (602) 968-2552 or fax (602) 968-0911.

- E-mail George Roman (bhloveguru@aol.com) or call him at (310) 289-5129, for his gold-mine list of speaker resources. This is no exaggeration. He has compiled a list that would take anyone else hundreds of hours to research. It includes names of professional organizations; directories of speakers, experts and seminars; speaker's booking services and bureaus; speaker's business products and seminars; and online research databases. Roman, a psychic and astrologer, compiled the list for speakers, authors and entertainers. At the time of publication, he was e-mailing it to people at no charge.

SELLING VIA INFOMERCIALS

Does your book deliver a huge promise to the masses? Can it solve a chronic problem that's deeply felt, even painfully felt by most Americans.

Will they become richer, skinnier, or more youthful looking by faithfully following the instructions in your book? Can your book show them how to finally buy a house with zero down? Can your book show a woman how to shrink from a size 11 to a size 7 in two months by adhering to your fitness plan? Does your new book promise good-tasting meals in less than 30 minutes? Will people find money and happiness in their lives by studying your book, *The Top 10 Behavioral Traits of Successful People*?

Does this sound like an infomercial? It should, because these are exactly the kind of books that do very well in long commercial formats.

Infomercials are largely the province of exercise equipment and household items which are designed to make life more convenient. Well-made infomercials cost anywhere from $50,000 to $250,000 to produce and air on national television.

Yet it is possible to produce infomercials as cheaply as $1,000 for 15 minutes and air on a tiny cable channel for $85. Will it work for your book? Good question. It's extremely rare to see a book advertised in an infomercial. If you are considering this medium, it's imperative to call other advertisers on the target channel to see what results they've received.

Before you invest any money in an infomercial, take note of Peter Bieler's key criteria listed in his book, *This Business Has Legs*:

1. Is your product right for direct response? Does it demonstrate well? If it's a service, is it going to have repeat business?

2. If you go with long-form, what format do you choose? A newsmagazine dominated by location reports; talk show with a host and guests; storymercial with a story line and characters; demonstration show; seminar with a speaker and an audience.

3. Does your copy strategy work? What compelling promise can you make about using the product that will make people want to buy it? Don't leave this to your copywriter. You know the product better than anyone.

4. Are you casting the right spokesperson? Celebrity or non-celebrity, male or female, young or old. The wrong celebrity is worse than no celebrity at all.

5. Is your offer effective? Have you looked closely at your payment plan, guarantee, price point, and premiums?

Infomercials work well only for books that are very clear in their benefits. Because this format is so expensive, it's wise to offer a collection of related books. Before investing *any* money, tread lightly. Marketing maniac Dan Kennedy once said that only one in 16 infomercials makes any money.

Shel Horowitz, author of *Marketing w/o Megabucks* (available by calling (800) 683-WORD)), offers these additional tips:

- If you air a long-format commercial at very cheap rates on late-night TV, obtain an automatic 4-number VCR programming code, and publicize the spot. Encourage people to tape your show and watch it later.

- Pick up a copy of *Electronic Retailing* magazine and contact some of the infomercial producers who advertise there. Address: 9200 Sunset Blvd., #612, Los Angeles, Calif. 90069; (310) 724-6458 (editorial); (310) 724-6457 (advertising). The magazine, *ResponseTV*, is also a valuable resource. Call (714) 513-8400 to order a sample copy.

- Make sure your ad is viewer-driven and includes a toll-free telephone number for easy ordering.

- Don't be overly coy with your format. Craig Evans points out in *Electronic Retailing* (September/October 1995) that if consumers think they're watching an information program and then find out it was designed to sell product, they'll feel betrayed, cynical and reluctant to buy.

- Once you've taken the trouble to create a first-class presentation, get as much mileage as you can. Consider mailing a video or audio cassette, CD-ROM, or floppy disk, to your prospects, for example. People are naturally flattered to receive electronic media in the mail (particularly if you attach a personalized letter).

ADVERTISING ON HOME SHOPPING CHANNELS

On September 24, 1994, 155,000 copies of *In the Kitchen with Bob* were sold to QVC watchers. Think of it. Never before in history were so many copies of one book sold in a single day. A year later, 1,495 sets of books on how to win at casinos were sold within *several minutes.*

About 158 million people tune into home shopping channels every day of the week, making it a challenge for these TV retailers to fill up hours and hours of programming. This has made the four major TV retailers hungry for new, unique, and unseen products. So what small publishers consider a liability—their inability to get books into general bookstores and in the mainstream media—is, in fact, an asset for home shopping television. These very same books will seem brand new and special to the viewing audience.

"We're constantly looking for new products to feed this machine because we've got to reinvent it every day," said Home Shopping Network Vice President John Pinocci in the February 1997 issue of *Nation's Business.*

"That leaves us open to—and motivated to—having small vendors and manufacturers present goods to us."

In fact, QVC has developed a special initiative called Quest for America's Best, in which they travel to each state to find new products.

How many books can you sell with one appearance on a home shopping channel? The luckiest publishers have reaped more than a million dollars with a single appearance on QVC, although on average about 3,000 books are sold. That's still terrific, considering it sometimes takes two to three years and heavy promotion dollars to sell that many.

What sort of books do well? The book's topic has to be timely or fit in with one of the TV retailer's upcoming themes. Like an infomercial, the book should be able to solve a deeply felt, chronic problem such as facing the prospect of cooking dinner every night. Authoritative books on child-rearing, however, don't do well.

In your letter to the TV retailer, focus on the benefits that your book can deliver for viewers. Those with demonstration possibilities do best. As always, make the lead catchy—focus on the rewards the readers will reap from your book as opposed to the simple fact that it was published.

Here's another key suggestion given in the *Nation's Business* article:

"Mail a homemade video to the network that clearly explains the product's 'magic' as well as its value."

Taking that advice to heart, Lisa Shaw, president of Litterature, plans to send a video of a pet birthday party that nicely shows off her pet greeting cards.

In general, publishers can expect a 50-percent discount with freight paid with the right for the TV retailer to return any unsold books. Returns average about 7 to 9 percent, well below the book industry average. If the TV retailer is confident that viewers won't return the book, they may offer a 55-percent discount with guaranteed no returns.

Here are the four major TV retailing channels:

- Home Shopping Network Inc.: 69 million viewers; P.O. Box 9090, Clearwater, FL 34618; (813) 572-8585, Ext. 4750.
- QVC Network; 59 million viewers; 1365 Enterprise Dr., West Chester, PA 19380; (888) 505-0872.
- Shop At Home Inc.; 20 million viewers; 5210 Schubert Rd., P.O. Box 12600, Knoxville, TN 37912; (423) 688-0300.
- ValueVision International, Inc.: 13.5 million (cable only); 6740 Shady Oak Rd., Eden Prairie, MN 55344; (612) 947-5200.

CONCLUSION

If a publisher has good business judgment, direct marketing can be one of the most satisfying parts of selling a book. Your success is dependent on your business savvy as opposed to market forces beyond your control. Likewise, you control your expenses. Just keep in mind, before investing substantial money in this channel, it is imperative to conduct small market tests to gauge your ultimate success.

20.

How To Sell And Publicize Your Book On The Internet

The only way to make sense out of change is to plunge into it, move with it, and join the dance.
ALAN WATTS

Coauthored by **Sam Wells**,
Coordinator of Online Publicity at Planned Television Arts

IF YOU HAVE ALWAYS FEARED THE INTERNET AND CONSIDERED IT THE BIG I-word (incomprehensible), now is the time to get over it. With nearly 40 million people now on the Internet (and that number is expected to double each year!), there is no cheaper and easier way to truly "target market" your book.

Many publishers originally get on the Internet to sell books, but find the secondary rewards make it worth climbing the learning curve. Their websites might garner unexpected attention from reporters or editors browsing the Web for story ideas. Likewise, books have been "discovered" and optioned for movies. There are even stories of foreign publishers finding a book on the Internet and offering thousands of dollars for foreign rights.

In this chapter, we'll first discuss the basics of establishing a "presence" on the Internet for your book—basically, a home page where people can order your book.

Secondly, we'll discuss how to get potential buyers to arrive at your doorstep. There are literally millions of Internet sites, so the odds that people will just happen by your site are slim. You must invite and direct them there. But your invitation must be extended with savvy. If you appear to be hawking your book to Internet users, you will get publicly "flamed"— that is chastised, ridiculed, and perhaps shut out of a particular Internet discussion group.

Finally, we will talk about generating publicity for your book on the Internet. Many reporters from large metro newspapers, magazines and television news stations scope the Internet for story ideas. We'll tell you how to find their e-mail addresses and how to write an e-mail that doesn't get dumped. Publicists say the Internet is one of their favorite venues because *most* reporters who are online personally open their own e-mail.

Ready for the plunge? Consider this just an introduction. We'll include lots of resources to help you further explore cyberspace.

WHAT IS THE INTERNET?

The Internet is basically a network system that connects computers throughout the world via phone lines, coaxial cable, fiber optics, and even satellite. The computer can be in your kitchen or on a university campus. An Internet user might want to visit the unclassified files of the Pentagon or the morgue of the *New York Times*. It's all there on the Internet.

All you need to connect to the Internet is a modem, communication software, and an Internet Service Provider (ISP), who might charge anywhere from $10 to $30 a month for unlimited use (it really pays to shop around).

What are the different aspects of the Internet? Here's a brief rundown:

Send and receive e-mail: The vast majority of ISPs give you a program to send and receive e-mail. This is, by far, the Internet's most popular function, partly because it's so easy. People who don't like to incur long-distance charges love this service. It costs as much to send an e-mail to

Africa as it does across town. (Make sure you ask the prospective ISP if there is a surcharge after receiving or sending a specific number of messages per month. There are still a few with such a billing structure.) In its simplest form, e-mail is easy to use, but there are subtleties for marketers which we'll discuss later in the publicity section.

Mailing list: A mailing list can serve as the primary forum for your Internet publicity efforts. It's like an electronic correspondence system where people post messages on a subject that they're all interested in, whether it's publishing books or breeding dogs. Participants send a message to one e-mail address, and everyone on the list gets a copy. Every mailing list has its own personality and can degenerate into vicious attacks on an individual for spamming (advertising on the list) or an obsession with trivial issues. It's difficult to say which is worse. The group's names and e-mail addresses are kept in a central file. Anyone can join a mailing list by subscribing via e-mail. The best sources of information about using a mailing list can be found on the Web. (The Rockefeller University Hospital website has a section that covers this topic rather well at http://clinfo.rockefeller.edu/manual/mlists.htm.) Once you subscribe, you receive copies of all messages posted to the list. You can even set up your own mailing list! Some lists are moderated, some are not. A moderated list is overseen by an administrator who may filter out messages he or she considers unacceptable (such as ads).

A warning about mailing lists: You may get HUGE quantities of e-mail that will eat up space allotted by your ISP in no time. Be careful not to subscribe to too many.

Usenet newsgroups: Usenet has a bad reputation and people desiring intelligent conversation have largely abandoned it because of the high incidence of spamming followed by vitriolic attacks on the perpetrators. A Usenet newsgroup functions much like a mailing list, only it's accessed in a different way. You must use a newgroup reader program that's provided by your ISP or commercial provider. Newsgroups are different in that you do not subscribe to them, and the ongoing discussion is not e-mailed to you. Many people prefer this to having thirty or more messages appearing in the mailbox each day. Newsgroups are analogous to an electronic bulletin board, where you use the newsreader software to "go to" read posted messages.

Internet Relay Chat (IRC): A chat group differs from newgroups and mailing groups in that it's immediate and interactive. It's a bit more difficult to use than newgroups because you'll need to learn a few commands. There are more and more programs available that are making this a less intimidating task. Again look to the Web for information on some great chat programs. Stroud's Consummate Winsock Applications (http://cws.iworld.com/) has it all. You name it—e-mail programs, chat programs, newsreaders—you'll find them all here. Most are freeware or whareware, meaning they want little or no money to use them.

Some people use IRCs for publicity purposes by sending private e-mail to a particular prospect who seems to need specific information.

The World Wide Web (WWW): This is the most user-friendly aspect of the Internet. In fact, thousands of Internet users never knowingly use Telnet, FTP or Gopher (described below), being quite satisfied with their results on the World Wide Web. Few people realize it, but when they use a web browser to access information on the Web, the program is actually performing Telnet, FTP and even Gopher functions in the background.

To get around the Web, you'll need a Web browser, which your ISP or commercial server will usually provide for you. To get to an address on the Web, you simply type in an address, which often begins: http://www. The browser will take you to the specified address or what's called a URL (Uniform Resource Locator). The web page may look like an ad or a magazine article. Websites often include "links" to web pages that feature a related subject. A link is usually text (called hypertext and is highlighted in some way) or a graphic; either way, you click on the graphic or hypertext to move to the desired site. Many publishers set up a home page (sometimes called a website) to market their books and establish links to related sites.

Telnet: The Telnet function lets you to connect to a distant computer and allows you to do anything that the distant computer can do: execute programs, retrieve files, "chat" with other users, play games, or gain access to huge databases. To log on in most cases, you'll need to know the user ID and will be assigned a password.

File Transfer Protocol (FTP): FTP is similar to Telnet in that it allows you to connect to a distant computer. But the primary function of FTP is to upload and download files rather than to perform any other functions. It's a popular feature for transferring files from one computer to another. A lot of people use a program called "Archie," which is a search program that locates the FTP sites that have copies of the files you are looking for. Look again to Stroud's Consummate Winsock Applications site (http:// cws.iworld.com/) for Archie, Veronica, Telnet, FTP, and Gopher.

Gopher: Gopher was an early use of the Internet and developed by the University of Minnesota. It predates, and is the textual equivalent to the World Wide Web. As you might suspect, Gopher goes for information on the Internet that you are looking for. "Veronica" is the program used to locate files housed at various gopher sites. The Gopher program presents a series of numbered menus. By making a variety of selections and searches, you are eventually provided with the file or text information you were looking for. It's possible to even create a Gopher server so people can find out about your book, though the vast majority of efforts are directed toward the Web.

WAIS (Wide Area Information Search): This function will search databases of text for a key word which you specify, such as "Hemingway" or "book marketing." But only documents that are indexed for WAIS will be searched. You can use WAIS by going through Telnet. Many of the more sophisticated search programs available on the Web are actually using WAIS databases in the background, freeing the user from learning to use this program directly.

INTERNET AND COMMERCIAL ONLINE SERVICES

Perhaps you're not online at the moment and wonder whether to sign on with a commercial online service such as America Online (AOL), Prodigy, CompuServ, GEnie, Delphi and others. Or perhaps you should simply sign on with an Internet Service Provider and connect directly with the Internet's World Wide Web.

America Online has emerged as the strongest competitor of all the online services; most of the others are either up for sale or close to biting the dust.

Why sign on with AOL at all? After all, an ISP is usually cheaper and has become the increasingly popular choice. And who can forget the AOL fiasco in early 1997 after it offered unlimited access for $20 a month? Thousands of users were left adrift because AOL lacked the equipment to handle the huge influx of customers.

There are predictions that commercial services may go by the wayside, but, for now, AOL can give you some extra features plus access to the Internet. If you're not an AOL subscriber, you can't get access to it. What will you miss? Perhaps an important channel for publicity, such as AOL's forums (equivalent to the Internet newsgroups) that are geared toward families, women, seniors, entrepreneurs, small business people, doctors, and many kinds of groups. They also provide a number of book related forums and "live chat" events that are perfect for publicity efforts.

SELLING BOOKS ON THE INTERNET

If you are like most publishers, you won't sell a lot of books on the Internet, but those that you do sell (at least off your own home site) will be at full retail price or close to full retail price with a fairly minimal investment if you play your cards right.

Veltisezar "Velty" Bautista sells one to five books a day off the Internet at full retail price. He lists his books both on his home page and with Bookzone, an Internet catalog. His buyers, who live as far away as Hong Kong and Japan, are even willing to pay postage.

"Probably because they feel that there's a thrill in buying books in cyberspace," he said. "What a great invention by mankind!"

There are several ways to post your book on the Internet. Many publishers establish a web page for their book where people can go to read the index, a sample chapter or two, a background on the author, book reviews, audio readings by the author, and ordering information.

Other publishers establish a presence on other book-selling sites or even in general catalogs related to their book.

Increasingly, publishers are doing both. They establish their own home page plus their book can be found on two to three other book-selling sites. At the very least, a publisher will ensure that their book is listed with the major online bookstores such as www.amazon.com. The listing gives them credibility and also a few orders at virtually no cost.

Most laymen refer to websites that sell books as "online bookstores," but payment to publishers for their books varies and falls into several categories, including:

- Online bookstores or resellers like Amazon.com offer more than one million titles and sell books only on the Internet. Amazon will sell to anyone, from individuals to libraries to bookstores. They discount the books on the site from 10 percent to 40 percent, depending on how much Amazon pays the publisher or distributor for the books. Amazon takes payment from the customer's credit card.

After Amazon receives an order, it either pulls the book from its existing inventory or passes the order to the publisher, which ships the books to the customer. Amazon takes the standard industry discount of 40 percent to 50 percent from the customer's payment and sends what's left to the publisher. Publishers pay nothing to have their book listed with Amazon (in fact, some publishers are amazed to find their books are online)!

Before you get too excited, many small publishers are totally frustrated with Amazon because it informs customers that it will take four to six weeks for the book to ship, even though these same small publishers have committed to a 24-hour turnaround. Amazon claims it's a programming problem, but it has left many a publisher outraged.

Many publishers say that while they don't rely on Amazon to sell books; it's one more outlet for sales and costs nothing. Others take the opposite view. They purposely direct Internet visitors to Amazon instead of taking an order directly because they view Amazon as a full-fledged partner who will reward their business with more visibility at the site.

You can visit Amazon at http://www.amazon.com to see if your book is already there. You'll see how browsers can read brief descriptions of the book, bits and pieces of reviews, and, best of all, other readers' opinions of the book. The full listing is absolutely free, but it's up to the publisher to supply book reviews, author comments, and excerpts from the book using Amazon's online instructions. For an additional $26, Amazon will put the book cover's image on the site.

- ReadersNdex calls itself an online book site for consumers who are browsing for books on the Web. All of the books listed on its site are available for purchase directly from the publisher or via its participating online booksellers (such as Tattered Cover Book Store, Stacey's Professional Bookstore, and more). ReadersNdex doesn't charge a transaction fee to the booksellers; it does charge a "modest annual subscription fee per title" ($250 for the first title and $50 for each additional title) to all participating publishers, said Stephanie Baartz-Bowman, sales and marketing manager.

ReadersNdex works with more than 75 publishers, some of which use ReadersNdex as their primary Web presence. Others use ReadersNdex as an alternative sales and marketing tool to their own website. ReadersNdex goal: to provide a marketing tool to online booksellers.

- There are many bookstores that also sell books on the Internet. Future Fantasy, for example, specializes in science fiction and the fantasy genre. It runs a bookstore in Palo Alto and takes e-mail orders off the Internet to supplement its existing business. It orders books from distributors, as usual. Powell's Books is another. It has the huge selection of Amazon, but isn't as user-friendly. It's located at http://www.powells.portland.or.us.

- Book catalogs charge a set fee for publishers to take up residence on its site. They pass the book orders along to publishers who receive 100 percent of the asking fee from the book customer. This has two advantages: publishers get more money and they get the list of customers, which, of course, makes a great mailing list for the next book.

There are general book catalogs and there are niche catalogs. BookZone, for example, has a general selection and is one of the oldest electronic book catalogs. It creates a "presence" for publishers. Consumers can key in a specific category of interest and read information about the book, excerpts, review blurbs, price, ordering information, etc. For an additional fee, it will also create independent websites for publishers, which are crosslinked to BookZone's listing.

It costs $129 for a publisher to be listed on BookZone's site. It sounds cheap, but not all publishers reap the investment.

"If you ask why, the answer is they're not doing any other marketing, making no effort at all to tell people about their books," said Mary Westheimer, BookZone president. "It all has to work together. Do we have publishers who do make back the $129?

"Absolutely. Our most successful publishers sell 600 books a year through us. You might say, 'that's not many books,' but that's at full price, and that doesn't account for the increase in bookstore sales, which publishers tell us frequently is an unexpected boon."

There are other advantages to being on a catalog site besides selling books, Westheimer said. "The exposure aspect is really so important," she said. "We get calls from publications such as American Express Traveler, and recently, from Warner Brothers studio. They were very excited about seeing a book on our site that they wanted to purchase rights to."

• Wholesale sites, like AllBooks, take orders only from bookstores, retailers, and libraries (essentially everyone but the direct consumer).

AllBooks was formed by a group of small publishers frustrated and maddened by exclusive distributors and national wholesalers. Its founders hope that its more favorable terms will lure bookstores and libraries away from the traditional channels of distribution.

AllBooks founders believe if their site catches on, everyone will win. They are offering better discounts than bookstores and libraries pay to distributors; they also offer a special discount for bookbuyers agreeing to nonreturnable orders. Generally, publishers receive 50 percent of the list price of every book sold.

Many of AllBooks publishers create their own web page with an excerpt of the book so that buyers can preview before they order.

If you're currently with an exclusive distributor, the orders can go through your distributor at your request. The downside, of course, is you'll get a bigger chunk taken out of each sale. Jacob's advice: Ask that the exclusivity clause be stricken the next time you re-negotiate your contract.

To sign up, go to http://allweb.net/books/. Click on the "publisher signup" button and fill out the form. You can use the system immediately.

Which Site Is Best For Your Book?

Before investing in a spot on a catalog site, shop around. The most important criteria is to find a good match between your book and the customers who like browsing on the site.

Ask about fees, the number of "hits" each catalog receives on an average day, the most popular genre of books that sell on the site. Fees and discounts cover a wide range. Be sure you also ask about the level of publicity done for the online outlets you are considering. How much do they promote themselves to get others to visit, and how often?

As a rule, sell your book(s) on the online bookstore or catalog where your customers are most likely to browse, whether it's new age, outdoor gear, recipe books, or perhaps a popular bookstore that can offer the most information on a given selection. Also, make sure your book is on the sites with heavy traffic (such as Amazon).

Test out the site by asking it to search for an author or book you know is there. If there are glitches, you may want to choose another online bookstore.

Teresa Marrone, who wrote books on wild-game cooking, goose hunting, and a back-country cookbook, heavily researched her options on the Internet. In the end, she chose to post her books on a site called GORP (the Great Outdoors Recreation Pages) that posts articles on the outdoors, and includes a listing of 3,000 outdoor-related books.

"I truly believe that I have gotten many of my online orders by people who found my pages simply while poking around on GORP as opposed to those who found me in response to a search through Yahoo or whatever, although I'm registered with most of them," Marrone said. "To me, it's like making a decision on where to put a print ad. If you are selling ski poles, you should advertise in a ski magazine; it's more effective than dropping inserts into a daily newspaper or leafleting cars.

"I also have my books listed with a couple of cyber-bookmalls because I feel people go there just to browse. So I feel you need to be in both types of locations."

Marrone's yearly Internet rent of $900 for a presence on the Internet has more than paid off with sales of 20 books a month—a total of about $2,640 after production, handling and postage expenses. And that's with absolutely no time spent promoting her book to discussion groups!

WHAT SHOULD A WEBSITE INCLUDE?

There's no better way to draw browsers to your site than by including a promise of free information. Not only will it lure surfers, it will also give a prospect confidence to order the book. Your sample chapters should be provocative, ground-breaking, and make the reader want to know more. Although this may seem obvious, but we've seen publishers include a sample chapter that was only tangential to the title of the book and a disappointing read.

Also, include:

- A cover page that includes a brief description of your book and pithy, glorious review quotes.
- An author's biography.
- A table of contents.
- Book reviews.
- A page of "cool links" related to your book topic.
- A method to order your book. For those customers who are uncomfortable sending their credit card number over the Internet, provide an 800 number to order by credit card and a mail-order form for

those who prefer to mail a check. Also, include a response mechanism that allows you to track how the customer found your website.

To Design Or Not To Design?

Should you build your own home page and set up the website yourself, or hire someone else to do it? Both tasks are time-consuming, and some people would rather put their efforts toward promoting and shipping books. Others like the idea because it means they can change their site as they see fit, add reciprocal links without any help, and learn a tremendous amount, which helps when a technical problem crops up.

If you want to build your own website, try these application packages: Pagemill for the Mac, or Frontpage for the PC. Both come with good tutorials and don't require any knowledge of HTML. Once your website is designed, you'll need to install it on your ISP's server. There are free programs that can do this: Fetch-it for the MAC (shareware) and Cupertino FTP for the PC (freeware). Michael Mathiesen's *Marketing on the Internet* goes into detail on setting up a website (it will also tell you how to set up your own mailing list).

You can also find lots of information about designing a website at http://www.wprc.com, a website promoter's resource center. Be sure that the website can track exactly how your customer found you on the Internet (your home page, a book cybermall, an Internet ad, etc.) Bautista checks his visits each day on the Internet and learned that his ads for his book on testing for the U.S. postal exam weren't generating any orders. He had posted the ads at the AOL Career Center and the Internet Career Center, but will pull them this year because they produced no results.

How Should You Price Your Book On The Web?

Typically, it costs a few more dollars to order a book off the Internet than to buy it in a bookstore because of the added postage. Would sales increase if there wasn't this price disincentive? Should publishers discount their book a little?

It's an interesting question. Historically, the people who bought books on the Internet did so because they lived in a rural area or foreign country with an incredibly slim selection of books. These customers gladly paid postage simply because they had no option.

Yet with the media hype surrounding Amazon, many traditional book shoppers have turned to online shipping. The panic about stolen credit cards has also abated somewhat. An interesting note is that 47 percent of Internet respondents to a Graphics, Visualization & Usability Survey said they have never purchased anything on the Internet. Yet this same survey said that 42 percent of respondents visit the Web at least once a week to find product information. This begs the question: does a user NOT buy on the Internet simply because he or she can save a few bucks by driving downtown? We think so. Consider seriously lowering your book price to accommodate postage in order to turn information seekers into buyers.

PUBLICIZING YOUR SITE

SETTING UP LINKS TO YOUR WEBSITE

You'll need to bring visitors to your book site via links that you'll want sprinkled on strategic web pages.

What is a link? Simply highlighted text (usually in blue) or a web button that will deliver the user to a totally different place on the Web once it's clicked. If you want to be totally accurate, the user isn't going anywhere—the file is delivered on command to the user.

Setting up links isn't difficult, but it is time consuming. Internet publicist Steve O'Keefe succinctly explains how to conduct a link campaign in his book, *Publicity on the Internet (Copyright © 1997 Steve O'Keefe. Excerpts reprinted with permission of John Wiley & Sons, Inc.).*

Your biggest challenge in setting up links, O'Keefe writes, is finding the specific websites on where you want to place a link to your own home page. Most beginners try to find these web pages using Yahoo or Alta Vista; these search engines, however, are in a sense too thorough, calling up a huge number of websites, many of them triplicate leads to the same website.

Instead, O'Keefe suggests trying to locate what he calls a SuperSite or a specialized *directory* for a specific subject. On it, you will find a gold mine of web addresses.

How do you find one of these SuperSites?

O'Keefe suggests using the "Galaxy" search engine http:// tradewave.com.html. Don't type in your subject word, but instead go the desired category and click. For example, if you've written a book geared toward police supervisors, find the category of "Community" and click on the subheading, "Crime and law enforcement." You'll get a listing of seven directories, including "The police pages" and "Police K9 Home Pages." (O'Keefe also suggests using the search engine called "Infoseek" for this exercise.)

Another source of directories: try the Subject Index Clearinghouse at http://www.clearinghouse.net. One other technique: type in link:mysite in the Altavista search engine to see who has linked to your home page. Go visit the sites because one might be a SuperSite.

Once you've found the addresses, make a visit to see if a link to your home page would fit in and exactly where the link should go. Many websites provide a list of "hot links"—places of special interests that are must-surfs.

Does the web page look perfect for a link-up? If so, take note of the webmaster (the person who created and oversees the page) and his or her e-mail address. Your next step: e-mailing a query asking the webmaster to add a link to the website.

O'Keefe explains the following elements of a "linkletter." It should:

- Compliment the webmaster on the link-list and ask if he/she wouldn't mind adding a link for your site.

- Include the name of your site (something catchy) and its URL.

- Cite the specific page on their site in which the link would fit. In-clude some fragment HTML linking text that they can cut or edit as they see fit. (HTML, or Hypertext Mark-up Language, is the special formatting instruction used to create a web page.)

- Your link should offer a reward for visiting the site, such as a sample chapter.

- If it seems appropriate, offer a reciprocal link.

Here's an example of what you might send to the webmaster:

Your page of publishing links is fantastic and I was wondering if you wouldn't mind adding one more? We've written a how-to book on guerilla marketing for independent book publishers. The site is called Bestsellers and has information on the book called, Publish to Win. *This link would work beautifully on your Writer's Websites page.*

I'd like to suggest the HTML linking text below. Feel free to cut as you wish. Please let me know if you'd like to link.

Anne Stanton and Jerry Jenkins

<a href: "http://www.publishtowin.com/>Bestsellers</a>
<p>For small book publishers who want to smash the Goliaths of the book industry, this book is an incredible resource. It gives you all the marketing tools every David must have. Check out our sample chapter on Selling and Publicizing Books on the Internet.

Include this letter in a file that you can send while visiting your desired link sites right online. Call it up, customize it, and send it. You'll save a lot of time this way. Avoid the temptation to bookmark the site and return later because that will double your work, O'Keefe suggests.

PUBLICIZING YOUR BOOK THROUGH "DISCUSSION GROUPS"

Posting to discussion groups (also called newsgroups, mailing lists, and forums) will be a huge part of promoting your book on the Internet. We'll discuss at the end of this chapter how to find the discussion group that's right for your book.

Before you begin making posts, however, first develop a "signature file" for the bottom of your e-mail messages. It is automatically appended below all correspondence that you e-mail from your Internet account. It's a business card of sorts that tells something about you and provides contact information. Every e-mail program has a unique procedure for creating a signature file. Just look up "signature" in the e-mail documentation or "help" file.

What should a signature file include? Your name, your company name, phone number, fax number, the title of your book, a brief tagline of what the book is about, and your book's website address. Your URL should be in hypertext to allow people to click it and immediately go to your home site.

Ready to launch a discussion group campaign? Steve O'Keefe, who specializes in publicizing books on the Internet, likes to the tell the story of how, in 1994, Laurence Canter and Martha Siegel flooded the Internet with ads for their legal services.

"The infamous 'Green Card Lawyers' stirred up some paying customers, all right. They also stirred a hornets' nest of anti-advertising sentiment on the world's largest computer network," O'Keefe wrote in an article that he posts on his home page, http://www.olympus.net/okeefe/pubnet. "Canter and Siegel received hate mail and death threats, had their Internet accounts sabotaged, and have been stalked across cyberspace. It appears that no billboards will be tolerated on the Information Superhighway."

Advertising on the Internet takes good judgment. Provide useful information and people will thank you. A well-placed review may even get the attention of a *New York Times* book reviewer, feature writer, or even lead to a rights sale of some kind. Yet if you post blatant self-promotion, you'll get ripped apart.

The books that benefit most from Internet publicity are on computers, business, careers, and cutting-edge fiction, O'Keefe wrote in his report.

"However, any book can benefit from Internet publicity because of the ease of targeting people by their special interests," O'Keefe wrote.

O'Keefe's outlines in his report this simple program for generating "heat" for your books on the Internet.

First, identify the discussion groups that would benefit from reading your book. Secondly, when a review is published on your book, call the author and ask for permission to post the review in full on the Internet. Once you have permission in hand, go to the various discussion groups and post the review (using your cut-and-paste function). Hang around the discussion group for a few days to see if there's any response or questions. Have information ready to send if anyone asks for it.

That's O'Keefe's basic plan: post news and reviews, then follow-up with advertising materials when requested. Of course, don't limit yourself to posting reviews to discussion groups. If you notice that the content of your book somehow relates to the discussion and would prove useful, talk about the specific chapter. For example, if the thread is about someone buying horses for children, perhaps you might mention that you've written a book about the subject and highlight something unique from the book: "If you absolutely require a gentle horse, I've listed a few measures to test the horse to see if it's inclined to bite or kick. These are three things that you can do. . ." Then tease the book a bit more by saying, there's lot more to consider, but you wanted to mention the basics.

REGISTERING YOUR BOOK SITE WITH SEARCH ENGINES

You'll need to register your site with several search engines so that when an Internet surfer types in a key word, your book site will show up in the resulting index.

Technically, there are two kinds of search engines. One is called a spider and the other is called a directory. A spider—Alta Vista is the biggest—simply matches a word with any page on the Web that has that particular word on the page. Typically, you don't have to formally register with a spider. If you're on the Web, the spider will find you. Every two or three days, a spider makes a sweeping search of the Internet; words of each site are stored on the spider's database. Typically, your site will show up on a spider because of this automatic search, but it's wise to register your book site if there's a way to do it.

Yahoo is a directory. When you register your website with Yahoo, you must specify the category it belongs in, i.e., cookbooks. So whenever somebody types in "cookbook," your URL will pop up.

There are more than 100 search engines on the Internet and it's possible to register on many search engines at once by using such one-stop registration services as "Submit It!" But O'Keefe believes that registering with a huge number of sites at once isn't always a good idea. It's optimal, he writes in *Publicity on the Internet,* to visit each individual search engine in order to check out the subtleties and adapt your copy to match. Individual visits often translates into your site getting listed faster, O'Keefe adds.

For a detailed discussion of the strategies and mechanics of registering your book site in these search engines, read Chapter 4, "The Registration Campaign," in O'Keefe's *Publicity on the Internet.*

CHATTING UP YOUR BOOK

It's more unwieldy than radio and doesn't reach near the numbers, but Chat Internet offers some interesting possibilities for publicizing your book.

O'Keefe writes in his Internet website report, *Booking a Chat,* olympus.net/okeefe/pubnet, about how to make an online appearance in a chat group. If you're interested, he suggests contacting the host and presenting your credentials.

What's out there for book authors? O'Keefe lists these opportunities.

- America Online has a Center Stage auditorium for which it books headliners. Prodigy has a similar venue. You might find a more receptive audience in smaller special-interest forums. All of CompuServe's forums have conference rooms, and America Online is starting to add more of these.

- CompuServe offers smaller, special-interest forums with "conference rooms." AOL is starting to add more of these.

- The World Wide Web is also coming up to speed. Many commercial websites are adding software to facilitate online chats. Sony Online at www.music.sony.com sponsored Michael Jackson's "simulchat."

- Hot Wired at http://www.hotwired.com—an online offshoot of the online magazine—has a couple guests every week in its "Club Wired" area.

- Book Stacks Unlimited, an online bookstore, has started holding author conferences in its "Book Cafe."

Even if you don't belong to these commercial online services, you can still access the chat. The host can provide guests with an I.D. and password (test before the big day and provide an emergency number in case of technical difficulties).

O'Keefe recommends providing the host with a brief introductory script, some sample questions, and instructions on how people can buy your book. This is important. Unbelievably, some authors fail to mention it.

Publicize your appearance on discussion groups. O'Keefe writes that this may draw a flame, and suggests softening the announcement by offering transcripts to anyone who won't be able to attend.

SENDING PRESS RELEASES OVER THE INTERNET

An editor at *Forbes* magazine saw a review that O'Keefe had posted and contacted him for a review copy of the book. It resulted in excerpts appearing in *Forbes*, which led to many other inquiries.

"But you don't have to wait for reporters to stumble over your discussion group postings—you can send them your news releases directly," O'Keefe wrote in an Internet report, *Book Publicity on the Internet*, posted on his home page.

Finding the media address of a reporter at a specific newspaper or magazine can be challenging. Here are some resources:

- Parrot Media Network: www.parrotmedia.com, a free and comprehensive source of media addresses, phone numbers, fax numbers, market data, and the names of key people of most TV stations, cable systems, radio stations, and newspapers of America. With a few clicks, it will sort out the newspapers in the top 10 markets or the top 100 radio stations. Glean a newspaper's circulation numbers, section editor names, get the names of radio show hosts, ask for radio stations by category: Christian, all-talk, country, etc.

- The Reporters Network claims connections to more than 2,000 reporters and offers a search engine that enables searches by specialty. Find it at www.reporters.net.

- A related site is webcom.com/leavitt/medialist.html. This spot gives you general e-mails for newspapers (ranging from the *Flint Journal* to the *Tampa Tribune*) when you're ready to propose a hot story idea. This site, however, wasn't updated at the time of publication and many of the addresses no longer worked. It also includes a Congressional e-mail list, television and radio shows, wire services and review syndicates.

- O'Keefe's site contains links to online publicity and promotion resources. Choose from 14 categories, including "Media Finders and People Finders." The URL is: olympus.net/okeefe/pubnet.

- Xpress Press offers a press-release delivery service to more than 750 media professionals and editors. Find it at www.xpresspress.com. This one takes time to peruse, but can link you to a myriad of journalism resources, magazines, newspapers and online magazines. Type in www.newslink.org/ajrdir.html.

Writing The Press Release

Think brevity and a grabby lead. You'll need to consider all the basics that you would with a normal press release, except scale it down. Use no mercy. Keep telling yourself that if they need more information, they can always ask (and be ready with information in a file to respond). Use common sense. When someone does ask for more information, don't get carried away by sending scads of publicity information by e-mail; it's cumbersome to read page upon page on a computer screen. Consider arranging an author interview with the journalist. Send what's required by regular mail if time permits. You should always ask if they can receive e-mail with files attached and what format works best for the recipient. If they don't know, save it in a "text with line breaks only" format so anyone can read it. Attaching a file allows you to quickly send formatted information created in your word processor such as press releases, brochures, manuscripts, etc.

Besides brevity, the rules for writing a press release are exactly the same as those covered in the publicity chapter. The press release must sound similar to a news story, leading with information that a reader would care about—in particular, the reader of the magazine you're trying to pitch.

A note: use *asterisks" or CAPS for emphasis because italics and bold aren't possible to use. Don't overdo.

The Mechanics Of Sending A Press Release

O'Keefe suggests that whenever you're mailing out a "snail mail" press release on your book, mail out an abbreviated form over the Internet at the same time. It's easy to do. Write all the addresses in the bcc (blind carbon copy) field, so that your recipients don't realize that you're also sending your release to 300 other media, press a button, and voila! You've just doubled your chances that your press release will be seen, O'Keefe wrote in *Publicity on the Internet.*

Don't make the mistake of putting the media addresses in the cc (carbon copy) field because everyone can see your complete media list, creating for yourself considerable embarrassment. Put the addresses in the bcc field, O'Keefe wrote.

Some address books let you assign group names so that you could address a message to "parent magazines" and it would be sent to every e-mail address in that group. This is incredibly time-saving.

INTERNET RESOURCES

You can find lots of free advice and tools right on the Internet.

- Jordan Cohen, publisher of the book, The Netwise Investor, has published links to information on the basics of website promotion. Go to his site at http://www.netwiseinvestor.com.

- Bookwire (http://www.bookwire.com) is a wonderful online resource for book publishers. The site includes a directory of online bookstores at http://thule.mt.cs.cmu.edu:8001/bookstores/.

- BookWorld, an exclusive national book distributor, has set up a Publishing Resources Center that features links to articles related to marketing books through newgroups. It also has e-mail addresses for newspapers, magazines and TV shows. You'll find it at http://www.bookworld.com/pubresources.

- BookZone.com has 17 pages of valuable Internet publicity advice, but your book must listed with the catalog in order to gain access.

BOOKSELLER SITES:

- Powell's at http://www.powells.com was one of the first to feature online ordering and a complete list of titles over the Web. Claims to be the largest independent bookseller in the world. Contact names: Kanth Gopalpur, Powell's Books, 1005 West Burnside, Portland, OR

97209, (800) 878-7323, ext. 295; For school and library books, call Barbara Blackburn, (800) 878-7323, ext. 244.

♦ A website of interest to publishers who can sell their books through specialty mail-order catalogs is http://www.buyersindex.com.

♦ Basement Full of Books at http://www.sff.net/bfob/: This website allows authors to list books that people can buy directly from them, including signed copies. Publishers can't list their books, but independent publishers can register as individuals.

GREAT RESOURCE BOOKS

♦ *The Book Lover's Guide to the Internet* by Evan Morris for $12.95 (Fawcett-Columbine) features information on where to look online for books, magazines, reference sources, bookstores, publishers, authors, discussion groups for writers and publishers, how-to information on improving your writing, and more. You'll find places to list, promote, and sell your book. A lot of publishers find the written word a lot less wieldy to use than fiddling around for hours on the Internet.

♦ *Publicity on The Internet* by Steve O'Keefe for $25.95. We've said enough already, but consider this selection a book-publicity bible.

♦ *Marketing on the Internet* by Michael Mathiesen at $34.95 is more technical than the first two, but easily comprehensible and will become a valuable tool as you explore the Internet in depth. Mathiesen will tell you how to set up your own newsgroup, ensure credit card security, and even how to create your own home page.

♦ Also, check out *Internet World*, the best of the family of Internet magazines.

LOCATING DISCUSSION GROUPS

♦ A search engine called DejaNews is primarily used to track down postings or authors of postings for newsgroups. Yet some people use it to quickly scan what a newsgroup is talking about without actually joining the group. Enter the subject of your niche market into DejaNews and up will pop names of relevant newsgroups.

- Also, go to http://www.liszt.com, which will do a search of more than 15,000 newsgroups and 65,000 mailing lists. Or go to http://www.tile.net/listserv/ and type in your keywords for a search.

- Still another route: to receive a catalog of lists, send an e-mail to mailserver@crvax.sri.com with the message "SEND INTEREST-GROUPS.TXT" in all caps.

- O'Keefe suggests Sunsite Search for Groups at http://sunsite.unc.edu/usenet-I/search.html—"the absolute best way to search for appropriate newsgroups" created by the University of North Carolina.

MEDIA SITES

Many publishers will make sure the authors of their books are listed in the various sites on the Internet where journalists check to locate experts and interview sources.

One such site is called FACSNET, developed by the Foundation for American Communications, the *Detroit News* and the San Diego Supercomputer Center. You can find it at http://www.facsnet.org/.

Another site is at www.GuestFinder.com. On this site, celebrities, experts, spokespersons, and entertainers pay less than $200 a year to be listed on the site (includes a photo, background info, suggested interview questions, e-mail links, contact information, and related subject links).

A FINAL NOTE

Publicity on the Internet can be enormously time-consuming and doesn't always pay off in sales. If you are reluctant to invest the time and aren't pinched for money, you might want to consider hiring a publicist such as O'Keefe (to find others, use a search engine and type in "Internet publicist." Also, ask for references on the PMA mailing list). These publicists have a few advantages: they are familiar with discussion groups, they know the various search engines and the people behind them, and they usually have access to all of the commercial services, such as Prodigy, AOL, and CompuServ.

21.

SELLING YOUR BOOK
PIECE-BY-PIECE
OR ALL IN ONE BITE

Big shots are only little shots who keep shooting.
CHRISTOPHER MORLEY

WHEN DISCUSSING SELLING OUT, IT'S ALL A MATTER OF DEGREE. IT CAN mean selling subsidiary rights. That means secondary rights or all rights short of publishing the book itself—making a book into a movie, a television show, an audio product, etc. The publisher and author often split the proceeds from these rights 50/50, but it's negotiable. A talented and well-known author can often command and receive a higher percentage. There is also selling the primary rights to a book, or the right to publish the book itself. Finally, an independent publisher may decide to sell out completely.

To the casual observer, it may seem a simple decision to sell a book for hundreds of thousands, maybe even millions of dollars to a huge publisher. But the decision is rarely that. There are not only emotional entanglements, but legal considerations as well. Here is a brief introduction:

SUBSIDIARY RIGHTS

FIRST SERIAL RIGHTS

First serial rights give a magazine or newspaper the right to publish an excerpt from a given book prior to publication. Most publishers try to negotiate *nonexclusive* first serial rights, meaning other media will be allowed to excerpt different parts of the book.

First serial rights may be sold by category: newspaper, syndicate, tabloid, and magazine (further broken down by type of magazine, i.e., health, women's magazine, etc.).

How much do first serial rights go for? It all depends on the book, the length of the excerpt, and the magazine. The most popular national magazines pay up to $200,000 for the hottest celebrity books. Small, niche magazines may pay no more than 10 cents a word. That may sound depressing, but remember: rights sales mean incredible exposure for the book. A rights sale to a niche magazine means exposure to your target audience. And giving potential readers a taste of your book in a non-advertising medium can translate into huge sales.

You'll need to deliver your sales pitch for first serial rights obviously before the book is published—three to six months prior to publication for magazines, which have a long lead time. If a magazine insists on exclusivity or a lengthy time before anyone else can excerpt the book, it should be willing to pay a higher fee. A magazine may also ask to include electronic rights in the negotiated fee. That is, it may want to reprint the excerpt on its web edition; this is a separate right, however, (an electronic right), and you should be able to command an additional fee. Wait until the magazine publishes the article before selling it for Internet publication (or publishing it yourself on the Web).

When negotiating a contract, be sure it specifies:

- Whether the magazine can modify or delete any of the copy in any way within the text.

- The amount the magazine will pay, and exactly when it will pay.

- Exactly what rights are being given.

Second serial rights give a magazine permission to excerpt your book *after* the book is published.

HOW TO SUBMIT QUERIES FOR MAGAZINE RIGHTS

Your first task is to identify those magazines that are most likely to be interested in the subject matter of your book. Write a query letter explaining why the book would be of interest to the audience. Suggest exactly where your excerpt would fit in the magazine; editors really appreciate queries that show a strong familiarity with their magazine. Send a manuscript to those magazines that respond with interest. Be sure to track who you queried and their response; follow up each query with a phone call. If a magazine doesn't make a practice of excerpting books, send a cover letter with a manuscript to the book editor and request a review.

Literary MarketPlace lists magazines and newspapers that feature books, along with contact information, circulation numbers, and the kinds of articles the magazine focuses on. Also, Ad Lib Publications offers two databases—the *Book Marketing No-Frills Data Files* and the *PR-ProfitCenter* data files. These files list nearly 9,000 newspaper and magazine editors, contact information, and whether or not they buy serial rights, along with the topics they're interested in writing about. For more information, call (800) 669-0773. You can also use the media lists mentioned in Chapter 9 and call the magazine editor to inquire whether they buy serial rights.

Don't jump at your first offer. Wait to see if anyone else is interested in buying exclusive first serial rights. There are some books that garner such demand that the publisher or agent can set up a rights auction. The publisher or agent sets the starting price based on the highest guaranteed amount offered on the book. The guarantor is given the last chance to bid at an agreed upon percentage—generally 10 percent—higher than the last, highest offer. This is called a "topping" privilege.

To run an auction, you'll need to set a closing date and a minimum opening bid. (If any of the buyers can guarantee they will pay at least the opening bid, they get to sit out the auction and receive the privilege of making one last bid a certain percentage over the highest offer [usually 10 percent].)

You can either have the parties submit their bids in writing or by the phone. As the bids come in, you'll need to call the lower bidders to see if they want to exceed the highest bid. Keep doing this until you're left with the highest offer. Then go back to the buyer with a topping privilege to see if he wants to top the highest bid.

There is also the possibility that the magazine isn't interested in excerpting the book, but is interested in writing about it in a column or running a short blurb on its forthcoming publication. If so, be sure that ordering information is included. And write a sincere thank-you note! After all, it's free publicity.

ELECTRONIC RIGHTS

It is important in the area of electronic rights to explicitly define what rights belong to the author and which rights belong to the publisher, wrote Jonathan Kirsch in *The Portable Writers' Conference*, edited by Stephen Mettee.

In one of the most comprehensive discussions available on the subject, Kirsch outlines the following categories of electronic uses:

- CD-ROM or "electronic books": Publication of a book on CD-ROM. The most popular CD-ROMs are encyclopedias and dictionaries, but some publishers have attempted to put books on CD-ROMs. Most have flopped.

- Fax on demand, where the publisher faxes part or all of the book to a customer for a fee.

- Subscription databases or online services: This allows customers, who subscribe to these services (such as Nexus), to electronically download information on their computers. This is common for newspaper and magazine articles, but not for books.

- Publishing on Demand: Similar to the above, customers can electronically download an entire book made available by the publisher.

- Multimedia: Includes any electronic adaptation of a book's graphics or text, such as in a video game.

The trend in the publishing world is that publishers seek to own and control rights for a complete electronic version of a book, or what's called a linear version of the book. The logic is this: a CD-ROM of a book is essentially an electronic book, and thus its use is a *primary* right, not a secondary or subsidiary right. The typical deal is that a publisher pays an advance to the author for specific electronic rights. The publisher agrees to pay royalties to the author, but only after the advance is recouped *plus* the cost to develop and manufacture the electronic version of the book, Kirsch wrote.

Authors typically reserve the nonlinear rights to the book, or the use of their book that isn't a "beginning to end" version of the work. Examples include: a video game based on a book's character or the book's plot; or information taken from the book and combined with other sources of information. Many authors demand the right to approve how their work will be used and ask that the book's title and author be explicitly stated with a copyright notice, Kirsch wrote.

Another issue to consider is when the publisher or someone else wants to excerpt all or part of a book on the Web for nonprofit purposes. Typically, publishers and authors agree that the publisher may excerpt a specific book on the publisher's web page (or book catalog) for purposes of promoting and selling the book on the Internet.

No one else can excerpt the book on the Web without permission from the *copyright owner*, who has exclusive control for the use and reuse of his or her book. There are certain exceptions, mainly that of fair use—"a safety valve for the First Amendment" which allows someone to use small portions of text, said Lloyd Jassin, an attorney who is currently at work on a book on copyright and libel law.

The copyright owner is justified in charging a fee for Internet use. How much? Basically, it's negotiable. Some publishers try to get whatever they can get. Others believe that excerpts published on the Internet increase exposure and they charge very little in exchange for a link to their web site.

There's an excellent forum on cyberspace law that explores the subtleties of copyright ownership and electronic rights. To join, send an e-mail to: Listserv@publisher.ssrn.com with the subject line saying "Subscribe." The body message must say: "Subscribe Cyberspace-Law Yourfirstname Yourlastname."

FILM RIGHTS

Of all the subsidiary rights deals, film rights (whether a movie for the big screen or television) can be the most lucrative *and* the most frustrating. Many an author has been tantalized with a production company's offer to "option" a book or magazine article, only to hear it was rejected a few months later. Do *not* get your hopes up until you literally see a signed check in the mail.

An "option" gives the production company the exclusive right to purchase an article, novella, or book for a movie project for a given period of time—anywhere from one year to five years. Options may range in price from $5,000 for a magazine article to hundreds of thousands for a novel by a big-name author. At the point of the option offer, the producer will also state the full purchase price—$60,000, for example. If the production company actually starts production on the film, it will apply the option price ($5,000) to the purchase price, and $55,000 will still be owed. Be forewarned that movie production companies produce only a tiny fraction of the magazine articles and books that they option.

AUDIO RIGHTS

Audio rights is a fairly straightforward sale. The difficult part is to find an audio company that publishes audio books in your genre. A complete list of the 100 or so publishing companies (many of these are major New York publishing firms) is published in R.R. Bowker's *Words in Print*. To find the best fit, visit audio stores to investigate the current products and request catalogs. Remember, not every book makes good audio. Use your common sense. A book on the best hostels in Europe would not make a good audio book. Uplifting, spiritual and fiction books do.

Once you think you've found the right company, send a book and query letter that describes the book's appeal, why you feel it fits in with the company's product line, the target audience, and the author's biography. Plus add anything that lends the book credence (awards, a testimonial by someone impressive, etc.). Advances for small-press books range around $5,000 and royalties between 5 percent to 10 percent. If you receive offers from two companies, don't just consider the money; consider, also, the marketing savvy of each company. Ask to see their promotional literature, how many retailers they market to, and the scope of their direct mail campaign. It's a good sign if your book will be in good company with nationally known authors.

The audio publisher may negotiate rights for direct marketing (mail order and telemarketing) or retail rights or both. If your publishing firm decides to delve into audio publishing in a big way, you may want to join the Audio Publishers Association, which focuses on increasing the visibility of audio books. For more information right to Jan Nathan, Audio Publishers Association, 627 Aviation Way, Manhattan Beach, CA 90266, or call (310) 372-0546.

SELL DIRECT OR HIRE AN AGENT?

Rather than try to sell rights directly—any rights—most publishers and authors use agents. Getting an agent's weight behind your book can be worth every penny of the agent's commission. An agent knows the right people to contact, how to appeal to them, and how much to squeeze out of a deal. Typically, agents will charge 10 percent for book club rights and mass market paperback rights, 15 percent for movie and TV rights, and 20 percent for serial rights. Another advantage of an agent is he or she will ensure a fair contract. The finer points can often be missed by an amateur.

In our estimation, an agent is *most* important when trying to negotiate a movie deal. Individual authors and unknown publishers very rarely get past the receptionist's desk of a movie production company. Movie producers know that good agents are selective about which books they represent and that well-respected authors almost always use an agent rather than going solo.

For a movie agent, call one of the major Hollywood agencies such as William Morris or ICM (International Creative Management); both have branches in New York City. A warning: these agents field hundreds of queries a week and can be extremely brusque, verging on rude.

For a list of legitimate agents, consult the *Literary MarketPlace* or contact the Writers Guild of America, West, 7000 W. Third St., Los Angeles, CA 90048. Telephone: (310) 550-1000. Or write to: Writers Guild of

America, East, 555 W. 57th St., New York, NY 10019. Telephone (212) 767-7800.

If you choose to contact production companies directly, the Hollywood Creative Directory sells a regularly updated list of production companies. For more information, call (800) 815-0503 or write: Hollywood Creative Directory, 3000 W. Olympic Blvd., Suite 2525, Santa Monica, CA 90404.

For a list of more than 550 agents that can represent you in the broad spectrum of subsidiary rights, a list can be purchased from The Jenkins Group, 120 E. Front St., Traverse City, MI 49684. Call (800) 706-4636.

WHEN IT'S TIME TO SELL YOUR BABY

The New York book industry sees the small publishing industry as a proving ground, so to speak, for best sellers. Stories abound of a New York house paying millions of dollars for book rights, which they could have originally bought for a song.

Publishers move on a book, not so much because of its sales to date, but because the author has proven charisma, a sense of her market, and the potential for even more sales. Hyperion Senior Editor Pat Mulcahy, for example, bought *The Girls with the Grandmother Faces* after author/publisher Frances Weaver sold 100,000 copies.

"You come with success on your side for sure," Pat Mulcahy told *Publisher's Weekly* in a May 22, 1995 article. "I was taken with the authentic voice of the writer and her humor. But the key for us here was that she had had so little bookstore distribution. She hadn't exhausted the field. It's an absolutely in-place situation."

There are lots of reasons why publishers decide to sell out. They get a huge multimillion dollar offer, or even a modest offer of $5,000. They find they'd rather write books than publish them. Sometimes health reasons get in the way of being able to market the book.

David Ramsey, publisher/author of *Financial Peace*, had sold 135,000 copies of his book before he decided to sell out to Viking Press.

"We spent a whole lot of time struggling with whether we should sell out or not," he explained. "We'll probably make less money with Viking unless we sell several million books because the spread is so good self-published. But Sharon, my wife, and I are more on a crusade to help people—our finances are set now—and we figured a whole lot more people will read and be helped by *Financial Peace* with Viking than if Dave Ramsey did it the rest of his life."

In his settlement with Viking, Ramsey obtained a commitment of Viking's intended marketing support. Viking delivered and the media attention exploded. Ramsey was immediately booked for appearances on the *Ollie North Show, 48 Hours, G. Gordon Liddy,* and was interviewed for an article in *People Magazine.*

Cash flow is the recurring answer from independent publishers when asked why they decided to sell out. They also said they wanted their book to reach thousands more people; something that's rarely possible to achieve as a micro-publisher, or even as a well-established small publisher.

The following story of The Hampton Roads Publishing Co. illustrates the dilemma.

Hampton Roads, a small independent press in Charlottesville, Virginia, found itself in what most publishers would consider a highly desirable position. It was faced with the prospect of a best seller.

Conversations with God was selling beyond what any book in its backlist stable had ever achieved—more than 10,000 copies a month. In the book, author Neale Donald Walsch laid his troubles at the doorstep of God and received some unexpected answers. Walsch's tale quickly captured the imagination of readers beyond the new age market, and Hampton Roads Publishing Company found itself with a cash-flow problem despite its record sales, said John Nelson, director of advertising and publicity.

"Bookstores don't pay you money for 90 to 100 days, yet we were expected to pay the printer within 30 days," Nelson said. "You get this printing bill due every month, but you're not getting paid for three or four months."

"What compounded the problem was that we not only had a runaway best seller, we had a runaway best-selling series. Neale had *Conversations with God, Book 2* in the works, and then we'd have the same problem compounded twice, trying to sell 25,000 to 30,000 copies a month.

"That would have been something we could have managed with a little better terms from our printer, which we were working on, and getting quicker payment from the distributor, which also could have been negotiated; but on top of all that, we had an author who was not satisfied to allow this to happen slowly. He wanted his message out quicker so he hired one of the best publicists in the country, Ariel Ford, who was telling us that she got Deepak Chopra on the *Oprah* show, and was guaranteeing she'd do that with Neale Walsch. So then we're faced with the prospect of major publicity and major publicity can generate demand in the hundreds of thousands. If we could have taken it slowly, we could have done it."

The pressure on the company's small staff of 10 was also getting intense, Nelson said.

"Had we not sold out, we may have self-destructed. We'd be putting all this pressure on people; it would have driven us all crazy."

Meanwhile, the New York publishing firms began putting in some highly vocal bids to buy the publishing rights to *Conversation*; one publisher put in a 7-figure offer. Despite the company's cash-flow problems, Robert Friedman, co-owner of the press with Frank DeMarco, was reluctant to let his "baby" go. Several times Friedman said it was like considering selling one of his children. If he did sell the book, he wanted the publisher to treat the book with the honor and understanding that it deserved.

It was a woman, finally, who swayed Friedman. Susan Peterson, a long-time publisher of metaphysical works, loved the book. As executive vice-president of Putnam/Berkley Group, she convinced Friedman and the author that Putnam would give the book tender, loving care. It could also give the book one other thing that Hampton Roads hadn't been able to accomplish: strong distribution in the chain stores.

"Putnam sold 400,000 copies in the first four months of release and a lot of it was in chain stores," Nelson said. "They've got a presence in chain stores that we didn't have. When we started selling well at 10,000 copies a month, the chain stores still wouldn't buy at the level that was required. They thought, 'This is a small press, they can't have a runaway best seller. That's not the nature of a small press.' We couldn't even get the bookstores to sell us end caps.

"Now the interesting thing about all of this; it's six months later, and it's now No. 6 on the *New York Times* Best Seller List and we're preparing *Book 2* for release in May 1997. Across the board, the distributors are buying at the level we want and the printers are giving us incredible terms so that we can manage it better. It's because Putnam established the mainstream appeal of the book."

Nelson wouldn't reveal the deal's terms, but said the two-year payoff was very lucrative, and was split with the author. In the short-term, however, the publishing house suffered from losing *Conversations with God*.

"We had an engine and when you have an engine, everyone comes to you and buys other books in the train," Nelson said. "So after we sold to Putnam, we had a mediocre fall season. They weren't buying our other books. We lost a substantial amount of money, while Putnam immediately reaped $3 or $4 million from *Conversations*."

Of course, the impending release of *Book 2* in May immediately turned Hampton Roads' profits around by early spring, plus money began flowing in from Putnam. The capital influx allowed Hampton Roads to prepare for the big sales numbers expected for *Book 2*.

"We have five more people than last year: a financial officer, an assistant bookkeeper, two full-time marketing assistants (added to the 3-person marketing staff), and another warehouse man. These are the people we needed. The financial officer alone is getting us terms we had never dreamed of, so it was a smart decision if you're just looking at the bottom line."

The obvious question is: If Hampton Roads knew it was a best seller, why couldn't it find investors or borrow the money?

Nelson explained that Hampton Roads couldn't find a lender even for this proven best seller because all of the books could be potentially returned.

The company did have investors offering large sums of money, but they wanted a piece of the company which was unacceptable to Friedman and DeMarco.

In retrospect, Hampton Roads cut a win-win deal. Its decision to keep rights to *Book 2* and *Book 3*, in addition to a companion guide to the original, *Guidebook to Conversations with God*, was key to its present success. Its advance sales on *Book 2* show promise that it, too, will achieve best-seller status. And that's with little spent on advertising and promotion. Plus, knowing the book had legs, Hampton Roads has been able to seek out advice from Putnam, which is savvy in matters like buying front-of-the-store display space.

"They've been magnanimous in helping us understand how to deal at this level," Nelson said. "We're a small press that stays on the cutting edge with occasional far-out stuff, and we'd like to stay on the cutting edge. We have established authors knocking on our door, and we'll be able to afford the advances. But we're committed to doing the books no one else wants to do."

SELLING OUT YOUR PRESS

Greg Godek has achieved notoriety in this country as the Romance King. He has written 10 romance books, but his best seller continues to be *1001 Ways to Be Romantic.* Over six years, he has sold 1.2 million copies.

In 1996, however, he sold out his entire Casablanca Press to Sourcebooks, a publishing company (specializing in gift stores), which is owned by his former national distributor, LPC Group. Godek declined to specify the terms he negotiated, but made it clear he'll reap back the rewards through continued strong sales as opposed to a multimillion dollar advance.

The question is why?

Godek said he wanted to join the two strengths of himself as a gifted marketer, and Dominic Raccah, president of Sourcebooks, who is a superb publisher. She *likes* handling inventory analysis, cash flow management, payment terms and returns, Godek explained.

"Let's face it," Godek said. "Publishing is the worst business, the most complicated, the most miserable. With returns and payment terms, you couldn't choose a more difficult business to be in. That's why many people fail. People who get into this are writers, visionaries, and dreamers and they get pounded with the realities."

Godek said he first wrote his book after teaching an adult education romance class for 10 years in Boston. He decided that he did indeed have a message to get out to the world about love and romance and how to take action on your feelings. The thought, however, of going begging to Random House turned his stomach and he decided to independently publish the book.

After three years of very strong sales, Godek, an all-or-nothing kind of marketer, decided to push the limit by doing something no one else had done before: a 2-year, cross-country book tour that would hit every state in the United States. He put the tour on wheels, outfitting a 36-foot Romance-mobile.

"The tour was the straw that broke it," he said. "Imagine putting yourself in a truck, going across the country and trying to run a business. Pay phones are a pain. I had to give up something."

Not only was Godek stressed from doing business from an RV, cash flow was a constant problem, as he had to fund press runs of 50,000 to 75,000 books at a time. Plus he was paying publicists more than $100,000 a year. With a 68-percent discount, he found it difficult to juggle money. Now that Sourcebooks owns the books, Godek receives a royalty, and Sourcebooks picks up the risk. For example, it pays for press runs and picked up the expenses of the tour and the publicity support.

Godek believes he and Raccah make an "amazing team."

"She's a brilliant publisher. I'm a prolific writer and very creative and want to be out front. Dominique wants to be the person behind the scenes supporting me."

Godek says the deal, unlike the kind he would have secured with a New York publishing firm, will allow him status as equal partner with control.

"I throw out title ideas, we go over the book covers together, I have a say-so. If Random House gave me $5 million and took away the control, I couldn't live with that."

22.

WHEN IS IT TIME TO GROW YOUR LINE?

EXPANDING A BOOK LINE IS A NATURAL STEP FOR MICRO-PUBLISHERS. The question is, when? Some publishers hesitate to invest energy and capital into more books, believing that their first book can live for years and years with enough time, promotion, money, and desire. Yet adding books and complementary products can create a synergistic effect for the entire book line, as the following stories will show.

Brian Jud's first book, *Job Search 101*, sold well to bookstores and libraries, to state governments, and to colleges.

He was prompted to write a second book after he received several requests from state governments to write a book on people's attitude toward unemployment. His second book, *Coping with Unemployment*, sold well to bookstores and governments, but not to colleges. His next venture was to translate *Job Search 101* into Spanish, which required all new distribution and promotion. Then he produced a video, *The Art of Interviewing*, which he sold through direct mail and catalogs.

After some research, he decided to expand his line once again. He found that college students didn't like to read a book on finding a job so he created a series of eight 20- to 30-page booklets, one on each segment of the search. He customized the books for colleges, printing their names on the cover with a minimum order and sold them by the thousands. The booklets sold well to state governments, too.

"I thought it was important to create a product line in order to be considered a serious author," Jud said. "My later books gave my first book—and me as the author—more credibility, particularly at trade shows and personal presentations," he said. "I was able to create a more complete catalog with all the books I sold."

Another advantage: Jud was able to sell his books as a package. For example, if a college wanted his newest job-search book, he could offer them reduced-price copies of his earlier books for their alumni association members.

As publishers peddle their books, they need to listen to what their book buyers would really like to see. Sometimes a request is very direct. Barnes & Noble, for example, told Jud they'd buy his first book if he changed the cover, which Jud himself had designed.

"I was able to get around my ego and make the sale with a new cover," he said. "Sabrina Farber was the buyer at the time, and I got her involved with the decision-making process on the second cover."

Sometimes publishers have found that creating a new product helps them improve upon an old one. In 1994, the Vermont publishing house, Images from the Past, published a book, *Remembering Grandma Moses*. It was originally written three decades ago by Beth Moses Hickok who, in 1934, was considering marrying into the Moses family. She was able to recreate the period as if it were yesterday thanks to her meticulous diary and letters written to her mother.

"It was really a pretty magic book," said Tordis Isselhardt, who heads Images from the Past. "Then I got to thinking we should make this available to the blind on audio. It's very inspirational, after all, that here is a first-time author in her 80s, who exemplifies the strength of Grandma Moses herself.

"To produce a 60-minute tape, we needed to add more material. So while still at the sound studio, we asked Beth about Grandma Moses—her cooking, her experiences in the kitchen, her marriage to Thomas Moses, and her own childhood. Then we pieced it all together like a narrative quilt."

Isselhardt will use some of the additional information gleaned from the audio recording to produce a second edition of the book.

"The project started from a desire to offer a recording for the blind, then it took on a life of its own. It will give us a chance to do a better job of marketing the book than we had in 1994," Isselhardt said.

For some publishers, it's often difficult to let go of the first book and to expand into new territory. Yet the market dictates when it's time. Cynthia and Sang Kim of Turtle Press realized early on that their first book, *Teaching Martial Arts, The Way of the Master,* appealed to an overly narrow audience so they purposely geared their second book to a wider audience. Still in the martial arts realm, the second book was fitness oriented and appealed to the millions of Tae Kwon Do practitioners worldwide.

Turtle Press has also published 30 videos, but Cynthia Kim admitted they simply fell into the market. Sang Kim had produced videos for another company, which proved so popular that the Kims decided to produce their own product.

"People would call and tell us they wanted this or that kind of video, and we'd listen. So it's very much customer-driven," Cynthia Kim said.

The Kims have published a total of 10 books in the last seven years, riding the crest of martial arts popularity. Their decision to grow was made easier by the quickly expanding market, thanks to the immensely popular children's programs, *Power Rangers* and *Teen-Age Mutant Ninja Turtles.* The Kims' last book, *1001 Ways to Motivate Yourself and Others* by Sang Kim, is the first to cross over into the mainstream market, Cynthia said.

"He's so good at motivating people because he's good at teaching. We felt that even if it didn't work in the mainstream, it would still have a big appeal in the martial arts market, which is very much focused on self-improvement and self-development.

"It wasn't a big leap for us because we were set up for that logistically and that's really important. We have a national distributor in place and whatever we send them, they say, 'Great! Go for it!'"

In addition to books and videos, Sang Kim formed a membership organization for marital arts schools. The reason: so many people were contacting him for advice, it was simply the most organized way to disseminate information, Cynthia Kim said.

Like Brian Jud, the Kims decided to rejuvenate their first offering by jazzing up the original black-and-white cover and adding a powerful photo.

"Packaging really helps sales," Cynthia Kim said.

So when is the effective life of a book over?

One way to objectively evaluate is your net sales—or sales after returns, said Greg Godek, who feels his book *1001 Ways to be Romantic* hasn't even approached the end of its 6-year, robust life.

"Track your sales over the years and look at your curve. What is it doing? Combined with that, ask yourself what have you been doing to market it? What are similar books doing? This is very critical. In the world I'm in, I look at John Gray's *Men are from Mars, Women are from Venus, Love* by Buscaglia and *The Real Rules* by Barbara De'Angelis. How are buyers reacting to this genre? Does the media still like romance, relationship books? Ask yourself, are you getting calls for interviews? Books on time management, for example, were hot in the '80s. Then people started yawning, and wanted something new. That's an indication you're on the downside of the curve."

In the mainstream trade, a book is very much alive for six months, said Cornelis "Cor" van Heumen of the Cate Cummings Publicity and Promotion Group.

"The book isn't necessarily dead after six months, it's just a long row to hoe and maybe not worth the effort if you don't plan right or if the weather goes against you. New age can be extended as much as two years because everyone is still catching up to all the information that's gone before. As is known, new age is not terribly new. The growing general interest is, though, with a desperate need for background to understand what it's hearing."

Essentially the publisher needs to offer something new when the media responds with, "Who else you got," without booking an interview, van Heumen said.

The publisher or publicist needs to be able to tell if the time is simply wrong for an interview or if the book's moment in the sun has forever passed.

A book, thought dead, can be revived with the right opportunity, van Heumen said. The book's subject may once again become topical, or maybe it was ditched in the first place for a reason completely unrelated to the quality of the book, such as the author was too ill to promote it when first published.

Tim Smith, author and publisher of *Buck Wilder's Small Fry Fishing Guide*, sold 80,000 copies of his book within the first 18 months of its publication date, most of the copies in Michigan. The beauty of expanding a book line, he said, is that the publisher can take advantage of all the lessons painfully learned from the first book. Smith, for example, originally put his Buck Wilder books into Orvis stores and bait shops.

"It was a waste of time because men don't buy books. Men don't buy *things*, in general. So that was one of the things we found out," he said.

Smith decided to publish a second book, *Buck Wilder's Small Fry Camping Guide*, after hearing repeatedly from people in the entertainment industry (who were interested in licensing the Buck Wilder character) that not every kid likes to fish.

"They told me that I needed to make him into a hiker, camper, make him into an outdoorsman who everybody can relate to," Smith said. "A publisher needs balance to their line. If you're going to publish a recipe book, *Cooking Scandinavian*, you'll find that you'll want to make yourself into a well-rounded cook, so that you're considered an authority. So you may take your cookbooks into recipes from the Middle East or Japan.

"Just listen to what people are telling you and your sales will continue to grow," Smith said.

Often when publishers expand a line, they seek to appeal to the same target audience in the same channels. This way they can build on what they know and don't have to invest in building a completely new mailing list or a media contact list. Nor do they have to produce completely revised brochures or catalogs. They've already invested in analyzing the particular taste of a market and its buying habits; by adding more books to their line, they can capitalize on that knowledge. There is a danger, however, of putting "all your eggs in one basket." If demand falls, all your books will fall. That is why many publishers choose at least two distinct line of books.

Ed Hinkelman, president of World Trade Press in San Rafael first published the *Importers Manual USA* in 1993; it was a giant book requiring an investment of $120,000 in research and development. Retailing for $87, it served as a complete reference book for importing to the United States and was targeted at both professional and prospective importers and exporters.

Hinkelman sold 6,000 copies of the book, and decided to embark on another ambitious project—a series of country business guides. Each book was a definitive encyclopedia of doing businesses in an emerging country such as China and Mexico.

"They're jam-packed, 300 to 500 pages each. No fluff. Each book covers 25 business topics, how to import, how to export. Financial institutions, opportunities, labor, and so on," he said.

He further expanded the line with a *Dictionary of International Trade*, and a series called *Passport to the World*, which covered the business culture and etiquette in specific countries.

Like Smith, Hinkelman had to learn a few lessons the hard way. Number one: bookstores are a terrible place to sell his books.

As his company built up the line, it also changed its strategy and "pushed like hell" for international distribution. That effort was successful, along with carefully targeted appeals in direct mail pieces and catalogs. The company also found a significant market in corporate sales; United Parcel Service, for example, buys thousands of Hinkelman's *Dictionary of International Trade* at a time.

As Hinkelman has expanded his line, he has applied consistent principles: his books appeal to an international audience, they are designed to have a shelf life of 10 to 15 years with updates, and they are comprehensive.

Hinkelman's advice is that before embarking on new projects, *research the market*.

"I bet a book could be done on how to do market research because very few people do it. Some publishers say they publish books on a hunch, and some are good with their hunches. But they're doing it with a lot more information than they're letting on; they're talking to customers constantly or talking to their distributors or the bookstore owners, managers and sales people on the floor. They know whether something has potential for success, and that's not a hunch and it's not a gut feeling. It's based on market research."

CONCLUSION

ED HINKELMAN, PRESIDENT OF WORLD TRADE PRESS, SAID HE GREW up believing that if you could build a better mousetrap, people would beat a path to your door. He found it wasn't true in the book industry, and his company came close to going belly up because of his naivete.

"I put so much emphasis in developing content that marketing took a back seat and almost became an ugly word. We were the content developers, the authors, we considered ourselves more important than *those* people. Now we're finding the right balance, and the balance is a lot of marketing."

He soon discovered that you can have a reasonably good book with very good marketing and turn a healthy profit. You can publish a dynamite product, but can easily go broke if it's not coupled with aggressive promotion.

We hope this book has enriched you with sound marketing advice. We thank the many publishers who agreed to share both their pains and triumphs. As you close the covers and think about any single point this book has made, it's this: it is totally insane to throw your books and promotional money willy nilly against a wall and hope that something sticks; that strategy will break your budget and break your spirit. But throw that money and those books with laser precision at the right people with a message they *want* to hear, and you'll sell books. A *lot* of books. Best of luck to you.

BIBLIOGRAPHY

Bieler, Peter. *This Business Has Legs.* New York: John Wiley & Sons, Inc., 1996.

Burgett, Gordon. *Publishing to Niche Markets.* Santa Maria, California: Communications Unlimited, 1995.

Cardoza, Avery. *The Complete Guide to Successful Publishing.* New York: Cardoza Publishing, 1995.

Corpening, Gene. *What the Self-Publishing Manuals Don't Tell You And You Didn't Know to Ask.* Granite Falls, North Carolina, 1995.

Dessauer, John. *Book Publishing; What It Is, What it Does,* 3rd ed. Dessauer Continuum Publishing Corp., 1989.

Geiser, Elizabeth, ed. *The Business of Book Publishing: Papers by Practitioners.* Boulder: Westview Press, 1985.

Horowitz, Shel. *Marketing Without Megabucks:* North Hampton, Mass.: Accurate Writing and More, 1995.

Jenkins, Jerrold, and Link, Mardi. *Inside the Best Sellers.* Traverse City, Michigan: Rhodes & Easton, 1997.

Kremer, John. *1001 Ways to Market Your Books.* 4th ed. Fairfield, Iowa: Open Horizons, 1993.

Mathiesen, Michael. *Marketing on the Internet.* Gulf Breeze, Florida: Maximum Press, 1997.

McHugh, John B. *The College Publishing Market.* Wilmington, Massachusetts: CMG Information Services, 1996.

Mettee, Stephen, ed. *The Portable Writers' Conference.* Fresno, California: Quill Driver Books, 1997.

O'Keefe, Steve. *Publicity on the Internet*. New York: John Wiley & Sons, Inc., 1997.

Poynter, Dan. *The Self-Publishing Manual*. 8th ed. Santa Barbara: Para Publishing, 1995.

Ramsey, Dave. *Financial Peace*. 3rd ed. New York: Viking Press, 1997.

Ross, Marilyn and Tom. *The Complete Guide to Self-Publishing*. 3rd ed. Cincinnati: Writer's Digest Books, 1994.

INDEX

ABOUT THE AUTHORS

 JERROLD JENKINS AND ANNE STANTON HAVE TEAMED UP TO PRODUCE a book that tackles the question of book promotion and marketing from a unique angle; it is written by an independent publisher *and* an experienced journalist. One has published several books and helped scores of publishers package and publicize their books. The other has received literally thousands of press releases and can testify to what works ... and what gets tossed.

Jerrold Jenkins has become known as the national "guru" of small press publishing. He publishes two nationally distributed magazines: *Small Press* magazine, the voice of small press publishers, and *Publishing Entrepreneur*, a nuts-and-bolts magazine that features how-to articles on publishing books profitably.

Mr. Jenkins is CEO and president of Jenkins Group, Inc., a company that services independent publishers, small presses, and information providers. Its book publishing division is Rhodes & Easton, which publishes numerous books a year, including the one you are holding. Other divisions offer the services of book packaging, editing, production and publicity to independent publishers. The Jenkins Group also formed a publisher's association—International Small Press Publishing Institute—which conducts educational publishing seminars across the country. Finally, the Jenkins Group compiles and markets data bases.

Mr. Jenkins is in strong demand as a speaker. He is frequently on the road, lecturing at National Speakers Association chapters, colleges and universities, writers' groups, and writers' conferences. He is frequently quoted in national newspapers and magazines about small press issues. He is also a member of the Advisory Council of the Small Press Center in New York.

Anne Stanton is an experienced journalist, winning state and national awards for stories about education, the environment, poverty, racism, and social policy. After working for nearly a decade as a full-time newspaper reporter and monthly news magazine editor, she focused her freelance efforts on the publishing field. In *Publish to Win*, she explains how to hit the media's hot buttons with well-written press releases and attention-get-  ting events. She has also drawn on her research abilities to cull the most effective marketing strategies from the nation's small press and independent publishers. Ms. Stanton now serves as book editor and assistant marketing director for Rhodes & Easton.

ORDER INFORMATION

PUBLISH TO WIN   **INSIDE THE BEST SELLERS**

One is about perspiration. . . the other inspiration.

Do you have a writer friend who is thinking of publishing a book or has already done so? If your friend is in need of inspiration, give the gift of *Inside the Best Sellers*, which features the inside scoop of 18 authors who have sold literally hundreds of thousands of books. Each one started with a book that was either self-published or published by a very small house. Full of human drama and rags-to-riches stories, this book reveals how the business of publishing has changed forever. **$21.95**

Do you have a writer friend who has just published a book or is seriously considering doing so? Then give them *Publish to Win*, an indispensable guide that features specific advice on promoting and selling books in a very competitive market. **$20**

Order your copies today!

Rhodes & Easton
121 E. Front St., Fourth Floor
Traverse City, Mich. 49684
(800) 706-4636

PUBLISH TO WIN

Cover design by Eric Norton

Text design by Mary Jo Zazueta in ITC Galliard with display lines in Arial

Text stock is 50 lb. Royal Antique

Printed and bound by Royal Book, Norwich, Connecticut

Production Editor: Alex Moore